Religion and Alienation

GREGORY BAUM

Religion and Alienation

A Theological Reading of Sociology

NOVALIS

ORBIS BOOKS
Maryknoll, New York 10545

Cover design: Pascale Turmel
Cover image: PhotoDisc
Layout: Dominique Pelland

Business Offices:
Novalis Publishing Inc.
10 Lower Spadina Avenue, Suite 400
Toronto, Ontario, Canada
M5V 2Z2

Novalis Publishing Inc.
4475 Frontenac Street
Montréal, Québec, Canada
H2H 2S2

Phone: 1-800-387-7164
Fax: 1-800-204-4140
E-mail: books@novalis.ca
www.novalis.ca

Library and Archives Canada Cataloguing in Publication
Baum, Gregory, 1923–
    Religion and alienation : a theological reading of sociology / Gregory
Baum. – Rev. ed.

Includes bibliographical references and index.
ISBN 10: 2-89507-800-9
ISBN 13: 978-2-89507-800-5

    1. Christian sociology. 2. Alienation (Theology). I. Title.

BT738.B383 2006   261.8   C2006-903343-9

First published in 2007 in the United States by Orbis Books,
Maryknoll, New York 10545-0308
ISBN 10: 1-57075-689-9
ISBN 13: 978-1-57075-689-4
Library of Congress Cataloging-in-Publication

BT738.B32 2007   261.5--dc22   2006018930

Printed in Canada.

We acknowledge the financial support of the Government of Canada through the Book Publishing Industry Development Program (BPIDP) for our publishing activities.

5   4   3   2   1   10   09   08   07   06

Contents

Foreword

When *Religion and Alienation* appeared 30 years ago, Christian theology was undergoing a radical transformation. In Europe, Johann Baptist Metz, Jürgen Moltmann, and Dorothee Sölle were fashioning a political theology that attempted to overcome the reactionary and nationalistic theologies that supported fascism and Nazism. In Latin America, Gustavo Gutierrez, Jon Sobrino, and Leonardo Boff were starting to give shape to a liberation theology rooted in the experiences of the poor. In the United States, James Cone and Rosemary Radford Ruether were beginning to articulate theologies that explored experiences of racism and sexism. In Canada, Gregory Baum was in the initial stages of developing a theology that was in dialogue with critical social theory and engaged in social, political, and cultural debates. Although Baum wrote *Religion and Alienation* to introduce students of theology and religious studies to sociology, the book now serves another purpose – it is the foundational text in Baum's 30-year project of bringing theologians together with critical social theory to forge lines of solidarity in the pursuit of social justice.

While many of these thinkers wrote about society and social injustice from a theological perspective, what stood out in Baum's *Religion and Alienation* was his willingness to explore the theological significance of the emergence of the sociological imagination in the modern age. Traditionally, philosophy had served as the dialogue partner of Christian theology. Along with others, Baum set out to discover what the social sciences could contribute to our talk about God. His audacious proposal in *Religion and Alienation* was that Christians could learn much about themselves, their churches, and their theology by studying sociology. In this second edition, Baum introduces new dialogue partners, most notably the Frankfurt School of Critical Theory and the political economist Karl Polanyi (1886–1964), who compel us to think about the social, political, and economic consequences of the gospel. These new dialogue partners are discussed in the all-new Chapter 11.

In one of the best papers ever written about Baum's work, Canadian sociologist Ray Morrow summarizes what Baum sees as the most significant advances from this dialogue.[1] According to Morrow, Baum sees the sociological imagination as giving us the ability to understand alienation as a product of injustice rather than an essential part of the human condition. It allows us to analyze the source of human suffering and distorted consciousness and to imagine a remedy. It makes Christians impatient with any theology that would make us passive or fatalistic about human suffering. The sociology of knowledge, and especially the critique of ideology, reveals the historical roots and social basis of all truth claims, including allegedly eternal and unchanging church doctrine and other theological

---

1   Raymond A. Morrow, "Straining After Universality: Gregory Baum's Theological Method and Contemporary Social Criticism", Annual Meeting of the Society for Socialist Studies, Learned Societies Conference, Queen's University, Kingston, Ontario, June 1, 1991.

claims.[2] For Baum, the sociological imagination awakens in us a sensitivity to the ambiguity of religion. Beyond the endless debates about secularization ("Religion: yes or no?"), Baum asks "What kind of religion?" Will we promote a religion that reconciles us to the death-dealing forces of the world, or one that inspires us to liberate ourselves from them and to act in solidarity with all who struggle against them? Finally, Morrow concludes that the sociological imagination persuades Baum that the Church's excessive privatization of sin has been an error. The classical notion of sin as a freely chosen act by a conscious individual violating divine commands is insufficient when dealing with the evils that emerge from the unjust nature of social institutions and structures. For example, many people today starve on a planet that can provide food for all – and not because those who eat are each and every one uncharitable and gluttonous. Rather, their starvation is the product of an international economic system that routinely excludes the hungry, while a neo-liberal ideology teaches the rest of us that their deaths are natural, necessary, and generally none of our concern.

In 1991, in what was supposed to be the farewell editorial of *The Ecumenist*,[3] the journal of theology, culture and society that he had founded in 1962, Baum wrote that the war in Iraq (the first one) was a covenant sealed in blood introducing a new global politico-economic order, led by the sole remaining

---

2   For an excellent analysis of how Church doctrine has changed in relation to modern society, see Gregory Baum's *Amazing Church: A Catholic Theologian Remembers a Half-Century of Change* (Ottawa/Maryknoll, NY: Novalis/Orbis Books, 2005).

3   *The Ecumenist* has been resurrected a number of times and is now published by Novalis at Saint Paul University in Ottawa, Canada.

superpower, a nation that spends as much on its military every year as the rest of the world combined.[4] His dark conclusions were indeed prophetic. The past fifteen years have not been kind to the poorest people on our planet. The West's "victory" over Communism was supposed to usher in a "New World Order" of prosperity and peace based on an ever-expanding free-market system.

However, the free-market utopia of the early 1990s never materialized. The Gulf War in 1991, the Balkan crises of 1991–2001, the Somalia intervention in 1993, the Rwanda crisis in 1994, military actions and sanctions against Iraq throughout much of the 1990s, and al-Qaeda terrorist attacks on US interests, which culminated in 9/11 and the "war on terror," exposed fatal flaws in the "globalization peace plan." Despite these setbacks, however, the George Bush, Bill Clinton, and George W. Bush administrations, in conjunction with the so-called G8, forged ahead with a policy of market deregulation and expansion. While economic indexes such as the Dow Jones, the FTSE, and the DAX hit record highs over the past decade and a half, developing countries such as Thailand, Mexico, Argentina, and Brazil struggled to maintain control over their own economies. And perhaps most serious of all, we are now confronted with losing an entire generation in Africa due to the scourge of AIDS. As Stephen Lewis, the UN Secretary-General's special envoy for HIV/AIDS in Africa, has argued in his book *Race Against Time* (2005), this humanitarian crisis remains of little interest to the richest countries in

---

4   Baum reproduces much of this important and dark editorial in the new edition of *Religion and Alienation*. See pages 223–226.

the world largely because to address it holds little economic or political gain.

The message of *Religion and Alienation* has never been more important. We fail as a church if we become complacent and allow church leaders, theologians, and pastors to return to distortions of the past, especially a privatized faith that confines itself to personal piety, a pastoral agenda that confines itself to the "spiritual" needs of people without regard for their physical well-being, and an inward-looking church concerned most with its purity and self-interest. This privatized faith is not politically innocent. It legitimates the individualism of the capitalist social order. In all of this, we risk losing the social dimension of the gospel, the good news that Christ came to feed the hungry and set the captives free.

We first encountered *Religion and Alienation* as students of Gregory Baum. Like many who studied with him, we marvelled at the way he could take complex issues, synthesize them, and then explain them in ways we could understand. Today, as university professors, we still marvel at how he can capture the core elements in the work of Hegel, Marx, Toennies, Durkheim, Weber, and Freud and communicate them to students. It is why we so often assign *Religion and Alienation* as required reading in our undergraduate courses. At the graduate level, we have passed it on to doctoral candidates to help them organize an enormous and unwieldy reading list in classical sociological theories of religion. We have used sections of it in public talks and adult education classes outside of the university to explain how modern society presents the Christian churches with unprecedented challenges and opportunities. Because it was so useful to our churches, communities, students, and ourselves, we pestered Gregory Baum to revise and republish *Religion and Alienation*. We are delighted that Novalis in Canada and Orbis Books in the United States have undertaken this important project.

Scott Kline and David Seljak
St. Jerome's University
Waterloo, Canada
June 2006

Preface to the Second Edition

In 2005, Novalis asked me to prepare a second edition of *Religion and Alienation*, a book I wrote over 30 years ago to introduce students of theology and religious studies to the ideas of the classical sociologists. My own studies had convinced me that the exploration of theology and religious studies demanded an ongoing critical dialogue with the social sciences. At the time, few theologians were engaged in this endeavour. This was soon to change. In a 1983 issue of the review *Concilium* (170[10/1983]2), I made this observation: "Over the last ten years, the dialogue of theology and the social sciences has come to be recognised in all branches of theology." This dialogue was especially important for theologians who believed that the Christian Gospel had an emancipatory message and was divinely intended to transform human beings and their societies. This practical orientation of theology was confirmed by the pastoral teaching of John Paul II that the mission of the Church included support for human rights and social justice and efforts to pacify and reconcile the deeply divided human family. Since teachers and students of theology try to reveal the meaning and power of the Gospel in the social and cultural conditions of the present, the initiation into the critical sociological reflection offered in this book has retained its relevance for today. For this reason I welcomed Novalis's decision to publish a second edition of *Religion and Alienation*.

Rereading my book after 30 years confirmed for me that my introductions to the important sociological thinkers – Tocqueville, Marx, Toennies, Weber, Durkheim and Mannheim – are still relevant. I therefore decided to leave those chapters as they were, except to improve the style to make them more readable. I discovered that 30 years ago I was not as sensitive to the women's movement's search for recognition as I am today. My extended report on the Church's effort to purify itself of the inherited anti-Jewish rhetoric and redefine its relationship to the Jewish people does not as yet acknowledge the shadow the Israeli-Palestinian conflict has cast on Jewish-Christian dialogue. But I am pleased that all the chapters emphasize the ambivalence of religion, its light as well as its dark side. The recognition of this ambivalence has become widely accepted in recent years, thanks to the rapid spread of fundamentalism and its problematic political consequences.

Since Chapters 10 and 11 of the first edition did not specifically deal with sociological authors, I decided to omit them in the second edition. The previous Chapter 12 has now become Chapter 10, with a new title. I also decided to omit the brief bibliography that followed each chapter: they listed the books I had studied at the time, but these no longer represent contemporary research. Attached to the Preface to the first edition was a short list of introductory readings: books on the history of sociology that were famous and are still being used by students. I have replaced this list with a short bibliography in two parts: i) books dealing with the sociological tradition, and ii) books by theologians in dialogue with sociology.

Totally new in the present book is Part II or Chapter 11, entitled "After Thirty Years." Here I compare the historical context in which the first edition was written with the present historical situation, and then turn to social and political thinkers who help me understand the social and cultural problems created by the globalization of the free-market economy. In critical dialogue with these authors, I try to formulate what Christian hope means in dark times.

I wish to thank Nancy Keyes and Anne Louise Mahoney, who graciously helped me edit the present book, and Jean-Marc Biron, SJ, the director of le Centre justice et foi of Montreal, who gave me an office at the Centre where I can read, think and write.

Gregory Baum
Montreal 2006

Preface to the First Edition

One of the best ideas I ever had was to take a two-year leave of absence from teaching to study sociology at the New School for Social Research in New York. I was interested in sociology largely because I could not understand why the Catholic Church, despite the goodwill of clergy and laity and the extraordinary institutional event of Vatican II, had been unable to move and adopt the new style of Catholicism outlined in the conciliar documents. I thought that sociology, as the systematic inquiry into society, should be able to answer this question. What I did not expect was the profound influence that the study of sociology would have on my entire theological thinking. I became convinced that the great sociological literature of the nineteenth and early 20th centuries records human insight and human wisdom as much as philosophical writings do, and that sociology ought to have a special place in the education of philosophers and theologians. I found that the sociological tradition contains basic truth that is absent from philosophical and theological thought, truth that modifies the very meaning of philosophy and theology. I am thinking here especially of the relationship between mind and society. While sociologists may differ in their understanding of this relationship, all of them in one way or another acknowledge that society (the institutions in which we live) affects our consciousness (the way we perceive reality and think about it). Thought, in other words, is socially grounded. I began to feel that the exclusion of sociological literature from philosophical and theological education has been a misfortune. What I want to do in this book, therefore, is to introduce the student of theology to the sociological tradition. My hope is that more theologians will turn to the sociological literature and enter into conversation with it.

Among the many things that impressed me when I read the classical sociological writings was the central place that the study of religion occupied in the work of the great thinkers. While theologians look upon the Christian religion mainly in terms of faith, hope and love, and frequently become uneasy about the Church's presence in the world, sociologists for the most part regard religion as a powerful factor without which it is impossible to account for the creation of culture and society. This certainly was the view of Max Weber and Émile Durkheim, even though neither regarded himself as a believer. Religion, however spiritual in appearance, has a social impact that may be hidden from the theologian but that sociologists make the special object of their attention. I cannot deny that the study of sociology gave me a new sense of the power and meaning of religion.

What also greatly impressed me in the sociological literature was the humanist perspective adopted by these great thinkers. They studied society to detect in the social institutions the trends that hurt and diminish human life, and they tried to create sociological theory that would promote social processes that promised to make society more truly human. Beginning with Alexis de Tocqueville and Karl Marx, the great sociologists were moralists. Since they distinguished themselves from Christian thinkers and from historical scholars who examined society in an interested way, in defence of specific secular or religious institutions, the sociologists insisted that they studied society in an objective manner. Their approach was value-free and scientific. They wrestled against inherited prejudice and personal bias. At the same time, they were committed to values. They had a vision of what human life ought to be like, and it was this commitment to a philosophical anthropology that enabled them, each in his own way, to detect the alienating or dehumanizing aspects of society and look for social processes that promised to deliver people from their plight. The theological reader is greatly impressed by the moral passion in the sociologists, despite their effort to be objective. This moral quality makes the classical sociological literature so different from most of the publications that emanate from the research institutes and sociology departments of our universities today.

This moral concern struck me as soon as I began my study of sociology. In "Personal Testimony to Sociology," an article I wrote two months after my arrival at the New School and published in the fall of 1969 in *The Ecumenist*, I expressed my amazement at the great concern for human life found in classical sociology and suggested that this moral concern was in fact the perspective from which these thinkers examined society. I continued to read the sociological literature from this angle, and while my reading convinced me of the validity of my approach, I discovered that my interpretation of the classical authors was not shared by many commentators. Why were there so many interpretations? I eventually came to realize that the sociological literature is always read from particular hermeneutical presuppositions and that the interpretation of the great authors depends, at least in part, on the perspective of the commentator.

In the well-known work *The Structure of Social Action*, Talcott Parsons presents the thought of the great sociologists of the nineteenth and early 20th centuries from his unique viewpoint: he finds in them the sociological insights that have prepared, piece by piece, the vast sociological synthesis produced in the 20th century, in which the original insights are interrelated, adjusted and harmonized. Parsons rightly regarded himself as one of the principal architects of this synthesis. When we turn to Robert Nisbet's beautiful book *The Sociological Tradition*, we are introduced to the same social thinkers from a slightly different perspective. Nisbet believes, as the title of his book indicates, that present among the various social thinkers was, despite their considerable differences, a basic agreement on the nature of society and the fundamental concepts, in terms of which the social reality must be analyzed. He therefore presented the sociological literature grouped around the fundamental concepts that emerged early in the tradition and were later modified and refined but never abandoned by it. If we then read Irving Zeitlin's interesting *Ideology and the Development of Social Theory*, we are again introduced to the classical sociological thinkers read from different hermeneutical presuppositions. For Zeitlin, the development of social thought reached a high point – a watershed, as he calls it – with the sociology of Karl Marx. From that time on, every sociologist worked out a theory of society with Karl Marx looking over his or her shoulder. Zeitlin persuasively argues that each social thinker has been, in one way or another, in conversation with Marx's ghost, and that the stance he has adopted in this conversation determined the manner in which he analyzed society. While I do not compare myself with these learned professors of sociology, I did feel that it was reasonable for me to read the same sociological literature from another perspective, one that I had adopted quite spontaneously and tested and confirmed by subsequent studies. Ernest Becker, in his *The Structure of Evil*, has adopted a very similar focus for his reading of the social thinkers of the Enlightenment. While I do not claim that this is the only perspective from which these authors can be read authentically, I do insist that the humanistic passion was a central dimension of their thought and that I am able to defend my interpretation of these authors against the commentators who come to different conclusions. Since a vision of human life that includes its destiny has an implicit theological a priori – an implicit theodicy, as Max

Weber would say – I have decided to call my book *Religion and Alienation: A Theological Reading of Sociology*.

In the course of the book I move from sociology into theology properly so-called. I try to make use of sociological concepts and insights to understand more clearly what Christian practice should be in the present and how we can more adequately formulate the action of the Holy Spirit in society.

I wish to thank my colleagues in two departments, religious studies and sociology, with whom I have engaged in lively dialogue over the years, especially Irving Zeitlin and Roger Hutchinson. I also wish to thank several of my students – in particular, John Mitchel, Donna Geernaert, James Reimer and James Pambrun – for letting me use their research in the writing of this study. I dedicate this book to two close friends with contrasting yet converging interests, Rosemary Ruether and Philip McKenna, with whom I have been in constant dialogue for a long time.

Gregory Baum
May 24, 1975
St. Michael's College, University of Toronto

A Short Bibliography

1) On Classical and Critical Sociology

Raymond Aron, *Main Currents of Sociological Thought*, 2 vols., New York: Doubleday, 1970.

Ernest Becker, *The Structure of Evil*, George Braziller: New York, 1967.

Randall Collins, *Four Sociological Traditions*, New York: Oxford University Press, 1979.

Peter R. De Coppens, *Ideal Man in Classical Sociology*, University Park, PA: Pennsylvania State University Press, 1976.

Anthony Giddens, *Capitalism and Modern Social Theory*, Cambridge, UK: Cambridge University Press, 1971.

Anthony Giddens, *Central Problems in Social Theory*, Berkeley, CA: University of California Press, 1979.

Graham Kinloch, *Sociological Theory: Its Development and Major Paradigms*, New York: McGraw Hill, 1977.

Graham Kinloch, *Ideology and Contemporary Sociological Theory*, Englewood Cliffs, NJ: Prentice-Hall, 1989.

Calvin Larson, *Major Themes in Sociological Theory*, New York: David McKay Co., 1973.

Don Martindale, *Sociological Theory and the Problems of Values*, Columbus, OH: Charles E.Merril Co., 1974.

C. Wright Mills, *The Sociological Imagination*, New York: Oxford University Press, 1959.

Robert Nisbet, *The Sociological Tradition*, New York: Basic Books, 1966.

Talcott Parsons, *The Structure of Social Action,* 2 vols., New York: Free Press, 1968.

Charles Pressler and Fabio Dasilva, eds., *Sociology and Interpretation*, Albany, NY: State University of New York Press, 1996.

Budford Rhea, ed., *The Future of the Sociological Classics*, London: George Allen & Unwin, 1981.

Larry Roy, *Critical Sociology*, Brookfield, VT: Edward Elgar Publishing Co., 1990.

Irving Zeitlin, *Ideology and the Development of Social Theory,* Englewood Cliffs, NJ: Prentice-Hall, 1968.

2) Theologians in Dialogue with Sociology

Michael H. Barnes, ed., *Theology and the Social Sciences*, Maryknoll, NY: Orbis Books, 2001.

Gregory Baum, *Essays in Critical Theology*, Kansas City: Sheed & Ward, 1991.

Don Browning and Francis Fiorenza, eds., *Habermas, Modernity and Public Theology*, New York: Crossroad, 1992.

Kieran Flanagan, *The Enchantment of Sociology: A Study of Sociology and Culture*, New York: St. Martin's Press, 1996.

Robin Gill, ed., *Theology and Sociology: A Reader*, London: Cassell, 1996.

Andrew Greeley, *Religion: A Secular Theory*, New York: Free Press, 1982.

Andrew Greeley, *The Catholic Imagination*, Berkeley, CA: University of California Press, 2000.

David Martin et al, eds., *Sociology and Theology: Alliance and Conflict*, New York: St. Martin's Press, 1980.

David Martin, *Reflections on Sociology and Theology,* New York: Oxford University Press, 1997.

Joseph McCann, *Church and Organization: A Sociological and Theological Inquiry*, Scranton, OH: Scranton University Press, 1993.

John Milbank, *Theology and Social Theory: Beyond Secular Reason*, New York: Basil Blackwell, 1991.

Paul Weithman, ed., *Religion and Liberalism*, Notre Dame, IN: Notre Dame University Press, 1997.

Robert Wuthnow, *Acts of Compassion: Caring for Others and Helping Ourselves*, Princeton, NJ: Princeton University Press, 1991.

I

Religion as Source of Alienation:
The Young Hegel

T he young Hegel, writing at Frankfort, was greatly concerned with the relationship of religion and alienation, and his thoughts, incomplete and fragmentary though they were, continue to appeal to contemporary religious thinkers. In his Frankfort manuscripts, published in English under the title *Early Theological Writings*,[1] Hegel anticipated modern theological literature arguing against traditional theism, against the outsider God, the God over and above history, the God out there. At Frankfort, Hegel went through a phase in which he negated reason as the norm of human history. Reflection objectifies life and hence, according to Hegel at Frankfort, inevitably falsifies life and becomes estranged from it. Thinking severs us from the sources of life: life must be lived, not thought. Thinking negates life. The riddle of life and its apparent contradictions cannot be mastered conceptually and then reconciled in a rational synthesis – they can be resolved only through commitment and action. Human life is unified through loving. This phase of Hegel's biography is not well known, for in his later philosophical system, he regained confidence in the power of reflection and the role of reason in overcoming the contradictions of life.

Of special interest to us is the essay "The Spirit of Christianity and Its Fate," in which the young Hegel, in an imaginative effort, presents the Old Testament as an example of alienating religion and the New Testament as the religion that recreates humanity in love. It is not likely that Hegel regarded his theological essay as a reliable interpretation of the Scriptures. It offered him, rather, a literary form for bringing out the alienating elements of religion and contrasting them with opposing religious trends that reconcile and liberate men. Since we are interested in the young Hegel's critique of religion, we shall pay little attention to the absurd projection of the negative account on "Jewish religion" and instead, in light of contemporary studies on Hegel at Frankfort, offer a systematic presentation of religion as source of alienation.[2] Let us follow the young Hegel in his analysis of the manifold alienations of human life. The supreme source of humanity's multiple alienation, Hegel then thought, was the conceptualization of the divine in inherited religion. Attempting to think and resolve by reflection the interrelation and co-existence of infinite and finite being, people have come to objectify the divine. They have created the "bad infinity," an infinite being over and above the finite world, extrinsic to and apart from human life and history. Hegel supposes that this was the religion of the Old Testament. Here God was the God over and above history, the divine stranger in the heavens, who ruled the earth and its peoples from above and intervened in their history only at certain moments. This view of God as stranger and object, Hegel thinks, has been adopted by official Christianity. In the Church, God is preached as the almighty supreme being in heaven who, while having no communion with the cosmos and human history, graciously enters the lives of men and women to help them in their predicaments; yet even then, this God remains the totally other, the divine stranger, the infinite object. It is this bad infinity, according to the young Hegel, that gives rise to the manifold alienations of human life. Hegel held that the separations and cleavages that dominate modern life as he saw it developing before his eyes were rooted in the inherited religion.

God as object and stranger does not exist. This was Hegel's solution. The bad infinity must be rejected. At the same time, Hegel did not fall into the atheistic language adopted by some contemporary death-of-God theologians. There was indeed a good infinity. Hegel affirmed an infinity, not over and against the finite world but in and through it, grounding it, energizing it, orienting its unfolding. Yet, this good infinity could not be conceptualized. It could never become the object of the mind. The mediation between the finite and the infinite was possible only in love, in action, in a life dedicated to overcoming the contradictions in human existence. For the young Hegel it was Jesus Christ who was the first to realize that the sky was empty, that the infinite was not a supreme being over and above him to which he was asked to submit, but a supreme mystery operative within him as source of his life, his love and his forward movement. Yet this mystery could never be expressed as a truth of the mind. God reveals himself in reconciliation and in sacrifice. It is by loving that people solve the riddle of life and achieve the unity beyond all estrangement, separation and contradiction. While the inherited religion was the source of alienation in society, Hegel held that present in this religion, in the person of Jesus Christ, was available a breakthrough to a non-alienating human life and an understanding of religion that saved people from the cleavages and contradictions of their society.

In *Early Theological Writings,* Hegel anticipates the radical rejection of extrinsicism in Christian theology in the Protestant and Catholic tradition.[3] The infinite is immanent in the finite, not by absorbing or destroying it but by assuring and protecting its finitude and existence. The infinite is in and through the finite, but never identical with it, never absorbed by it, never exhausted by it. The infinite grounds the finite, orients it and defines its ultimate future. The mode of God's immanence is, therefore, not identity but transcendence. Pantheism is here clearly rejected. Following Hegel, Christian theologians, impatient with the extrinsicism of traditional theism, have been able to affirm God's immanence in human life and history without in any way weakening the sense of God's transcendence. Their theology is often called *panentheism.* Transcendence is here the mode of God's presence. Some theologians – I am thinking, for instance, of Maurice Blondel and Leslie Dewart – followed the lead of the young Hegel in asserting that the divine mystery manifests itself only in and through human action and becomes available to the mind only as people reflect on what they are doing. God is the never objectifiable mystery implicit in human love and commitment.

The young Hegel held that the inherited religion was the source of a threefold alienation: man's alienation from nature, from himself and from his fellow man. But before we proceed, we must take a critical took at the strange vocabulary Hegel adopted in contrasting alienating and reconciling religion. He identified alienating religion with Judaism. Following the dominant Christian tradition of projecting onto Jewish religion all the antitheses of salvation – blindness, infidelity, legalism, etc. – Hegel read the Old Testament, in particular the story of Abraham, as the typical expression of bad religion; here God appeared as object and stranger in an unqualified way. None of Hegel's allegations was based on careful scriptural scholarship. His constant reference to Judaism in *Early Theological Writings* was a literary device to describe the alienating religion of Christian orthodoxy. What Hegel did not realize – as no theologian did until fairly recently – was that by using Judaism as a symbol of unredemption, he perpetuated an image of a living people that created prejudice and contempt for this people and gave rise to the desire to see their religion suppressed. This is a significant instance where Hegel's insight into the alienating power of religion did not go far enough: he did not discern in the Christian language that negates Jewish religion a source of domination and a legitimation of violence. Hegel manifested the same blindness in regard to the subjugation of women in society and alienating religion's contribution to this situation.

Hegel's "The Spirit of Christianity and Its Fate" is a brilliant and imaginative tour de force. Our interest in this essay is quite limited here. We find throughout the essay descriptions of three distinct, though interrelated, types of human alienation produced by religion. Through the worship of a God conceived as object and stranger, we read, people become estranged from the nature to which they belong, from themselves as persons, and from one another as friends and fellow human beings.

Let us first look at humankind's estrangement from nature. If God is object and stranger, if God is conceived of as separated from people and our world, then we must turn away from our environment in order to find God. Then we no longer expect to find God in nature, but in separation from nature. We no longer reach out to discover an inner harmony between humankind and our natural environment; we no longer trust in a common light shining through human life and the cosmos. As people abandon this hope, they seek salvation from a God who is a stranger over a strange world. The world is no longer home. Nature becomes an object of fear and a source of danger. Instead of searching for the proportions in nature that are congenial to human life and exercising creativity in nature inspired by confidence, people begin to oscillate between the fear of nature and the desire to dominate it. People acquire fear of the foreign environment and a sense of impotence, the inability to transform this environment into a garden. Our creative spirit no longer finds in nature the laws and purposes within which we can become active and through which we can elevate nature. This fear gives rise to the will to dominate nature and make it serve our independent purposes. The loss of creativity leads to the search for power. The rule for our dominance over nature is not a measure within nature which is like unto us, but our own advantage, our profit, our strength against our enemies. The fear of nature thus gives rise to the exploitation of nature and its eventual destruction. Because we are unable to find God in nature, we look upon nature purely and simply as an object – a foreign object to be ruled and conquered and eventually destroyed. Hegel foresaw what we have come to call the ecological crisis.

Hegel continues this analysis to show that the false self-elevation of humankind over nature actually makes humankind fall into nature and become almost indistinguishable from it. For as we separate ourselves more and more from nature, we begin to look upon nature as an enemy, as opposed to our own life purposes, and become obsessed with the quest for survival. Surrounded by a hostile environment, we define ourselves in terms of conquest. Abandoning the spirit and adopting the struggle for survival as the principle of our life, we become in fact like an animal. Surrounded by enemies, we eventually invoke the God who is object and stranger to us and our world, asking God to protect us from the onslaught of our enemies and to suppress their power. We create for ourselves a harsh divinity who curses our foes and crushes their strength. We inscribe in our God the image of all our hatreds and, by doing so, make for ourselves a God who protects and promotes our wars, our dominations, our conquests. Falsely separating ourselves from nature, we unwittingly become assimilated to nature's destructive trends. Hegel describes here what in modern times has often been called the return of the repressed. Since Hegel's day, social thinkers have greatly extended the critique of people's alienation from nature – that is, from their natural environment or from their body and sexuality. Sometimes these forms of alienation have been attributed to the practice of religion.

Closely related to humankind's alienation from nature is our alienation from ourselves. If God is object and stranger, Hegel proposes, then we do not look for an inner harmony in our existence; we expect no transcendent melody to sound in our heart nor a light to shine in our lives that gives meaning to our existence. If God is over and above human life and history, then the only light we expect comes from a foreign source. In this way, people become estranged from their own depth. They no longer listen to the voice speaking within their lives. They turn to listen to the orders from a stranger who rules from afar – *ein Fremder über Fremdes*. People then no longer expect to discern in their own experience, their own consciences, their own sensitivities, the measure of life and a light that transcends their finitude and limitation; the light is sought outside of themselves. The transcendent principle is then the object over against us, the external principle that governs us according to a wisdom foreign to us. Here we come to look upon ourselves as empty, as being nothing at all, as having no certain ground within ourselves on which to stand and from which to face our life. People define themselves, rather, as servants of a foreign God, bent on obeying his law.

Here humankind loses its freedom. We become basically dependent and enslaved. Even the freedom we yearn for is in reality a false freedom of independence from others and even from God. Instead of discovering ourselves in the lives of others and in the mystery of life out of which we and these others draw our vitality, instead of enjoying a freedom that unites us with others and with the world and its infinite life, we find a freedom of alienation that separates us from others and makes us secretly yearn to become independent from God. This resistance to God only strengthens the urge to create a divinity that is ever more lordly, more powerful, the stranger in heaven who forces us into submission. Soon we experience ourselves as impatient, as obstinate, as the sinner before this God. Since our personal inclinations all go counter to the demands that the divine stranger makes on us, we are pushed into an abiding sense of guilt and a complete rejection of ourselves. The yearning for salvation before this all-powerful God only intensifies the destructive game of servile submission, secret protest and guilty self-repudiation.

What made people objectify the divine in the first place? Why did they create for themselves a foreign divinity in a distant heaven? The young Hegel thought that these projections were due to people's refusal to love and to live a reconciled life. The inability to love made them regard reason as the highest faculty and approach the divine mystery as an infinite object of the mind. This objectification of the divine gave rise to an ongoing destructive dialectics that enslaved humankind, estranged it from itself and from others. Hegel makes the biblical story of Abraham the proper parable of alienation. Abraham left his family and his country. His inability to love and live a life reconciled to friends and to the land impelled him to become a stranger in a strange land and there, out of his alienation, bring forth an objectified divinity, a strange God who was not present to the people and their land but who imposed his government on them from above. This God then imposed his rule on Abraham himself and made him the creator of a religion that has become a source of alienation in the world. The divinity worshipped by Abraham – and it is likely that the young Hegel at Frankfort here included the God worshipped by the Christian Church – was an expression of humankind's self-rejection and estrangement from humanity and the human environment.

In Hegel's *Early Theological Writings*, bad religion was a human projection compulsively produced out of humankind's inability to love. People project the worst of themselves, their self-rejection, unto the cosmos. This theory of religion is much more subtle and profound than Feuerbach's theory, proposed four decades later,[4] according to which religion was people's projection onto the cosmos of what was best and highest in them. God, for Feuerbach, was the projection of our greatest dreams and deepest aspirations; God represented our unrealized possibilities in terms of love, goodness and beauty. Karl Marx refuted Feuerbach's cheerful and superficial atheism; he accused Feuerbach of not asking what evil operative in human life makes people create projections and prefer unrealities to the real. For Hegel, long before Marx, projections were always inversions. They turned the right order upside down and hence generated confusion and destruction. To the extent, therefore, that religion is a projection of human life, it is produced not by the noblest in people but by the worst in them, by their inability to love and the subsequent rejection of themselves. Since the divine stranger has to keep all of our enemies in check, he becomes the symbol of all that we hate and at the same time the lord to which we desire to submit. God is produced out of the negation of the best in human life, and this God in turn intensifies this negation, strengthening people in their self-hatred and fostering the exploitation of the environment. The deliverance from this projection, as we shall see, is not offered by an effort of the mind and the advent of Enlightenment philosophy but by a life of love, sacrifice and reconciliation.

Finally, the bad infinity estranges us from others; it undermines the unity of the human family. The refusal of love that generated the objectification of God as object and stranger perpetuates itself in the hostile camps which this refusal has created. The divine lord protects the failure of love that has produced his image in the continuity of antagonistic groups and classes. We will then be unable to seek the mystery of life, operative in and through people, calling them to be friends and enabling them to bridge their differences. We will then be unable to seek the divine mystery in the other person, friend or foe, enabling them to bring forth gestures of reconciliation over inherited differences and barriers. God as object and stranger is related to people only as master. He is the supreme lord, aloof, extrinsic to life, existing apart from us as independent subjects; and we can find God only by obeying him as a subject obeys a ruler. God is master, and we are his servant. The only unity that people in this situation can hope for is the unity of being ruled by this divinity, i.e., the common submission to a divine stranger. The structure of human life thus becomes one of domination.

Bad religion promotes the structures of domination in human history. Domination, not communion, is the key to human unity. The master–slave relationship that characterizes the divine–human encounter is projected upon the whole of humanity, and people are made to define their relation to one another in terms of master and slave. Peoples and groups are related to one another through power imposed on them from above. Love becomes confined to fewer and fewer men and women, for on the larger scale people become imprisoned in unbridgeable relationships of unequal power. God as object and stranger becomes the legitimating symbol for all regimes of domination. The king of kings in his rule over the world establishes and sanctions the princes who exercise government and, through their laws, impose order on people estranged from one another, on people caught in their own selfish activity, doubtful of their power and mission. Alienating religion, according to Hegel, divides the human family into rulers and the ruled.

By way of summary, we note that the three alienations produced by bad religion – alienation from nature, from oneself and from other people – are profoundly interrelated. While they can be distinguished and described separately, they affect one another and intensify the burden of separation. In some way they are all due to the refusal to love and to the objectification of the divine as the stranger above history. Since God is no longer a mystery to be encountered in nature, in one's own depth and in the human community, individuals begin to fear nature and seek to dominate it, mistrust their own experiences of life and seek security in submission, and perpetuate the divisions of humankind in abiding structures of domination. The three alienations feed upon one another. While, for the sake of clarity, one should never speak of alienation unless one specifies from what exactly people are being alienated, in view of the interrelationship of the various forms of alienation, it is also reasonable to speak of alienation without referent. Alienation then refers to the structures of separation, which prevent people from enjoying their powers, from living up to their destiny, and from participating in the unitive forces of love and truth operative in their midst.

We note in passing that in his mature philosophical work, Hegel greatly extended his understanding of alienation.[5] In the perspective of history that he adopted in his mature work, the various forms of alienation from which humankind has suffered, and still suffer, are not simply understood as structures of domination to be overcome but also as stages, as counterweights to previous errors, as necessary evil, and as such as exercising a positive role in humankind's total evolution towards freedom. Alienation is not all bad; without it, people would not have become aware of the hidden contradictions in their lives and acquired a new consciousness transcending present errors without abandoning present truth. Yet the radicalism of the young Hegel, especially his analysis of religion and alienation, remains of lasting interest.

Contemporary theologians admire Hegel's openness to the negative critique of religion without fearing that authentic religion will thereby disappear. We have already indicated that the young Hegel recognized good religion (i.e., religion that was capable of de-alienating human life). For if the divine mystery is present in and through the finite reality – Hegel thought that this was in fact revealed by Jesus Christ – if, in other words, the divine is present in nature, present in one's own personal depth and in the community at large, then religious openness to God will lead to reconciliation. If people listen to the divine call and act in keeping with the divine impulse, they will discern the harmony between themselves and nature and thus create a garden in this world; they will get in touch with their own depth and be reconciled to the sources of their vitality; and, finally, they will learn to overcome the divisions of humankind and be reconciled to others through the common sharing of truth and love, marvellously operative in mankind.

We have already mentioned that Hegel's account of good religion in his early writings (as well as his reflection on religion in his mature work) has profoundly influenced modern theologians, Protestant and Catholic. A growing number of them have come to speak of God, and listen to God, as the non-objectified and non-objectifiable mystery present in people's lives, as ground out of which they come to be and as horizon towards which they move, as orientation operative in their lives and as vitality out of which they act. This has come to be the form of Christian piety for many believers today. This transformation of awareness is not simply due to the influence of Hegel and theologians who followed him. To explain this transformation we must turn to the sociology of culture. Through technological developments and democratic institutions, people came to realize their responsibility for their collective existence. Christians asked themselves in fear and trembling what kind of society the citizens were creating. Instead of a piety focusing on eternal life, they now sought a spirituality that allowed them to take their historical situation with utmost seriousness and inspired them to realize the will of God in history. They now experience the God in whom they believed as a mystery of immanence calling and enabling them to become responsible agents promoting social justice, universal solidarity and environmental care.

What seems excessive in Hegel's analysis of bad religion, and here few contemporary theologians follow him, is his claim that religion has *caused* alienation in personal and social life. Does religion have so much power? Does religion influence the shape of culture and the form of society, or is it simply a spiritual realm mediating the encounter between God and humans? Can we attribute alienating effects to religion? Or is it more correct to say that, at the worst, bad religion confirms the alienation generated by society?

Certainly, Karl Marx regarded Hegel as hopelessly "idealistic" when he attributed to the symbolic structure of the mind power over the concrete conditions of society. In the English-speaking world, philosophers and educated people in general have tended to follow Marx in his evaluation of German Idealism; they have regarded as outrageous and contrary to common sense the idealist claim that the structure of the human mind enters into the production of the historical and cosmic reality. People tend to take for granted that the world is a given, a finished object confronting the human mind, and that true knowledge consists of the mind's conformity to the reality existing outside of itself. The mind reflects reality; it does not create reality. Facts are facts, and it is the mind's task to discern and recognize them. German philosophers, perhaps more than others, have had great difficulty with this common-sense approach.

Already Kant insisted that the experience of reality is always mediated through the human mind, that the world out there is never encountered in the raw, and that facts simply as facts are not accessible at all. Contrary to common sense, the reality we encounter, including the facts, is already ordered by the human mind, and the world to which we belong is in part the result of our creativity. The human mind enters into the creation of the world. What does this do to objectivity? Kant held that the categories of the human mind were the same everywhere and that the regularity and stability of the world were safely grounded in the mind's identical structure. It is well known that Hegel went much further; for him, the human mind itself was historically constituted. The mind was not a given, not identical throughout human history, not an absolute on which to ground the stability of the world. The way people saw the world depended on their social and cultural tradition, and even the structure of the mind, mediating the experience of the given, was inherited from the particular tradition to which they belonged. Hegel attributed great creativity to the mind – this is the meaning of Idealism – for not only did the individual mind mediate the experience of the world and make life meaningful for the person, but the individual mind also belonged to a collective mind, produced by a particular social and cultural tradition, and hence was itself derived from the creativity of previous minds. For Hegel, mind was the creative principle in the world and its history. All this may sound rather strange to common sense. Yet this was the intellectual background from which Hegel attributed so much power to religion. Religion, as a special symbolic structure of the mind, had the power to produce alienation or, if faithful to divine revelation in Jesus Christ, to reconcile humans to one another and to themselves.

Hegel's idealistic philosophy makes good, concrete sense, however, if it is read as a treatise in sociology. For sociologists, following Hegel, have attributed great power to the symbols of the mind. Sociologists had to acknowledge that the experience of the world is mediated through the symbolic structure of the imagination. By symbolic structure they mean the framework of the mind, through which people open themselves to the world and through which they respond to it. The symbolic structure of the mind makes people see the world in a particular way, orient their lives and act in it in a particular direction, and thus mediates the given present into the future yet to be made. Man's self-symbolization creates the reality in which he lives and which he is. We note that the symbolic structure of the mind is not freely chosen; it is inherited from a particular tradition and appropriated through participation in the community. Sociologists have no objection, therefore, to speaking of a collective mind. For the social and cultural conditions in which people live do create among them a common consciousness or mindset in which the individual participates, lives his or her life and exercises personal creativity. Sociologists, then, have no difficulty in accepting that the human mind is historically constituted. It is not simply a given; it is not identical in all ages and in all cultures. Mind has always been produced by a people and their history.

Sociologists also like to adopt a dialectical language when speaking of the interrelationship between personal consciousness and collective mindset. On the one hand, the common mindset is a given into which children are born and socialized by parents and school; on the other hand, sufficient freedom remains in persons to acquire a new self-understanding and, in conjunction with others who have undergone the same conversion, to transform society and eventually even modify the common mindset. In this process, institutions play a powerful role. For institutions not only assure the physical survival of a people, they also embody its collective self-understanding and hence mediate the common consciousness to the next generation. Institutions create the continuity of a tradition. The power of religion operates through the institutionalization of symbols. We are here anticipating thoughts that shall be developed at greater length in subsequent chapters. Hegel's idea that religion as a form of consciousness is able to affect the social structure in which people live makes him a forerunner of the sociological tradition.

In this chapter we have looked at religion as cause of social pathologies. In the following chapter we want to look more closely at humankind's institutional life and ask the converse question: Can religion be an expression and a consequence of social alienation?

2

Religion as Product of Alienation: The Young Marx

After looking at Hegel's analysis of religion as the source of alienation, we shall now turn to a very different sort of analysis. The young Marx looked upon religion mainly as the product of alienation. Marx did not altogether neglect the dialectical relationship between mind and society, but against the intellectual trend of the young Hegelians of his day, he emphasized almost exclusively the role of institutions in the creation of humankind's self-awareness. The significant insight of Marx was that society produces human consciousness. "Consciousness can never be anything else than conscious existence, and the existence of men is their actual life-process.... Life is not determined by consciousness, but consciousness by life.... Consciousness is from the very beginning a social product, and remains so as long as men exist at all."[6] Yet according to the sociological reading of Hegel presented in the preceding pages, it would be quite wrong to think of Marx as in direct opposition to Hegel. For both Hegel and Marx were concerned with the objective, social, institutional factors in the creation of culture and consciousness. What characterized Marx was simply his exclusive preoccupation with economic and political structures and his almost complete neglect of the cultural and symbolic factors.

The young Marx developed his idea of religion as a product of man's self-alienation when he responded to the religious atheism of Feuerbach. In *The Essence of Christianity*, Feuerbach had presented a theory according to which religion was the projection of humankind's highest aspirations unto the cosmos. As children still ignorant of their own powers project their own unrealized potentialities onto their parents and invest them with the dreams of what they themselves want to do and be, so have people in the days of their immaturity projected their highest aspirations, their dreams, their potentialities, onto the cosmos and venerated as divine what was actually their own destiny as human persons. This, very briefly, was Feuerbach's theory. God was the symbolic language for expressing people's as yet unlived powers and talents, the great human future, the perfection of human life to be achieved by human creativity. Feuerbach, we note, did not regard religion as an insignificant cluster of superstition; he attached great importance to it. It was, for him, the imaginative expression of humankind's glorious destiny. If understood correctly and divested of its theistic interpretation, it was a reliable account of the meaning and power hidden in human life. It was the task of Enlightenment to make people aware that the magnificent world of religion did not speak of God but of humanity. To the extent that people projected their highest aspirations unto the divinity, they emptied themselves of their own powers, regarded themselves as impotent and in need of help, and became estranged from their own life and destiny. Religion as understood in the days of humankind's immaturity was an alienating power. But through the conversion of the mind produced by Enlightenment, religion could come to reveal its own power and initiate people into the greatness they were to achieve in their history. From Feuerbach's viewpoint, traditional religion, by defending belief in God, was cause and promoter of humankind's alienation from its own depth and power.

Feuerbach's religious psychology is quite uninteresting compared to the Hegelian version we examined in the last chapter. For Feuerbach, God is the projection of the highest in humanity, and the reason why we engage in projections is simply due to our immature state. Feuerbach's psychology was naive. There was, for him, nothing of the inversions and distortions associated with psychological projection that we find in the Hegelian theory. According to the young Hegel, we recall, people objectify the divine implicit in life itself as a divinity above and apart from life – that is, they project the divine as a stranger in heaven who, as the projection of the best in humankind, becomes the worst for humankind. For this divinity transforms the universe into a world of fear and offers peace only to the extent that everything and everybody submit themselves to God's domination. Born out of the refusal to love, God signifies everything of which we are afraid and guarantees a universe of order and punishment. Hegel anticipated depth psychology when he describes how these projections, inspired by self-centred wishes, actually achieve the very opposite of what was wished. While God appears as the projection of the highest, in actual fact God is the projection of the lowest, the most hateful in humankind: namely, its refusal to love, the wish to stand alone, and the will to interrupt fellowship.

Karl Marx rejected the religious atheism of Feuerbach not because of its imperfect psychology, but because of its lack of sociological understanding.[7] While Marx agreed with the atheistic option of Feuerbach, he complained that Feuerbach did not pay adequate attention to the social reasons why people project the best within themselves onto the cosmos. What are the social conditions that drive people to make projections? If these are not analyzed, if the cause of these compulsive dreams is not found in the social order, then the Enlightenment advocated by Feuerbach will be followed by other projections. It will not do to unmask the illusory character of religion unless this is accompanied by changes in the social order, overcoming the frustrations that prompt people to create illusions. Feuerbach simply unmasked the symbolic world of the feudal order, but what he substituted in its place was the symbolic world of universal reason, characteristic of bourgeois society. It is an idealist illusion, Karl Marx held, to suppose that Enlightenment alone could achieve significant changes in people's lives. For religion and mental life in general are largely reflections of people's actual social and institutional realities. Hence, consciousness is changed not so much by new arguments as by transforming the social institutions in which we live. Feuerbach's atheism was not good enough. It was based on the idealistic illusion that intelligence alone can change the human reality, the illusion that Marx regarded as the ideology of the new ruling class. Atheism, for Marx, was acceptable only if it included a sociological analysis of the contradictions in society that made people create religious illusions. Atheism is acceptable only if it leads to a radical transformation of the social order: "The secular base (of religion) must be understood in its contradictions and revolutionized in practice."[8]

For Karl Marx, then, religion is the product of social alienation. The discrepancies in the social institutions inflict burdens on people, diminish their humanity, distort their self-understanding as human beings, and eventually create false consciousness in them. What takes place is a distortion of awareness, according to which the present social order becomes the measure of reality. People then generate ideals that protect this falsification of perception. First among these ideals is religion. Religion persuades people that the present ordering of society is the acceptable order, and it directs their yearning for happiness away from the human to the divine world. Religion becomes, therefore, the heavenly image of the society to which people belong, but it is an inverted image since society constitutes itself by domination and injustice and hence inverts the truly human values. "This state and this society," writes Marx, "produce religion which is an inverted world consciousness, because they are an inverted world."[9] Religion is thus the measure of society's social ills. Religion is the product of alienation and, once produced, protects and fosters this very alienation.

Humankind's self-alienation was a central topic for the young Marx. He analyzed it from various viewpoints, and to this day scholars are not in agreement on how to combine the various lines of thought into a single theory. Added to this is the difficulty that the mature Marx no longer used the word "alienation." It is not clear whether his later analysis of the contradictions in the social and economic institutions deals with the same dehumanizing effects that he had previously discussed under the title of alienation. It is not our purpose to enter into this discussion. In this context we are interested in Marx's analysis of labour as the source of humankind's multiple self-alienation.

In the "Economic and Philosophical Manuscripts,"[10] the young Marx analyzed the dehumanizing effect of modern industrial society – that is, of labour in the factory, of external labour as opposed to creative work. His perceptive treatment of human alienation often anticipates, in a few insightful paragraphs, later sociological and anthropological theories dealing with the alienating effects of modern life. The anticipatory value of these early manuscripts recalls the anticipatory power of Hegel's early theological writings on religion and alienation. While Marx analyzes alienation from the bottom up, and Hegel, in his early writings, mainly from the top down, both of them are quite ready to acknowledge the dialectical relationship between mind and society. For this reason, there is no need to read one author as invalidating the other. It may very well be true that religion – bad religion, to use Hegel's term – is both the product and the source of alienation.

Marx begins his analysis with the denunciation of the factory system of his day. He regards the industrial mode of production, operated for the sake of profit, as the source of a specific alienation that affects first of all the workers and is eventually communicated to the whole of society. In the factory system, men, destined by nature to creative work, are convicted to dehumanizing labour, the nature of which Marx carefully analyzes. At the same time, the exploitation of the workers is the source of wealth for the owners of industry. Marx insists in his early writings that it is not private property that produces labour and its dehumanizing conditions; alienating labour produces private property. The rightful gain of which the workers are deprived constitutes the wealth of the owning class. Property is defined by the young Marx as alienated labour. "Capital is not only accumulated labor. Capital is power of command over labor and its products. Capital is stored-up labor."[11] Private property, we note, does not refer to the possessions people have or should have to protect their independence and enjoy themselves. This positive nature of property is affirmed in Marx's early writings. But private property understood in its negative sense is the product of labour imposed on men and women in the factory. This labour does not enhance the lives of those engaged in it, yet it produces power and wealth for those who own the means of production. Marx's critique of labour, then, applies to all industrial forms of production, operated for the profit of the owners, be they private persons, large corporations or even the state itself. It thus also applies to the state capitalism adopted in communist countries. It is no wonder that Marx's early writings, so important for the New Left, were not appreciated in the communist world.

In his early writings, Marx's analysis of alienated labour remains very close to the actual experience of workers. What he offers us is a perceptive anthropological study of how the human person is transformed by being a worker in a factory. Marx here anticipates the critical thought of subsequent social thinkers. Marx has the profound conviction that alienation is not natural to human life, that it is imposed by the institutions in which people live, and that human life is destined to be free and express itself in creative activity. Marx reasons here from an anthropological a priori that is ultimately, so it would seem, theological.

Marx's analysis on the alienation produced by labour includes the threefold alienation from nature, from personal life and from human fellowship. Marx must have been aware that his analysis of humankind's productive life recalls the young Hegel's analysis of alienating religion. Marx specifically compares money to a powerful divinity operative in life, omnipotent, capable of transforming enemies into friends and reversing people's judgment on the significant issues of life. "The power to confuse and invert all human and natural qualities, to bring about fraternization of incompatibles, the divine power of money, resides in its character as the alienated and self-alienating communal life of man."[12]

Labour inflicted on people in the factory alienates them from nature. Their own body becomes a stranger to them. They become unable to experience their body as medium of participation in culture and enjoyment; the body becomes for them purely and simply an instrument for work. The mental life of the worker is wholly oriented towards moving his body in accordance with the strenuous pattern set by his mechanized tools. The labour devours his energies. The exhausting activity, regular and unrelenting, deadens his imagination and obscures his intelligence. Eventually his body itself comes to resemble a mechanical instrument. The perfect worker is the one who repeats the same motions, at the same intervals and at the same speed, adapted to the rhythm of the machine. By avoiding useless gestures and free-floating thoughts, the worker becomes one with the machine he operates. The perfect worker shaped by the industrial system is the one who resembles the machine. "The more value he creates the more worthless the worker becomes; the more refined his product the more crude and misshapen the worker; the more civilized the product the more barbarous the worker.... The more the work manifests intelligence the more the worker declines in intelligence and becomes a slave of nature."[13]

The worker finds it impossible to be at home in his place of work. Work for him is not in any sense a fulfillment of his desires; he works because he wants to survive. "The alien character of work is clearly shown by the fact that as soon as there is no physical or other compulsion it is avoided like the plague," says Marx.[14] Yet so destroyed is the worker's capacity for enjoyment and his freedom of imagination that he is unable to feel at home in life even when he returns from the factory. The worker feels himself freely acting only in the basic functions of eating, drinking and sexual intercourse, but since these activities are genuinely human and sources of joy only in the context of a fully human life, they only intensify his alienation from nature. The natural activities that are meant to express human happiness easily deteriorate into frantic animal functions. The worker has been made a stranger to his body and to the natural environment in which he lives.

In a deeper sense, industrial labour alienates the worker from himself because the product of his hands is removed from him and made the source of wealth and power for the lords of labour. Marx contrasts the creative work of the craftsman, who builds pieces of furniture, with the labour of the industrial worker, whose work is largely mechanical and repetitive and who never sees the product of his hands. The worker has no claim on his own work. What he produces in no way belongs to him. It is shipped away as commodity and enriches the masters of industry.

The worker sacrifices his body and his vitality in the factory; he gives the best he has, yet all of his human energy is stolen from him. When he goes home at night, his forces are gone. He has objectified himself, but the objects have been removed from him. This situation differs from that of the tired craftsman who in the evening looks at the objects he has made. Factory work for the profit of another is alienating; it is, in Marx's terminology, "external work." The work is external to the worker because it does not flow from his own creativity and because it does not humanize the environment to which he belongs. External work or forced labour estranges the worker from his deepest self.

Marx's analysis, based on the inhuman conditions of industrial production in the nineteenth century, is in many ways still applicable to the conditions of work in the 20th century. For even if factory work has been lightened through a complex labour-saving technology, the great amount of work that is being done in industry and administration is still external labour, is still the source of personal frustration, a waste of human talent, and avoided like the plague except under pressure. The work of most people in modern society still contributes to the building up of wealth and power to which they have no access. Marx's analysis of the alienation due to external work has an abiding validity. Does work by the sweat of one's brow belong to our natural condition on this earth? The biblical story did not think so; it regarded such work as a curse and a punishment. Nor did Karl Marx. Marx based his critique of society on a humanistic understanding of humankind's social existence and on the conviction that human fulfillment and happiness were in fact the destiny of humankind. Again it is hard to overlook the implicit theological a priori.

As the alienation of labour proceeds, according to the Marxian analysis, labourers lose their personhood altogether; they become like the things they make, a commodity. They become part of the factory system, including the raw materials, the products, the machinery. Management looks upon the workers as numbered items in the industrial process; they are evaluated in terms of costs and production. According to Marx, the workers themselves eventually lose their sense of being persons. They accept themselves as being a thing, a priced object, a piece of equipment to be manipulated, a number in a ledger. Since the workers themselves are bought and sold, they come to regard as objects their fellow workers who labour with or compete with them, but who have ceased to be persons in their own right. The workers have become alienated from their fellow human beings. Their relationship to others is determined by their place in the industrial process. Alienating labour thus reifies the workers' relationship to others. What takes place is the breakdown of friendship, of community, of common dreams and values. The workers find them- selves in a universe of manipulation that destroys the common human fabric, out of which personal life is created. While they work, sweat and suffer together, the workers are strangers to one another. Forced labour has removed them from their common humanity.

At this point, Marx expands his analysis of alienation from the class of workers to the owners of industry. Their wealth, their form of life, is derived from the exploitation of the working class. Relying on Hegel's famous analysis of the master–slave relationship in his *Phenomenology of the Spirit*, Marx shows that the slavery of the slave is inevitably communi- cated to the master. By having power over the slave, the master becomes slave himself. For by defining himself as master, and not just as person, the master links his self-understanding and his lifestyle to the slave; he makes himself dependent on the slave; he cannot affirm his life without the slave and thus he falls into the very bondage that he imposed on the slave. Slavery enslaves the slave as well as the slave-holder. Thus, for Marx, the labour that turns the workers into objects ruled by the laws of industry also affects the lords of industry, for they too define their lives in terms of objects, production, merchandise and economic competition. Members of the owning class also reify their personal relationships; they become slaves to their routine, they are devoured by their acquisitive preoccupations, they are estranged from their own depth and from their fellow men. Their lives are determined by profit. The masters of labour eventually come to share in the alienation that labour inflicts on the worker.

For Marx, the symbol of the total reification of human life is money. This quantification of life begins with factory labour and culminates in a society wholly dominated by the quest for money. All values and all dreams are assigned a price. Money becomes the visible sign and seal of the manifold alienation due to labour: "Money, since it has the property of purchasing everything, of appropriating objects to itself, is, therefore, the object par excellence. The universal character of this property corresponds to the omnipotence of money, which is regarded as an omnipotent being. . . . Money is the pander between need and object, between human life and the means of subsistence. But that which mediates my life mediates also the existence of other men for me. It is for me the other person."[15]

Money, as object par excellence, transforms everything into itself. Since money assures my life, my independence, my power in the world,

I tend to equate self-affirmation with the money I own. In my relationship to others I realize that they too have a price and that they can be
manipulated like objects. Money can overcome division and strife, make
ugliness attractive, and draw us to those whom we consider repulsive.
We ourselves and those with whom we associate are equally subjected
to the supreme value of money, which sums up in itself all the power
and virtue in this world. Money is the omnipotent ground and source of
human existence, bringing forth a multitude of beings and transforming
all things into itself. "Since money, as the existing and active concept of
value, confounds and exchanges everything, it is the universal confusion
and transposition of all things, the inverted world, the confusion and
transposition of all natural and human qualities."[16] Money as stored-up,
depersonalized, alienated labour is the agent of universal alienation. It is
the divinity of modern society.

Marx has described for us a threefold alienation of humankind due
to labour: the alienation from nature, from oneself and from human fellowship. He wants to persuade us that as this alienation becomes deeper,
it is felt less. The first alienation induced by labour is painful. The body
hurts. The labourers know that their bodily condition frustrates their
powers, their inclination, their very nature. The second level of alienation
removes them so much from the core of their personal existence that they
may become quite numb and unresponsive to the oppression inflicted on
them. Their imagination now fails to formulate for them the conditions
of their misery. At the final stage, when the workers – and with them the
owning class – have become objects in the process of production, the
alienation creates in them a false consciousness, in which life appears no
longer as it is but inverted, ruled by the omnipotence of money. At this
point, people may no longer be aware of their alienation. The truly alienated may be quite cheerful. Those whose consciousness has been totally
falsified will not experience their life as painful, will not feel that their life
ought to be different; on the contrary, they will accept the present conditions of existence as the measure of what life is meant to be. Precisely
because workers bear their pain in their body, they are less likely to be as
alienated as the bourgeois who are physically comfortable. Middle-class
people are vulnerable to false but cheerful consciousness as workers
are not. The beginning stage of alienation is painful, and for this reason
enables people to discover the extent of their enslavement and possibly
even to organize political forces to transform the conditions of life. In
other words, the early stage of alienation has a positive role to play in the

evolution of society. The complete alienation of the comfortable classes, made happy by money and security, blinds them to the truth and plays no positive role in the humanization of society.

Marx brings out an aspect of alienation that has influenced the thought of subsequent sociologists and psychologists, but has often been neglected by the more popular understanding of alienation. For Marx, alienation, or at least certain forms of it, is an ambiguous phenomenon. Alienation is not all bad. For while alienation expresses the loss of man's humanity and as such has negative effects on people's lives, it may at the same time have some positive effects. As alienation excludes people from life, damages their powers and pushes them to the margins of society, it is capable of making them more aware of the injustices of society. Alienation prevents people from being totally identified with their society; they are thus able to transcend the given social order and overcome the false consciousness the society induces in its members. Prophecy is possible only among the alienated. To be estranged, to be marginalized, to be deeply hurt by the system offers the possibility of analyzing more correctly the discrepancies and inequities of the social order.[17] For this reason, Marx held that the workers whose alienation was physically painful are able to come to true consciousness, while the comfortable classes whose false consciousness is more total, and who are situated at the centre of society, are caught in their blindness, unless they are willing to identify themselves with the working class and take upon themselves the pain of the deprived.

Despite his sympathy for Marxist thought, the Protestant theologian Paul Tillich observed in his major study of socialism that Marx's understanding of the working class was self-contradictory.[18] Workers, for Marx, were the class most alienated from their humanity and at the same time the most insightful class with the potential of overcoming the contradictions of society. Tillich's point is that Marx did not understand the rootedness of human beings in a religious culture, and thus failed to recognize that the emancipatory struggle of working people was sustained by their commitment to justice and the protection of their community, values inherited from their religious culture.

We have mentioned several times that Marx regarded religion as the product of the alienation inflicted on human life by the contradictions of the social order. We have analyzed in some detail the alienation due to the external labour imposed on humankind. Marx thought that people who are unable to find themselves and their happiness in the world tend to create another world for themselves in which their true destiny appears. Religion is, therefore, humankind's self-awareness so long as we have not found ourselves. Religion is the measure of our earthly misery. The alienation present in the social order produces religion as an inverted world consciousness, inverted because it is based on an inverted world. Religion tells the story of our injustices to each other, but tells it in such a way that it legitimates the present order and creates a hope for justice that remains forever illusory. "Religion is the general theory of the world, its encyclopedic compendium, its logic in popular form . . . its enthusiasm, its moral sanction . . . its general basis of consolation and justification. It is the fantastic realization of the human being inasmuch as the human being possesses no true reality."[19] Religion is, therefore, always false consciousness, reflecting and protecting the injustices of the present social order. For Marx, religion was the supreme legitimation of the structures of domination in human society.

How can the alienation inflicted upon people by external work be overcome? How can people free themselves from the multiple alienation despite its religious legitimation? The Marxian reply to this is clear: only through radical social change. It is not by new theories but by changing the social conditions of life that human consciousness is transformed. What kind of change did the young Marx advocate? He argued that the means of production should not be in the hands of the few; it should be collectively owned by the many. He advocated the democratization of economic and industrial life so that workers could participate in the ownership and the management of the industries. He envisaged that people's daily work would not produce wealth for the few or for the government but instead sustain the well-being of the whole community. If industries were no longer run in order to maximize production and increase the profit of the owner, and by this the state itself, but in order to provide goods and services necessary for the well-being of the community, then the style of work would express the workers' care for the people as a whole and assume a more humane character. This vision differed greatly from that of the later political Marxism that introduced the state-ownership of industries and did not allow workers to assume responsibility for the organization of labour.

Marx's idea of ideology has made a lasting contribution to the sociology of knowledge. Ideology in the Marxian vocabulary does not refer to a *Weltanschauung,* a system of ideas that offers a total world interpretation. Ideology for him is always something false. He defines it as a distortion of the truth for the sake of social interest, a symbolic framework of the mind that legitimates the power and privileges of the dominant groups and sanctions the social evils inflicted on the people without access to power. According to Marx, every community of people generates, in a largely unconscious process, a set of symbols that protects its position of power, affirms its identity over against its competitors, and makes it easier for the government to rule. For Marx, as we noted, religion is always ideological: it legitimates the existing order despite its injustices and consoles the victims with promises of future happiness. Culture and philosophy are also largely ideological in character. The dominating ideas, Marx argued, are the ideas of the dominating class.

Since Marx's day, the concept of ideology has been detached from the specifically Marxist presuppositions and become a central category of sociological analysis. While Marx restricted the source of alienation to the order of industrial production, and hence understood ideology as a hidden defence of actual economic power relations, sociologists have become aware of ideological trends in culture and religion that legitimate other forms of power and sanction forms of social evil not derived from the economic order. Secondly, while Marx held that the oppressed class alone was free of ideology, and that true consciousness was available only to the workers who had become aware of their exploitation (and to those members of the middle class who were in solidarity with the workers), later sociologists regarded the formation of ideologies as a universal phenomenon and hence applicable to all groups, including the economically exploited. Ideology, in this modified Marxian sense, has become an important concept in the sociology of knowledge. It is generally recognized today that all manifestations of culture and religion contain ideological trends – trends that protect the interests of society or groups within society.

This modified concept of ideology has been adopted by Christian theologians in their effort to gain a critical understanding of their religious tradition. It is the task of critical theology to discover in the proclamation and explication of Christian doctrine the ideological trends that distort the truth of revelation for the sake of legitimating the dominant social and economic values and assuring the triumph of the Church and the power of the ecclesiastical government.

A startling example of ideological deformation in the history of Christian doctrine, an example in no way derived from economic pressures but from purely ecclesiastical interests, is the persistent anti-Jewish bias present in Christian teaching almost from the beginning. We shall deal with this ideology in greater detail further on.[20] Because of the Church's conflict with the synagogue and because of the Church's need continually to justify its messianic reading of the Scriptures, Christian preachers and teachers accompanied the proclamation of the Gospel with a refutation of Jewish religion and the negation of Jewish existence before God. The Church regarded itself as the true Israel, the chosen people of God, that had replaced the original, the unfaithful Israel. Christian writers tried to persuade their readers that the people of Israel had never understood the prophetic message, not even in the days of the prophets; that they had never known God, that they had always lived in blindness and infidelity; and that by refusing to believe in the Gospel they had doubly excluded themselves from salvation. Within this ideological framework, the Jews eventually came to symbolize the enemies of God and all that is unredeemed and inhuman in the world. This monstrous ideology, closely associated with Christian preaching, communicated an anti-Semitic bias to the whole of Western culture. While Nazi anti-Semitism did not have religious roots and hence is not the product of Christianity, it did prolong the Church's ancient symbolism. By linking Nazi propaganda to the ancient anti-Jewish tradition, Hitler was able to make the Jews the scapegoat for the troubles of his country and rally a good deal of Christian support for his cause, at least in his early years of political power. Only since the extermination of European Jewry have Christian theologians been willing to submit the Christian tradition to an ideological critique, discover in it the many-levelled anti-Jewish themes, and try to formulate the Christian message freed from distortions and false negations. It is the task of theology, as we shall see later on, to liberate the Church's life from the various ideologies that distort the Christian message.

Karl Marx, as noted above, restricted his understanding of ideology to the legitimation of political and economic power so that he remained quite unaware of other ideological trends. In particular, he never confronted the anti-Jewish ideology present in Christian tradition and Western culture. Even though he came from a family of Jewish origin and knew of the hundred ways in which society excluded Jews from participation, he refused to analyze this form of injustice. When he was asked to defend the emancipation of the Jews in Germany against the arguments of Bruno Bauer, Marx wrote two papers, published under the title "On the Jewish Question,"[21] in which he supported the political emancipation of the Jews and at the same time advocated their human emancipation by demanding that they give up their religion and their identity. Since Marx interpreted the plight of the Jews in purely economic terms and assimilated their liberation to the universal emancipation from capitalism, he was unable to confront the anti-Semitic ideology that pervaded his environment and deal with his own prejudices acquired from his identification with the dominant society. In the second part of "On the Jewish Question," Marx drew a picture of "the Jews" according to the hostile stereotypes of his day.[22] Since Marx believed that humans were basically defined by their location in the economic system, he overlooked the religious, cultural and national factors that determine people's identity: a failure – as we mentioned above – explored by Paul Tillich.

One has to admit that after the French Revolution, the European churches strongly supported the aristocratic socio-political order and served as the sacred guarantors of the *ancien régime*. This is the religion that Karl Marx encountered. He never made a careful study of the history of religion. He never asked himself whether religion had always and everywhere exercised the same legitimating function. It was the German sociologist Max Weber, as we shall see in Chapter 7, who demonstrated that while the successful religions tended to offer an ideological defence of the existing order, they also produced religious currents that were a source of social criticism, offered a new vision of the future and supported the transformation of culture and society. Max Weber demonstrated that religion is not always a dependent variable, but often acts as an independent force. Religion is never purely and simply the reflection of society; it also contains within its traditions critical and creative elements. In a set of important essays,[23] Max Weber demonstrated that even in the same religion and the same period of history, religious commitment has different political meanings, depending in part on the social class of the believers. That is why it is impossible to make quick generalizations about the social function of religion. In each case, a careful study is required. Marx failed to do this.

There is, however, a beautiful passage in one of Marx's early essays that recognizes something operative in the religion of the oppressed classes that goes beyond ideology. "Religious suffering," Marx writes, "is at the same time an expression of real suffering and a protest against real suffering. Religion is the sigh of the oppressed creature, the heart of a heartless world, and the soul of soulless conditions."[24] Then follow the oft-repeated words that do not live up to the description of religion that preceded them: "Religion is the opium of the people." Opium is the expression of real suffering; it is a consolation sought because of frustrations imposed by the social order. But opium is not a protest against suffering. Opium may be the sigh of the oppressed creature, but it is not the heart and soul that intuit, in the midst of an unjust and exploitative world, what human life is meant to be like. Marx admitted that in religion is preserved the conviction that human life is meant to be different from its actual oppressed condition. Man's destiny is to be fulfilled in happy community.

Marx himself was gripped by a profound faith in the destiny of humankind. This was the source of his social passion. The analysis in his early writings of humankind's self-alienation was inspired by this humanistic vision of the future. The preceding pages have shown that his analysis transcended the conditions of politics and economic life; it had a more universal human meaning, based on the anthropological distinction between external labour and creative work and on the implicitly theological conviction that humanity is destined to be free.

In our first two chapters, we have chosen sections from the work of the young Hegel and the young Marx to study the relation of religion and alienation. Each author has made us sensitive to opposing viewpoints; each author has anticipated future developments in social science. While Hegel concentrated on religion as the cause of alienation, and Marx on religion as the product of alienation, there is no need to read the two thinkers in an antithetical way. Both authors readily acknowledge the dialectical character of human history, where mind and society interact in a complex manner not reducible to a simple cause-and-effect chain. We also note that neither the young Hegel nor the young Marx regarded alienation as an anthropological necessity. For them, human life in society was not necessarily alienating; alienation was always the product of disabling factors, and it was humankind's destiny to free itself from these oppressive forces. This view differs from the position taken by some 20th-century thinkers that human life, in virtue of its social character, is inevitably alienating. We find this position in existentialist philosophers and in social thinkers as far apart as Sigmund Freud and Peter Berger.[25]

In this chapter we have taken exception to the reductionism of the young Marx – that is, to the reduction of human consciousness to its political and economic base and the consequent neglect of cultural and symbolic factors in the constitution of human history. Yet we saw that even Marx alluded to the prophetic or critical role of religion. Religion, we conclude, is always and inevitably an ambiguous phenomenon. Since the time of Hegel and Marx, this point has been amply demonstrated by sociologists. There are many trends and layers in one and the same religion. It may be possible for the student of religion to discern alienating trends in religion (trends producing alienation-from-above) that interact with alienating social forces (producing alienation-from-below), but it is also possible to discern in religion – and this is what we hope to do in this book – creative, de-alienating currents that initiate men and women more deeply into their humanity and nourish the dream of a more humane social order.

3

Alienation in Industrial Society:
Ferdinand Toennies

At the end of the eighteenth century, a new world came into being. The movements associated with the Industrial Revolution and the French Revolution translated the rational ideals of the Enlightenment into social institutions. The application of science and technology to the processes of production created a complex factory system. With it emerged a new successful class, built on industry and commerce, and a new servant class of workers drawn into the urban centres from various parts of the country. The Industrial Revolution changed the conditions of life for large sections of the population. The owning classes desired to extend their enterprises and increase their power. They sought to improve the conditions of life in terms of comfort and efficiency, acquire an ever higher standard of living, maximize the role of science and technology in society, and expand the market at home and in distant lands. At the same time, the working class, unprotected by social legislation, entered a world of exploitation and powerlessness.

The democratic revolution, with its ideals of equality and freedom, made people realize that society itself was not a given, that it was man-made, that it could be subjected to criticism, reorganized and planned in accordance with the wishes of its citizens. All inherited institutions now became problematic. What emerged was the vision of a new society, rationally constructed, sustaining the personal well-being of the citizens and their growing expectations of life. This vision produced the hope that through science, technology and continued democratization, the citizens would gain control over the conditions of their lives, solve the problems that produce conflict and suffering, and initiate an earthly realm of freedom and happiness. The modern conversion to reason, it was believed, made historical progress inevitable.

Modernity regarded itself as the high point of world history, as the enlightened age, in comparison with which the preceding ages were undeveloped and had value only as preparation for the present. The successful classes, the bourgeoisie and the intellectuals associated with it, gave enthusiastic support to the liberal world in the making. Created at first in certain parts of Europe and North America, modern society eventually spread through the whole of Europe and North America and entered the other continents. While the optimism of early modernity has disappeared and the irrationalities of the system have become manifest, we still belong to this modern world; we still rely on the spread of industrialization, advocate the spirit of competition, praise the democratization of society, honour utilitarian values, and trust that science and technology will solve the problems of society.

The nineteenth century also produced thinkers who criticized modernity. We have mentioned Hegel and Marx, both of whom despised the individualism and the social conditions produced by the new society. A group of social philosophers, eventually known as "sociologists," recognized the dangerous and destructive trends present in modern society. In his book *The Sociological Tradition*,[26] Robert Nisbet has presented the ideas of these thinkers. He showed that by comparing and contrasting the new society with the preceding one, these thinkers created concepts for understanding the social reality. This comparative method generated sociology. The new social science was created by thinkers who observed the effects of the modern society on the people and examined how these effects differed from the human condition in the old order. The malaise with the new society prompted the sociologists to analyze the impact of institutions on human life and denounce the dehumanizing trends operative in the new urban centres. These critical thinkers created a countervailing current in the intellectual life of the nineteenth century. While the temper of the age rejoiced in the achievements of the scientific age and liberal society, the sociologists produced analyses that were critical of modernity and, for this reason, have retained their relevance to this day. They rejected the rationalistic understanding of human life and regarded as absurd the attempt to construct society on purely scientific principles. With Hegel and the Romantic reaction against the Enlightenment, the sociologists recognized that woven into the human community are values, symbols, dreams and expectations. These sustain society; without them, society would eventually disintegrate.

Auguste Comte, the French social philosopher who invented the term "sociology" and who is sometimes regarded, unjustifiably, as the father of sociology, was rather untypical for the subsequent sociological tradition. Writing in the first half of the nineteenth century, Comte, imbued with the spirit of rationalism, proposed the famous law of the three stages. According to this evolutionary principle, culture and society move away from religion and the non-rational aspects of human life to rational and demonstrable truths. He tried to show that this evolution passed through three phases:[27] "the religious age," when people accepted religious explanations of life's unsolved problems; "the philosophical age," when people sought purely rational and speculative explanations of life; and "the scientific age," when people had a scientific grasp of the laws operative in the world and sought to recreate society according to human needs. Comte called his theory of inevitable progress "positivism." He repudiated religion and philosophy as shadows belonging to a former period of history and trusted that science – empirical social science – would lead the modern world into freedom and true community.

While Comte fully embraced the scientific Enlightenment, as a sociologist he had an insight into the nature of society that contradicted his positivistic approach. He proposed the idea, subsequently influential in sociology, that society needed symbols to assure its cohesion and sustain its survival. The stability of society demands that people possess a symbolic language allowing them to celebrate their common values and dreams. Comte became convinced that the new social order, based on science, would have to deal with the non-rational factors of social life. He therefore created a new religion, the worship of future humanity, which expressed in symbolic form the destiny of society and provided inspiration for the social engagement of the citizens. Comte combined in a curious and contradictory way the rationalist approach of the Enlightenment, holding that religion would wane under the impact of modern science, and the sociological approach, critical of the Enlightenment, recognizing the indispensable role of the symbolic order.

Auguste Comte was not typical of the sociologists. Beginning with Alexis de Tocqueville, a contemporary of Auguste Comte, the French and German sociologists criticized the harmful effect on modern society exercised by rationalism, scientism, utilitarianism and individualism. These thinkers did not share the fashionable philosophies of progress. They recognized and measured the forces in the new society that impoverished human existence. While they used different terms, they offered remarkably similar comparisons between the old aristocratic order and the new liberal society emerging in parts of Europe and North America.

On his visit to the United States in the 1830s, Tocqueville observed what he called "the new individualism" created by the liberal, egalitarian society. While human selfishness was a vice that had always existed, the new individualism that separated people from their community and urged them to promote their own well-being was looked upon as a virtue.[28] Tocqueville feared that this new virtue would undermine the cohesiveness of the social order and destroy the authoritative traditions of the past. Even if their reasoning was different, the French and German sociologists were all disturbed by the demise of social solidarity. Karl Marx himself lamented that the free-enterprise society was undermining the traditional values, leaving only "the cash-value."[29]

The critical social thinkers, we said, offered very similar comparisons between the old order and the new society. They invented concepts that typified social life in the two different historical situations. What they sought were not detailed descriptions but useful models that would allow them to contrast the old order with the new society and gain insight into the effects of social institutions on human life. The models proposed by the German sociologist Ferdinand Toennies have become widely accepted, and are still used in sociological literature. Toennies called what was typical of the old order *Gemeinschaft* (community) and what was typical of the new order *Gesellschaft* (society). How did he define these two social models?

Toennies defined Gemeinschaft in terms taken from family life: it is natural, inherited and spontaneous. The bond of Gemeinschaft precedes deliberation and choice. One is born into the community and accepted by it as part of the order of nature. Gemeinschaft refers to a community where people live in reliance on one another, have a sense of belonging together and are keenly aware of their common bond. They experience their shared identity more strongly than their individuality. People here know themselves to be a community where each has a place of honour, where authority and inequality are taken for granted, and where each is deeply identified with the entire social order. Gemeinschaft existed in communities of feudal times that continued for centuries, where each family had its place and where the families together constituted a closely knit social body, even though they belonged to different levels of authority and prestige. Gemeinschaft is characterized by common values, a common vision and a common religion. Here people live out of a spiritual and intellectual tradition that they have inherited, hand on by their mutual interaction and protect by a common vigilance.

Toennies defines Gesellschaft in terms derived from free associations. Here the individual precedes the group. Here persons, after deliberation and free choice, have decided to form a society, defined its function and purpose, and determined laws that regulate their interaction. Gesellschaft is not natural but artificial. It is a rational construction by people who regard themselves as equals. Here the members are aware of their own individuality and have only a weak sense of belonging together. They say "we" only in certain clearly defined circumstances. Here people pursue their own advantage, seek personal success and look upon their neighbours as competitors. What unites the citizens is not a thick social bond of shared values, but a thin legal bond determined by contract. The legal bond is experienced by people as a necessary burden and not as an integral dimension of personality.

Toennies's book *Gemeinschaft und Gesellschaft,* published in 1887, was subsequently translated into English as *Community and Society.*[30] In it he made a detailed analysis of what was typical in the two types of society – the traditional, close-knit old order and the liberal, contractual system – and then constructed a social psychology that would show the effect of these institutions on people's own self-understanding. Toennies was convinced that the Gesellschaft model illumined the nature of modern society. The industrialized urban centres drew crowds of people away from the social matrix of their origin, the village or the small town; they became uprooted, socially isolated, competing with one another, each promoting his own well-being. The bond that united people in this society was largely contractual. Severed from their cultural tradition, people became increasingly preoccupied with pragmatic purposes and the immediate tasks of daily life. While the new urban population strives for a more comfortable life, it suffers the loss of its cultural inheritance. Cut off from the social matrix, people become alienated from their own humanity.

Typifications of societies can be found in authors who preceded Toennies. Hegel himself foresaw the disappearance of what he called "the ethical society," in which people defined themselves in terms of their collective inheritance, and the emergence of an individualistic social order, in which people acquired a highly personal consciousness and where a person experienced himself over against society and possibly even over against himself. Toennies builds on his predecessors. In his book, which has become a classic, he created a socio-psychological typology that remains an arsenal for critics of modern society.

It is worth noting that the value-free style of Toennies's book did not reveal to the reader whether his critical analysis of liberal society was made from a conservative or a radical point of view. His description of the impoverishment of life produced by the industrial society in fact became a source for both conservative and radical critics. Some people read the book as if the author yearned for the old feudal order and wanted to persuade his contemporaries to resist the spread of modernity. Toennies's book has even been accused of providing the Nazi movement in the 1930s with good arguments for the regression into tribalism. It is fair to say that this ambiguity is found in a good deal of the early sociological literature, since it revealed the ill effects on human culture of individualism, rationalism, and the money- and profit-orientation of modern society. This is especially true of German social thought. From the end of the eighteenth century on, German thinkers produced intellectual reactions against the rationalistic Enlightenment that could be read as nostalgia for the past or the yearning for a more radical future. It is quite true that Toennies drew an idyllic picture of Gemeinschaft and fostered conservative sentiments in many of his readers; yet he was a socialist (not a Marxist) who hoped that from the seeds of Gemeinschaft that survived in modern society would emerge a new form of social life, fraternal, egalitarian and liberating.

At this point it is important to emphasize that Toennies's account of Gemeinschaft and Gesellschaft is not a historical description of existing societies. There are no social groups that are simply Gemeinschaft or others that are simply Gesellschaft. There are always some contractual elements in social groups typified as "communities" and some communal elements in social groups typified as "societies." What Toennies did – and here he followed the example of previous writers – was to construct social models that would bring out the essential nature of the old and the new society and guide the researcher in his empirical observations. Already, 50 years earlier, Alexis de Tocqueville had written that in his study of American society, he was looking for "the image" of America, the set of basic institutions and their cultural impact, so as to learn "what we have to fear or to hope from its progress."[31] Later, towards the end of the nineteenth century, Max Weber called these models "ideal types."[32] Ideal types are intellectual constructions produced by exaggerating the dominant characteristics of a social group. They are useful as guides for the observation and analysis of existing societies. By focusing on the dominant characteristics, they allow the sociologist to predict future social trends. Ideal types are heuristic devices. Thus Toennies had asked himself to what extent the industrialization of Germany transformed society into Gesellschaft and to what extent Gemeinschaft characteristics were able to survive. These are questions that continue to be asked by sociologists who study the entry of industrialization in traditional societies.

In his famous book, Ferdinand Toennies tried to show that to the two social forms of life correspond two distinct anthropological principles. The personal principle of life and action operative in people living in Gemeinschaft he called "natural will," and the corresponding principle of life and action of people living in Gesellschaft he called "rational will." In a detailed analysis stretching over several chapters, Toennies showed that the coming into being of people in traditional communities follows the organic model of nature. People grow. Their natural inclinations are extended by sharing in the common life. Participation in custom, in common memories and in religion creates in them feelings and inclinations that become second nature to them. The socially induced inclinations are grafted onto people's personal nature and give rise to spontaneous actions that are in harmony with their own personal nature as well as the well-being of the community. Personal inclination and common good move in the same direction.

By contrast, what is operative in the self-constitution of people in a society is rational will.

> The theory of Gesellschaft deals with the artificial construction of an aggregate of human beings which superficially resembles a Gemeinschaft insofar as the individuals live and dwell together peacefully. However, in the Gemeinschaft they remain essentially united in spite of all separating factors, whereas in the Gesellschaft they remain essentially separated in spite of all uniting factors. In the Gesellschaft, as contrasted with the Gemeinschaft, we find no actions that can be derived from an a priori and necessarily existing unity; no actions, therefore, which manifest the spirit and the will of the unity even if performed by the individual; no actions which, insofar as they are performed by individuals, take place on behalf of those united with him. In the Gesellschaft such actions do not exist. On the contrary, here everybody is by himself and isolated, and there exists a condition of tension against all nature.[33]

In Gesellschaft, the basic anthropological principle is rational will. Actions are not spontaneous; they are based on deliberation and discrimination. They are freely chosen and endorsed because they seem useful and important in regard to the elected end. Since action takes place subsequent to critical judgment, people look for an understanding of their historical reality that is reliable and readily available. They wish that the human situation be measurable. There is thus an inevitable cultural trend in Gesellschaft that translates quality into quantity and the manifold values handed on by tradition into measurable unities that can be easily evaluated and judged. While in Gemeinschaft the natural will was operative within the activity of people, in Gesellschaft the rational will precedes the action, keeps itself apart from action, and retains an ever critical distance. What emerges in Gesellschaft is a different type of human awareness. The "I" emerges out of the "we." More than that, the ego-consciousness separates itself from life and action; it is stripped of all feelings and spontaneous reactions and becomes an empty, critical thinking mind. The thinking that defines this personal identity, according to Toennies' analysis, is not contemplative reason, the reason that seeks to be in touch with the whole of reality, but purely pragmatic reason, the reason that imagines the outcome of the action taken and compares it with the end and purpose regarded as useful and important.

In Gesellschaft, the relationship between people becomes quantified. Trust and mutuality gradually disappear. What takes over in these relationships can be defined in terms of money, and what is precious in the life of society can be bought. "Every man becomes in some measure a merchant."[34] The market becomes the perfect image of contractual, liberal society. "In Gesellschaft every person strives for that which is to his own advantage, and he affirms the actions of others only insofar and as long as they can further his interest. Before and outside of convention, and also before and outside of each special contract, the relation of all to all may therefore be conceived as potential hostility or latent war."[35] This war of all against all is restrained by the market conventions and contractual arrangements and tamed into a system of general competition. Competition becomes a vague symbol of unity, but by an inevitable logic the contractual bond as signified by money is increasingly weakened by the hostility of all against all, and open war is never far below the surface.

Following the same principle, mastery and slavery will be determined in this system by those who possess the money: the industrialists and the merchants associated with them. Although Toennies was not a Marxist – he wrote at a time when Marxism had not yet acquired a unique place among socialists – he came to the conclusion that the modern, liberal society would, according to a logic built into its basic structure, eventually divide the population into two classes of masters and servants.[36] While Toennies did not advocate class conflict as a weapon, he agreed that the logic of Gesellschaft would eventually turn the state into an instrument protecting the masters in society and perpetuating the oppression of the slaves – those who have no access to power. In Gesellschaft it was ultimately domination that would constitute the unity of the people.

Toennies draws a parallel between the personal and the social. Just as in Gesellschaft a man's personal life is brought under the domination of a separated, critical ego incapable of embracing personal life and arriving at decisions that spring from life itself, so will society eventually be ruled by a separated power, foreign to the innate forces of social life, imposing decisions that did not emerge from the common life but were derived from interests inevitably at odds with the life of the whole. What Toennies describes in his famous book is the gradual alienation of man, inflicted on him by modern, capitalist society, an alienation from his own depth, from his feelings, his nature, his spontaneity, his truly human pains and joys as well as his alienation from his brothers and from the community.

What, according to Toennies, is the effect of Gesellschaft on religion? For the German thinker, religion is the celebration of the common values and sacred laws that constitute the community. Religion, he writes, "even in the state of highest development, retains its hold and influence over the mind, heart and conscience of men by hallowing the events of family life: marriage, birth, veneration of elders, death. And in the same way religion hallows the commonwealth, increases and strengthens the authority of the laws."[37] Many years prior to Émile Durkheim's work, Toennies came to the conclusion that "the religious realm especially represents the original unity and equality of a whole people, the people as one family which by common ceremonies and places of worship keeps up the memory of its kinship."[38]

What, then, was the effect of Gesellschaft on religion? Toennies tried to show that the separating or alienating factors operative in modern, contractual society destroy the common bond that holds people together and therefore inevitably undermine religion. In Gesellschaft, the minds of people are united simply by public opinion, by norms and rules that emerge from science and common sense and from reflections that intend to improve the conditions of life. Yet the logic operative in Gesellschaft, which transforms the contractual society into a group defined by general competition and a thinly disguised state of war, also transforms public opinion as the embodiment of rational intelligence into a set of rules and conventions that protect the market, private property, and the power of those in charge of industry and commerce. Public opinion, in Toennies' analysis, now remains perpetually external to people. It cannot become part of them as religion had been in the Gemeinschaft. Public opinion promotes alienation. It separates people from their life energies, from the bonds of friendship and love, from the values inherited from Gemeinschaft, and it undermines the sway of religion in their hearts.

To avoid misunderstanding, it is good to recall at this point that these reflections on Gemeinschaft and Gesellschaft are not descriptions of existing societies; they deal with ideal types. Thus, while Toennies showed that Gesellschaft tends to eliminate religion and replace it with public opinion, he admitted at the same time, in a language that anticipates the work of Durkheim a decade later, that even in modern contractual societies "all regulations and norms ... retain a certain semblance to the commands of religion, for, like those, they originate from the mental ... expression of the spirit of the totality."[39] In particular, Toennies noted that "the 'binding force' of contracts does not detach itself easily from trust and faithfulness in the consciousness of men." This phenomenon was also observed by Durkheim: from it, the French sociologist came to the conclusion that even modern, individualistic society remains grounded in a set of shared values.[40] Toennies did not go quite that far. Yet Toennies admitted that certain elements of Gemeinschaft remain operative in societies dominated by Gesellschaft trends, and he regarded these seeds as a source of inspiration for the creation of a more humane society. The ongoing transformation into Gesellschaft, he wrote, "means the doom of culture itself if none of its scattered seeds remain alive and again bring forth the essence and the idea of Gemeinschaft, thus secretly fostering a new culture amidst the decaying one."[41] Toennies believed that the traditional religions were unable to overcome the alienating forces of modern society and hence were unlikely to survive, yet he never discussed future developments created by the religious seeds. Like many sociologists after him, he had little trust in the innovative power of religion.

Toennies, it should be added, also saw a positive side in the Gesellschaft trend. He argued that man's alienation from his humanity, induced by modern institutions, was not without some positive aspects. We saw that for Toennies the two types of societies produced different states of human interiority and self-awareness. Thus the inwardness of people living in Gemeinschaft is "conscience": here people are profoundly identified with a tradition and its values, share a common perspective and, rooted in a common life, are able to distinguish between good and evil and engage in selfless action serving the community. By contrast, the inwardness of people living in Gesellschaft is "consciousness": here the thinking self, separated from others and from its own vital functions, experiences itself as standing over against the world, other people and even its own bodily presence, and is capable of submitting all of these to a critique. Toennies writes: "Consciousness is the freedom of the rational will in its highest expression."[42] "Consciousness implies self-criticism, and this self-criticism turns as much against one's own practical blunders as conscience against one's imagined wickedness. Self-criticism is the highest or most intellectual form of rational will, conscience the highest or most intellectual form of natural will."[43] What Toennies describes as the uniquely modern consciousness, namely man's self-definition as a thinking self over against the rest of reality, is the consciousness already anticipated by Descartes in his cogito-argument and analyzed by Hegel in its relationship to modern rational institutions. Toennies did not deny the achievement of this typically modern consciousness, which is able to bend back over itself and make its own life and development the object of its reflection. Toennies' own sociological work, his self-critical analysis of the culture to which he belonged, was after all a product of this very consciousness, and he had no intention of abandoning it. What he wanted to show, however, was that this new consciousness had been acquired at a great price. A certain alienation from the sources of life was the condition for the rise of man's critical self-awareness. A degree of alienation, then, has positive meaning. While it separates people from their vital and cultural inheritance, it also enables them to see more clearly what goes on in the world and in themselves. This faculty of self-criticism Toennies had no intention of giving up.

We have treated Toennies's thought at some length because his theory of alienation was adopted by many sociologists, especially in Germany. Toennies did not in fact use the word "alienation" – he preferred to speak of man's "separation" from his own depth and his fellow human being. Nor did Toennies use the word "secularization," even though his analysis of the inevitable waning of religion in a Gesellschaft-type society constitutes a theory of secularization that was to become common among European sociologists. Max Weber, while making Toennies's analysis of society more nuanced, essentially followed him in his evaluation of the modern world. For Weber, the critical, rational trend, expressed in varying degrees in the institutions of modern life, leads to a growing "rationalization" of culture and to a consequent "disenchantment of the world."[44]

Max Weber's analysis, we note, concentrated on the effects of the growing bureaucracy.[45] He showed that the modern search for more co-ordinated, efficient and controlled social processes tends to expand the bureaucracies, create new hierarchies, demand ever larger numbers of staff members, multiply the rules and legal requirements, and create more careful division of competences and the corresponding delineation of powers. Weber thought that the drift towards rational authority, observable in industrial society, would lead to the extension of bureaucracy to all areas of social and political life: it would create institutions in which very few independent decisions are made, except at the very top, where all transactions were carried out according to written instructions, and where the employed staff members had hardly any personal contact with one another or with their clients. The reform movements in society, which seek to submit the life of society to more rational standards, would inevitably increase the extension and weight of bureaucracy and hence create organizational patterns more rigid and depersonalizing than the preceding ones. Weber's study of bureaucracy over a wide variety of cultures convinced him that the instrumental rationality that dominates the industrialized world would transform the whole of life into "an iron cage";[46] human life would become dreary, flat and unimaginative, with no room for passion, prophecy or religion. No inspiration, Weber feared, would survive in modern society. He anticipated much of what Herbert Marcuse was to say 50 years later regarding the "one-dimensional man."[47] Even though Toennies was an atheist and Weber an agnostic claiming to be religiously unmusical, both sociologists interpreted the waning of religion as a sign of the decline of culture.

We note that Toennies's and Weber's theory of secularization was quite different from the theories of Comte and Marx. Comte, we recall, held that the truth of science would deliver society from the primitive explanations of religion and philosophy. Comte rejoiced in the power of scientific reason and trusted that it would produce the humanization of society. He looked forward to the disappearance of religion. Both Comte and Toennies saw an inner contradiction between religion and modernity, yet Comte regarded the advent of the scientific age as the fulfillment of humanity's ancient hopes while Toennies feared that the spirit of modernity would estrange people from their happiness and destroy their inherited culture.

Both thinkers expected the decline of religion, but they interpreted the meaning of this decline in opposite ways.

Marx's analysis of the modern world resembles Toennies's in many ways. Both thinkers were critical of liberal society; both described the alienating and oppressive effects of individualism, competition, the profit system and the market economy; both foresaw class conflict; both interpreted civil or bourgeois society as a system of domination. Yet on a more basic issue, Marx and Toennies were far apart. Marx looked upon history as internally oriented towards human liberation – in this he resembled Comte – while Toennies wanted to be a value-free sociologist who studied the development of societies without invoking any overall purposes and trends in world history. Marx, moreover, believed that his analysis of modern society produced scientific concepts that enabled him to render an account of the existing society and discover the laws according to which this society would develop in the future; Toennies, by contrast, presented his social analysis not in scientific concepts but in reliance of ideal types, thus arriving at much more scientific conclusions. Toennies may well have agreed with Marx's multiple analysis of alienation, yet in his own analysis Toennies did not restrict his attention to the economic factor but took into account also factors of institutional and symbolic life. While he held with Marx that institutions create consciousness, he did not use this insight to reduce the independent role of cultural factors. For Toennies, human history was an open development without a defined future; at the same time, not sharing Marx's evolutionary faith, he was afraid that society was imprisoned in the present. Finally, Toennies repudiated the class struggle as a strategy of reform: he argued that the class struggle was ultimately based on Gesellschaft principles and hence would generate a mindset not of brotherhood but of domination. Toennies was a communitarian socialist who hoped that out of the return to small communities and other forms of shared life a more human society would be created.

As far as religion is concerned, Toennies does not follow Marx at all. While he recognized that religion exercised a legitimating role in society, he never reduced it to ideology in the Marxian sense. As we saw above, Toennies anticipated Durkheim: he saw religion as the symbolic celebration of society's ideals and common values, and even though, as an atheist, he did not accept its ontological reality, he still regrets the waning of religion as a sign of increasing alienation and the breakdown of culture. While Marx's spiritual anguish was the exploitation of the working class, which he made the starting point of his reflections, Toennies's anguished preoccupation was the decline of culture and the alienation of human life, on all levels of society, from its vital resources.

In the judgment of Toennies and the German sociologists after him, modern industrial society leads inevitably to the secularization of life. This view was also shared by many sociologists in England and North America who otherwise did not follow the peculiarly German intellectual trend that regarded technology, capitalism and utilitarian democracy as a system leading to cultural decline and the loss of human values. We shall discuss the theories of secularization in a subsequent chapter. At this time, I propose a few observations to place into historical perspective the pessimistic view of modern, liberal society found in Hegel, Marx, Toennies and Weber. This consistent negation of modernity is characteristically German. What are the reasons for this?

There was, first of all, the German reaction to the French Enlightenment, constituting a cultural and intellectual movement at the beginning of the nineteenth century that was curiously linked with the national struggle for liberation from the Napoleonic conquest. The German lands were more traditional than Western Europe; they were less industrialized; they were divided into small dukedoms and principalities, still firmly set in the aristocratic age, with the hereditary strata of peasants, craftsmen, small merchants, the clergy, the princes and, working for them, the bureaucrats in their chanceries and the professors and students at various universities. Apart from a few cities, there was no strong bourgeoisie in Germany. There was no social base for liberalism. The new ideas coming from France undermined the German tradition; they appeared foreign to Germans of all estates. The Germans did not believe in reason unless feeling was taken seriously as well; they did not believe in the individual unless he or she was understood as embedded in a living tradition and community; they did not accept that all people were equal unless room was left for the recognition of particular traditions and cultural pluralism; they did not believe that collectivities were constructed out of isolated individuals, but strongly held that groups of people were organic unities, alive by a common spirit, having a history of their own and a destiny to which to respond. In a famous article, "Conservative Thought,"[48] Karl Mannheim showed how this conservative response of the German people to the rationalist Enlightenment and its creative expression in the writings of their thinkers produced a new mindset or consciousness with a dynamic understanding of history, of reason and of human community, an understanding that generated a critical intellectual movement of its own, sometimes called the German Enlightenment. Hegel and Marx belonged to this movement, but so, generations later, did Nietzsche and Freud. Conservative and radical thinkers agreed in their critical evaluation of modern liberal society. It is within this trend that the German sociologists were situated.

German intellectual life at the end of the nineteenth and the beginning of the 20th century was a vigorous, creative movement of scholars, in line with the German Enlightenment. They strongly reacted against the scientific positivism that had been influential in Germany in the second part of the nineteenth century and, more especially, against the empirical, naturalistic, utilitarian thought that Germans associated with Anglo-Saxon culture. Some historians have looked upon this brilliant period of German scholarship as an intellectual turning point that might have given European society a new direction and a chance to overcome the forces that were pulling it apart.[49]

Other scholars, without denying the extraordinary creativity of these German thinkers, have tried to situate their work in its social environment and concentrated on the social implications of their intellectual achievements.[50] A theory has been proposed that the contempt of German scholars for modern society was a response to the rise of industrialism in Germany beginning in the 1880s, and the creation of a successful bourgeois class that threatened the power and prestige of the traditional intellectuals. According to this theory, the German scholars feared that modernity would endanger the inherited values and, with them, the entire social order in which they exercised authority. Relying on Toennies and other German scholars, the educated German public made a distinction between *Kultur* and *Zivilisation*, between a (superior) culture stressing the spiritual, literary and aesthetic aspects of life and an (inferior) culture dominated by science, technology, commerce and democratic politics. Many Germans of this period looked upon their country as the bearer of Kultur (*Kulturträger*), and saw in this vocation the origin and justification of their political ambitions. The distinction between Kultur and Zivilisation became an ideological instrument used by the traditional elites to stop the entry of democratic forms into social life and defend the authority of the inherited order against the pressure of the rising classes. The same distinction also served as a legitimation for the political aspiration of the imperial government against Western Europe, especially England, looked upon as a society of merchants (*ein Krämervolk*).

This cultured contempt for modern society was also used by the German churches to defend their power and prestige and protect their members from the impact of the secular spirit. In an angry outburst against the bourgeoisie, Max Scheler, a brilliant religious philosopher, produced a not quite believable tour de force, a book entitled *Ressentiment*,[51] which interpreted the irreligious temper of the day as an expression of resentment on the part of the bourgeoisie. He argued that the successful middle classes, entrapped in utilitarian concerns and deprived of higher values and ideals, were envious of the flights of the spirit and begrudged the passion and surrender experienced by religious people. Conscious of the emptiness of their lives, the bourgeoisie resented the spiritual richness of believers. While Scheler's bold proposal was not widely accepted, the secularization of industrial society continued to preoccupy scholars in sociology, philosophy and theology.

4

The Ambiguity of Religion:
A Biblical Account

The preceding chapters introduced the complex relationship of religion to society and culture. While we may not wish to follow the one-sidedness of the authors cited, we suspect that their different viewpoints contain a good deal of truth. Much of what they have written corresponds to our own experience of religion and society. There are indeed alienating elements in religion; there are ideological trends in religion legitimating the existing power relations; and finally religion is often the glue, the common bond, that keeps a community together and inspires its cultural self-expression. If all these things are true, then religion must be a many-levelled, complex and ambiguous reality.

Before we deal with the ways in which social thinkers have tried to analyze the ambiguity of religion, we want to turn to the biblical account of good and evil in religion. This chapter will be mainly theological.

The Bible paints a highly ambivalent picture of religion. The faith of the people is ever threatened by various religious trends that undermine their openness to divine truth and falsify their understanding of the human world. It is possible to read the Scriptures as a textbook of the pathology of religion. The prophets of Israel offer us a critical description of several corrupting religious trends: we learn from them to distinguish idolatrous religion, superstition, hypocrisy, legalistic religion, and finally religion as source of group-egotism and collective blindness. So vulnerable is the religion of God's people that it is in constant need of redemption; the believing community remains in need of the divine Word, which continues to judge its religion and renew it in terms of faith, hope and love.

While the ambiguity of religion and its ongoing need of redemption are a commonplace for biblical scholars, this need has been minimized or even forgotten by Christian teachers and theologians. The claim that in Jesus Christ the ancient promises have been fulfilled and the final age of the world has arrived has led the Church to look upon itself too un-critically as God's holy people and to ignore the ambiguity of its piety, its teaching, its life and practice – in short, its religion.

First and foremost are the repeated prophetic warnings against idolatrous religion. This warning belongs to the core of biblical teach-ing; it is summarized in the first commandment that God alone is to be worshipped.[52]

The very creation of Israel had been an act whereby the people were separated from the surrounding tribes involved in the worship of false gods. Yet the chosen people remained vulnerable to idolatrous trends. The prophets continually urged them to renew their dedication to the Holy One of Israel and abandon their attachment to other gods, to idols and images, and to the worthlessness surrounding them. "Hear the word of the Lord, O House of Jacob. What wrong did your fathers find in me that they went far from me, and went after worthlessness, and became worthless?" (Jer 2:4-5). The prophetic preaching against the idolatrous trends in the religion of Israel was not aimed exclusively at the worship of false gods: it also included the repudiation of world views that were incompatible with faith in the true God. At the time of the Maccabees, the temptation of idol worship was present in the surrender to the pagan humanism of the dominant culture that undermined the faith of Israel (1 Mc 1:43). In the New Testament, the warning against idolatry continues. The condemnation of idol worship was then aimed not so much at the veneration of false gods and demons as against the universal tendency in humanity to forget the creator who revealed himself in the works of his creation, and instead to elevate a part of this created order and wor-ship it as if it were divine (cf. Rom 1:18-32). The apostle Paul regarded this idolatrous trend as so powerful and central in human history that he derived from it the fall of culture and society into sin, violence and estrangement from all that is good and holy. Idolatry in this wider sense remained a constant temptation in the Church. Either Christians serve the Lord, or they become slaves and venerators of created realities such as money (Mt 6:24), personal gain (Col 3:5; Eph 5:5), political power (Rev 13:8), or envy and hatred (Ti 3:3). Faith in the true God implied the radical repudiation of the divinizing trends operative in culture and religion. To believe that Jesus is Lord meant that nothing in the created order, neither people nor ideas, can ever lay claim to be an absolute and demand unconditional loyalty.

While the warning against idolatry holds a central place in the Scriptures, it has not been central at all in Catholic preaching and teaching. In the Church's teaching, idolatry tended to be equated with the worship of false gods and hence did not refer to a sin commonly committed in a monotheistic religion. There was no reason, then, why the Church should warn people of the idolatrous trends in their piety. This neglect of the biblical perspective was largely due to the Church's institutional self-interest. For if idolatry be understood as the absolutizing of the finite and the elevating of a part to be the ultimate measure of the whole, then the Church's unmitigated claim to absolute truth and ultimate authority becomes problematic. From the biblical point of view, the Church itself could become an idol. Church doctrine and ecclesiastical authority promote idolatrous trends in religion whenever these institutions no longer present themselves as serving the divine Word and as mediating a divine mystery that transcends them. The Church becomes an idol whenever it identifies itself with the kingdom of God. The Church is tempted by idolatry when it wants to multiply the absolutes and regard its teaching and its hierarchy as the ultimate norms for judging all forms of Christian life and faith. It is no wonder, therefore, that the Protestant Reformation, in its struggle against the medieval Church, made the biblical warning against idolatry central in the proclamation of the Gospel. To this day, one of the most admirable characteristics of Protestantism is the ardent desire to discern the idolatrous trends in culture and ecclesiastical life. Yet even in the Protestant churches there is no structural guarantee against idolatry. Religion remains forever vulnerable to idolatrous trends. In the Catholic Church, it was Vatican Council II that clearly distinguished between the Church and God's promised kingdom. In doing so, it encouraged a critical trend among Catholics to discern the idolatrous elements in the life of their own Church.

Second, we find in the Scriptures a denunciation of superstitions that distort the true faith of Israel. The Scriptures repudiate astrology (Jer 10:2; Is. 47:13), necromancy (1 Sam 28:7-25), soothsaying (Ez 21:21, 23; Zech 10:2), and magical practices of all sorts (Ex 22:18; Lv 20:6, 27; Dt 18:10). Even the wearing of amulets, a superstitious practice to ward off evil spirits, was strictly forbidden (Gn 35:4; Jgs 8:24; Is 3:20; 2 Mc 12:40). The reason why these practices were so vehemently repudiated was that they were a sign of fear, and hence symbolized the waning of faith. These practices, moreover, recalled the ways of idolatrous religions; they invested with saving power the coincidental and the worthless. The New Testament continues to warn the faithful against magical rites of any kind (Acts 13:6-10; 19:13-19; Gal 5:20; Rev 21:27). Superstition is here regarded as the breakdown of truth. It is inspired by fear of the unknown and the suspicion that the universe is hostile and malevolent. According to the Scriptures, the universe belongs to God and reflects God's goodness.

Such is the ambiguity of religion that superstitious practices are almost inevitable. Superstition is present in the transition from faith to credulity. The manifestations of the sacred in history have always inspired people to surround them with protective ritual separating them from the profane aspects of life, and, following a tendency that is hard to resist, the gestures intended to serve the holy and keep it unalloyed acquire themselves sacred authority and become the object of veneration. The ambiguity of religion is such that the celebration of the sacred is never wholly free from superstitious trends. Faith in God's power is only too easily accompanied by a credulity that sees divine guidance behind historical coincidences. It is not always easy to decide whether a certain practice or a certain belief is based on God's self-revelation in history or whether it is simply the product of human credulity. To most contemporary Christians, the widespread belief in the verbal inspiration of Scripture and hence in its inerrancy appears like superstition; for here, faith in God's Word recorded in Scripture is transmuted into credulity in regard to the written text. Catholics have begun to ask themselves whether the belief in the infallibility of the Church and its hierarchy is part of their faith grounded in God's self-revelation, or whether it represents a fading away of faith into an all-too-human credulity. Catholic theologians seek criteria for distinguishing between the authentic response of faith to God's Word and the superstitious extension of faith into wishful thinking.

Conversely, the radical efforts on the part of religious leaders to root out all forms of superstition have usually led to such a rational and critical approach to life that religion itself began to decline. For when people can no longer accept their religious community and its liturgical gestures as bearers of divine grace, they fall into individualism and separate themselves from the sources of faith. There is then no pure religion. It remains ambiguous and thus always in need of redemption.

A third corrupting trend present in religion is hypocrisy. The ancient prophets and Jesus himself revealed the nature of hypocrisy and denounced its destructive effect on the believers, individually and collectively (Is 29:13; Eccl 1:29-30; 32:15; 36:18-19; Mt 6:2, 5, 16; 23:5-12). Believers are hypocritical when their words and gestures do not correspond to their hearts. Hypocritical religion is play-acting. We assume a role to which we are faithful, but we separate ourselves inwardly from the meaning of this role. We go through the motions of religion in order to deceive the public. The hypocrite undertakes public penances and assumes gestures of faith in order to be seen by people. In other words, hypocrisy is an attempt to use religion to advance one's position in life: it is a manipulative abuse of religion. It is easy for people to recite religious creeds and join in religious celebrations to protect their role in the community, enhance their authority, and derive the benefits the community bestows on its dedicated members. Jesus recalled the preaching of Isaiah: "They have honoured me with their lips, but their heart is far away from me" (Mt 15:7; cf Is 29:13). According to the biblical account, this self-serving use of religion may be due to purely personal ambition or, more often, to the interests of a particular class. The preaching of Jesus stressed that hypocritical behaviour protects the power of the dominant groups and enhances the respect given to them by the ordinary people. Hypocrisy is a particular temptation for those who exercise authority in religion.

Again we notice religion's inevitable ambiguity. The practice of religion itself produces the occasion for hypocrisy. Since religion is a communal activity, since in religion people are responsible for one another, it may at times be necessary for a person, especially if he exercises a position of leadership, to give witness to the common faith and celebrate the common hope, even if he is unable at the time to endorse these interiorly. This sort of fidelity to the community, disregarding personal doubts and hesitations, may sustain people's hope and nourish their personal faith. Yet such public witness can also lead ecclesiastical leaders into hypocrisy. For while the intention behind their testimony may at first be simply to strengthen the community of faith, the fact that their words enhance their authority in the community may in the long run define the dominant motive. Since we can never fully escape the ambiguity of religion, we remain forever dependent on God's mercy.

The fourth corrupting trend in religion, carefully analyzed in the Scriptures, is legalistic religion. The prophets of Israel and Jesus himself provided us with a detailed critique of legalism. Legalism, we note, cannot be equated with fidelity to a way of life, to liturgical rules, and to the norms in which a religious community embodies its ideals. The fidelity of the believing Jew to Torah does not represent what the Bible means by legalism any more than the loyalty of the Christian represents the ethos of the apostolic community. Legalism is, rather, the religious attitude that makes observance the end of religion. Legalism substitutes observance for holiness (Am 4:4-5; Is. 1:11-16; Lk 18:9-14; Mt 20:1-11; Lk 15:25-30; Rom 2:17-24). For the legalist, the laws and rites of religion are the ultimate norms of life; what he forgets is that laws and rites are meant to be symbols mediating inward transformation and new life. The legal structure of biblical religion was to establish people in a way that would deliver them from selfishness and group-egotism and lead them to communion with their God. The legalist deformation of religion concerns itself with the outside or the surface of human existence. It concentrates on observance. It makes obedience to the law the ultimate sign of religious surrender and remains unconcerned regarding the inward meaning of the law. Legalism creates a mask of conformity which makes the believer holy in his own eyes and thus prevents him from coming to self-knowledge. Legalistic religion stresses willpower, and it is this very stress on personal effort that makes the legalists unaware of their real feelings, of their own brokenness, and hence of their need of redemption. Legalists tend to think that it is possible for people to make themselves holy if they only try hard enough. They remain unaware of God's gratuitous presence to human life, bringing people to critical awareness and supporting their faithful action. Because they think that holiness is within people's grasp, legalists tend to despise the people who are less observant than they are. They elevate themselves above the sinner, the outsider, the non-conformist. Their reliance on themselves, coupled with lack of self-knowledge, makes it difficult for them to surrender to God's grace: they do not live by faith.

Legalists, in the perspective of the Scriptures, entertain a false understanding of God. God, for them, is an exacting lawgiver, a stern master who confronts his people with a set of rules, expects them to live up to these rules, and promises to reward them if they are obedient and punish them if they disobey. Yet this is a caricature of biblical religion. For the message of both Old and New Testament is that God is the redeemer of his people, that God has taken the initiative in a covenant of mercy, and that the way of life divinely revealed – first in the Torah and then, for Christians, in the Gospel – is the road that leads to fidelity and abundant life. The God of the Scriptures has power over the human heart. Hence, along with the commandments, God offers the inward help enabling people to respond to them in faith. In the New Testament in particular, we hear the good news that God is present and active in our history; that the divine mystery reveals to us the sin of the world and undergirds our actions of hope and love; that we are alive by a principle that transcends our own, limited powers; and that we have access to the life of holiness by relying on the divine grace operative within us.

Legalistic religion, we should add immediately, remains a dimension of the Christian life. While the great theologians of the Church, particularly St. Augustine and St. Thomas Aquinas, have stressed the radical difference between holiness and observance, and while even the teaching of the Council of Trent, especially in the session on justification, tried to remove the suspicion of legalism from Catholic teaching, the ordinary preaching and the official teaching in the Catholic Church do not pay much attention to the critique of legalism so central in the Scriptures. Even in Protestantism, which began as a vehement protest against the hypocrisy and legalism of the medieval Church, there is an ever-present need to be delivered from the ambiguity of religion and the legalist mentality. The roots of legalism are situated in the human psyche, for the legalist mentality is found even in people who have little to do with religion. Unfortunately, religion readily lends itself to a legalist misunderstanding. The reliance on ceremonies and commandments too easily leads to a false trust in the legal elements of religion, even when they are meant to proclaim and protect God's liberating presence in the religious community.

There is, however, an element of New Testament preaching that has prevented the churches from making the opposition to legalism as central as it was for the Hebrew prophets. We shall look at this element more closely further on. It is worth mentioning at this point that the vehement preaching of the early Church against hypocrisy and legalism, following the preaching of Jesus himself, was usually presented as a polemic against the group of people called the Pharisees. The books of the New Testament, confessional documents with a strong polemical message, describe the Pharisees as hypocritical and legalistic men with so much eloquence that to this day hypocritical and legalistic religion is called "pharisaism" in the language of Christians.

Modern scholarship has demonstrated that the New Testament has drawn a caricature of the Pharisees.[53] The Pharisees were actually a radical party of reformers in Israel who made Torah and the faithful life the centre of religion and the primary locus where people encountered their God as a living reality. This new spirituality made the Jewish community independent of the temple worship in Jerusalem and undermined the authority of the hierarchical priesthood; it also gave the people a sense of peace and self-possession in an age of oppression and delivered them from the feverish messianic expectations that pervaded occupied Israel in the century before the Christian era until the destruction of Jerusalem. The Pharisees had created a Judaism centred on daily practices, the study of Torah and peaceful community life. It was the Pharisees' rejection of the apocalyptic mood and eager messianic hopes that made them impatient with the claims of Jesus. The Pharisees were the most powerful movement in Israel, and after the destruction of the temple and the waning of apocalypticism, they represented the sole spiritual force in Judaism. Rabbinical Judaism is derived from the Pharisees. The Church's conflict with the Synagogue was, therefore, mainly with the heirs of the Pharisees, and it was for these polemical reasons that the early Christian writers projected onto the Pharisees the various corrupting religious trends Jesus had denounced in his preaching. This polemical caricature of the Pharisees has had tragic consequences for the image of Judaism in the Christian tradition; it has also had damaging consequences for the Christian Church, which was led to believe quite falsely that Jesus' preaching against hypocrisy and legalism was not a message addressed to the community that believed in him, but a denunciation of Jewish religion. It was this false identification of "Pharisaism" that prevented the churches from submitting their life and practice to the preaching of Jesus against hypocrisy and legalism. As we shall see further on, the Church's unwillingness to come to self-knowledge and confront the ambiguity of its religion made it project the repressed elements of its own life onto the community of Israel that preceded and accompanied it.

The fifth corrupting trend of religion, recorded in Old and New Testament, is the falsification of people's self-understanding, which is designated by the biblical words of "blindness," "deafness," or "the hardening of hearts." The ancient prophets and Jesus himself repeatedly revealed to people that they no longer saw themselves as they were: they had blinded themselves to reality, they clung to illusions that flattered them and protected the worst tendencies in their social life. The ironic phrase of Isaiah, repeated by Jesus, depicts the prophet as the one who drives the people's false consciousness to the breaking point: "Hear and hear, but do not understand; see and see, but do not perceive. Make the heart of this people fat, and their ears heavy, and shut their eyes, lest they see with their eyes, hear with their ears, and understand with their hearts, and turn and be healed" (Is 6:9-10; Mt 13:14-15). The people, we are told, made false use of the signs of election in their midst, the temple and the symbols of the covenant (cf. Jer 7:4), to persuade themselves that they were indeed God's chosen people and to remain ignorant of what was actually going on among them. This notion of "blindness" remained central in Jesus' preaching. The self-interest of groups, classes and peoples, we are made to understand, can be accompanied by so much self-delusion that they remain wholly unaware of the purposes, the motives and even the actions that determine their collective existence. The Bible describes here what Marxists were later to call false consciousness.

The people are blind when they misinterpret divine election as a guarantee that they are superior to others, have an elevated place in history, and are destined to triumph over their enemies. This misinterpretation prevents them from being aware of the danger in which they live and of their own infidelity to the divine promises. The divine election, commissioning the people to be a special witness of God's truth and generosity in history, becomes in the minds of stubborn and hardened men an election to a privileged status that grants them power over the destiny of others. This deafness leaves the religious community vulnerable, for it is no longer able to listen to God's Word, nor is it open to conversion and renewal. The people then regard themselves as a holy community, and their ministers as a holy priesthood. Their basic concern has become the protection of their privileges. They have so falsified their self-understanding that they do not see the games of power and the structures of domination at work in their community; and they do not notice how much these alienate ordinary men and women from the freedom and power to which they have been called.

Again, we notice the inevitable ambiguity of religion. For while religious people, following the Scriptures, desire to be seeing and recognize the structures of evil present in their midst, they also want to praise the special mercy, of which they are the recipients. They do experience themselves as guided, as having a light available in their lives, as being in the truth. But as soon as they express these convictions and lay claim to a truth that transcends the confusion generated by society, they create a language that easily gives rise to an exaggerated belief in divine guidance and hence to false consciousness. Contemporary Catholics, to give an example, who no longer accept papal and ecclesiastical infallibility are searching nonetheless for a language that expresses their faith in the Spirit guiding the believing community and making life-giving truth available to those who seek God's Word. There is no safe language in religion.

The inevitable ambiguity of religion demands that it remain open to an ongoing critique.

The preceding remarks on idolatry, superstition, hypocrisy, legalism and collective blindness offer a summary – a partial one – of the pathology of religion revealed in the Scriptures. What is the response of the faithful to these corrupting trends in their religion? The biblical keyword is here "conversion." From the beginning of the prophetic literature through the entire Bible, God calls his people to return to him, to seek his face, to repent of their sins, to be converted anew, and to enter into the peace and reconciliation to which they have been called. "Cast away from you all the transgressions which you have committed against me; and get yourselves a new heart and a new spirit. Why should you die, O house of Israel? For I have no pleasure in the death of anyone who dies. Be converted, then, and live" (Ez 18:31-32). This conversion to which the people were called demanded a recognition of what they were doing, an acknowledgment of how far they had removed themselves from the will of God, and a willingness to return to greater fidelity to the divine promises. The prophets of Israel addressed the people as if they were involved in collective sin and suffered from communal blindness; the prophetic message was meant to raise their common consciousness, to make them aware of what they refused to look at, and to open them to the summons of the divine Word. The prophetic call to conversion was to make Israel aware of the corrupting trends in their religious life and enable them, if they so wanted, to return to the authentic religion revealed by God.

This call for conversion remains central in the New Testament. In the preaching of John the Baptist and that of Jesus himself, the message of repentance and forgiveness was aimed more directly at individual believers, even though the social dimension of conversion was not entirely overlooked. Personally and collectively, people were called upon to recognize the truth about themselves, which their self-delusion had hidden from them, and to open themselves to the imminent coming of God's kingdom. In the apostolic preaching, conversion (repentance, metanoia) remained a central theme. Since the ambiguity of life marked the Christian community as much as any other, the faithful would remain in need of conversion until the day of God's final victory. They were to listen to God's word and submit to his judgment so that they be converted anew to the source of life. Conversion here means a change of heart or a raising of awareness.

It is curious and yet characteristic that, until recently, "conversion" in the language of Christians usually referred to the conversion of people to the Christian faith or even to the Catholic Church. While, in the New Testament, conversion and baptism were indeed the door by which people entered the Christian community, it was never supposed that conversion took place only once in the Christian life. Because of the ambiguity of religion, conversion remains a dimension of the Christian faith. By confining the meaning of conversion to the acceptance of the gospel faith, the Christian community forgot that the call to conversion was addressed to its own members. In this context, the word "repentance" acquired a purely moral meaning; people were asked to repent of their sins – that is, of their immoral actions. What was forgotten was that repentance referred to much more than that; repentance, the equivalent of conversion, included critical awareness, the acknowledgment of the repressed, and a new openness to the hidden truth. It was above all the biblical renewal of the 20th century that restored to the Christian churches a deeper sense of conversion. Today Christians are beginning to be aware that the call to metanoia is to make them see more clearly the ambiguity of life and religion and become open to God's healing and elevating grace.

We have suggested that the Church as a whole has not made the religious pathology indicated in the Scriptures central in its own preaching. There are many sermons against superstition and hypocrisy, but very few dealing with idolatry, legalism, and false consciousness. The Church has tended to look upon itself as the redeemed community, as the holy church in which the messianic promises have been fulfilled, as the very plenitude and embodiment of Christ extended through space and time. If a community identifies itself as Christ's mystical body, how much self-knowledge is available to it? Understanding its own life exclusively in terms of the redemption offered in Jesus Christ, the Church has largely lost the sense of the ambiguity of religion.

Protestants have taken the biblical teaching on the ambiguity of religion more seriously than Catholics. Yet when contemporary Protestant theologians, following the lead of Barth and Bonhoeffer, make a radical distinction between faith and religion and pretend that the Christian Gospel creates faith but not religion, they also evade the challenge raised by the biblical teaching. Christianity is community, worship, way of life, religion. It may be useful, at certain moments, to deny that Christianity is a religion. One may wish to stress the divine initiative operative in people's conversion to God and denounce the emptiness of self-willed religious ceremonies; or one may wish to emphasize that God is present in day-to-day secular life and not confined to specifically religious moments. But it is quite unacceptable to deny altogether that Christianity is a religion. Whether we follow the sociologists who understand religion mainly in terms of worship and the worshipping community, or those who prefer to define religion in terms of symbol systems directing people's lives and giving meaning to their existence, Christianity in whatever form is a visible religion. Theologians who insist that Christianity is only God-inspired faith, hope and love, and that the visible, social expression of these attitudes is always and inevitably a betrayal of the Gospel, prevent Christians from coming to a critical self-understanding and, in the long run, weaken in them the sense of responsibility for their own communities. The ready acknowledgment that the Church is sinful through and through, characteristic of certain Protestant currents, is as unhelpful for the emergence of self-knowledge as the corresponding Catholic trend to deny altogether the sinfulness of the Church.

To understand why the Christian Church has not given more weight to the biblical critique of idolatry, legalism and collective blindness, we must again refer to the Marxian notion of "ideology." Ideology, we recall, is the deformation of the truth for the sake of social interest. For Marx, this social interest was always and inevitably economic power. But this is far too narrow a view. Collectivities defend powers and privileges apart from the economic order, and by doing so distort their vision of reality. Needless to say, these distortions take place through mental processes that remain largely unconscious. When the Scriptures speak of collective blindness – we recall our preceding analysis – they refer to a social phenomenon that may be properly called ideology. According to the biblical account, the social sources of the corrupting religious trends (abstracting for the moment from the psychic sources) are the protection of the community against hostile forces and the defence of its power elites. The corrupting trends tend to attach people uncritically to their tradition, protect them from coming to self-knowledge, defend the authority of the dominant classes, create a false sense of superiority over others, and produce dreams of victory over outsiders. It is easy to see that this biblical critique of ideology made the Christian Church uncomfortable, especially since it regarded itself as the messianic community. For ideological reasons, then, the Church did not integrate the biblical critique into its preaching. In fact, the Christian Church created a special myth that protected it from confronting Jesus' critical preaching; this myth was the repudiation of the

Jews. Since this myth has been so important in the Christian tradition, we must deal with it at this point.

Almost from the beginning, the Christian Church projected the critical preaching of Jesus, especially his denunciation of hypocrisy, legalism and collective blindness, unto the scribes and Pharisees, the temple priests, and the undefined collectivity called the Jews. Thus the 23rd chapter of Matthew, which offers a brilliant analysis of ideological religion, is an accusation almost exclusively addressed to the Pharisees. It is they who preach, but do not practice; they who bind heavy burdens, hard to bear, and lay them on men's shoulders; they who do their good deeds in public to be seen by men; they who wear clerical stoles and fringes; they who love the places of honour at feasts and public celebrations; they who like to be called by high titles; they who traverse the sea to make a single convert and introduce him to their own oppressive religion; they who keep people from the kingdom of God; they who attach so much importance to legal and canonical regulations that they neglect the weightier matters of the law, namely justice, mercy and faith; they who are blind guides, straining out a gnat and swallowing a camel; they who cleanse the outside of the cup while inside they are full of uncleanliness; they who are like whitewashed tombs, beautiful outside but dead within. Chapter 23 then draws a line of continuity from the Pharisees to the disobedient sons of Israel who opposed and killed the prophets in the past. The Pharisees are heirs of unfaithful Israel: they now fill up the measure of their fathers. The chapter ends in the final condemnation of the generation of Jerusalem: upon them will come all the righteous blood spilled on earth. Their house, the house of Israel, will be forsaken and desolate.

There is, however, one section in chapter 23 that reminds the reader that the critical preaching of Jesus was originally applied by the early Christian community to its own self-understanding, in particular to the form that leadership should take in the Church. How should the leaders in the new community be called? "You are not to be called teacher [rabbi], for you have one teacher and you are all brethren. And call no man your father on earth, for you have one Father who is in heaven. Neither be called masters, for you have one master, the Christ. He who is great among you shall be called your servant" (Mt 23:8-11). This text fits obviously into a discussion within the Christian community, but by making it part of a sermon that is almost exclusively addressed to the Pharisees, the original meaning is almost completely concealed. Jesus' preaching against the pathological effects of legalism, clericalism and group-egotism was projected onto the Jewish community; the Christian Church, deprived of these principles of self-criticism, left itself unprotected against the ambiguity of religion.

We have already mentioned that the polemics of the New Testament against the Pharisees distorts the nature and function of this group of men in the history of Israel. Recent scholarship has brought out the spiritual and humanistic character of the Pharisaic revolution. While Jesus himself and possibly his early disciples used harsh, prophetic language to denounce the corrupting trends in the religion of their own people, later Christian preachers, speaking no longer out of an identification with Israel but out of a situation of conflict with the Synagogue, repeated the same words as a judgment pronounced by outsiders on the religion of Israel. In this manner, Jesus' prophetic exhortations acquired a different meaning: they were used as a weapon against the Pharisees and eventually against the entire Jewish people.

Why this polemic against the Jews? Since the Christian community saw in Jesus the fulfillment of the divine promises made to Israel, and hence read the Hebrew Scriptures from the viewpoint of the new covenant, it was necessary for them to argue against the Jewish reading of the same Scriptures, especially against the interpretation of the Pharisees, based on the ongoing validity of the old covenant and the continuity of the Jewish tradition. In her book *Faith and Fratricide*,[54] Rosemary Ruether has shown that from the very beginning, the Church accompanied the proclamation of Jesus as the promised Christ with arguments invalidating the Jewish reading of the Scriptures. She called this refutation "the left hand of christology." It was this left hand that generated the anti-Jewish polemics. For the refutation of the Jewish reading was not restricted to exegetical and hermeneutical arguments; it included attacks upon the Pharisees, the most influential of the Jewish interpreters. Early Christian preaching presented the Jewish teachers as blind guides who had never understood the Scriptures. And as it became increasingly clear that the Synagogue as a whole would not follow the Christian interpretation, Christian preachers began to claim that Jewish religion had never understood the Scriptures, that the Jews had read them according to the letter, that their view of the ancient covenant had been carnal, that they had always been unfaithful, and that they had never known God. Only in Jesus did the Scriptures reveal their spiritual meaning. The Jews, on the other hand, were a blind people, hard-hearted, legalistic, carnal and devoid of spiritual insight.

Let us take a brief look at how this polemics progressed in the early Church. The continuity between the contemporary Jewish opposition to the Gospel and the ancient religion of Israel, already alluded to in the 23rd chapter of Matthew, became a fully developed theme. St. Paul split the entire history of salvation down the middle by distinguishing between the history of the divine promises and the human response to them in faith, and the history of the law and man's servile obedience; Paul then identified the Christian Church with the tradition of promise and the Jewish religion with the law devoid of divine grace. In chapters 3 and 4 of Galatians, he developed the dichotomy between the spirit of faith and the works of the law, between the spiritual and the fleshly understanding of the Scriptures. Abraham, we read, was saved by the divine promises and by his trust in God's word, and he was told that the nations would be blessed in him since it was by faith in the divine promises, extended through Jesus, that the Gentiles were to be saved. Torah was introduced as a prison to heighten the sin in Israel. Those who live under the law, therefore, are estranged from the divine promises. Paul recalls the story of Abraham's two sons, one born from a slave woman, born according to the flesh, the other born from a free woman, born according to the promise. Now "these women are the two covenants" (Gal 4:24). Mount Sinai bearing children for slavery corresponds to the present Jerusalem, the Jewish religion, "for she is in slavery with her children," while the spiritual Jerusalem is free, she is the mother of Christians. For purely polemical purposes, the biblical critique of legalism has here been projected onto the Jewish religion. What Paul forgets is that in Jewish religion, Torah had not been separated from the divine promises at all. The obedience to the common law of life was understood by the best Jewish teachers as a personal response to God's covenantal love. Again, by applying Jesus' critique of legalism to the understanding of Judaism, the Church deprived itself of the critical principles for dealing with its own structures of authority.

The picture becomes complete in John's gospel. The fourth gospel was written long after the devastation of Jerusalem, when the surviving religion of Israel had become almost exclusively identified with pharisaic Judaism. For this reason, one must suppose, the author of the fourth gospel transforms Jesus' preaching against ideological religion into a polemics against the Jews, against the entire Jewish people. The Pharisees are hardly mentioned as a special group. The opponents of Jesus are simply "the Jews," and this identification is so complete that the author almost forgets that Jesus himself and his disciples were members of the same Jewish people. In the fourth gospel, Jesus speaks to "the Jews" about "their law," as if he did not belong to them (cf. Jn 8:17).

In the 5th and 8th chapters of John's gospel, we find the negation of the entire Jewish religion. Here Jesus addresses the Jews in the following way: You have never heard God's voice, you do not have his word abiding in you (cf. 5:37-38); you search the Scriptures because you think that in them you have eternal life (cf. 5:39), but you do not have the love of God within you (cf. 5:42); if you believed Moses you would also believe me, but you do not believe his writings (cf. 5:46-47); you judge according to the flesh (cf. 8:15); you know neither. What nourished this unrelenting Christian contempt for the Jews? The original polemics began as the left hand of the christological proclamation; but it is impossible to account for the demonization of the Jews, taking place in subsequent centuries, simply with reference to the conflict between two communities: the winning church and the struggling synagogue. A sociological analysis alone will not do, for the anti-Jewish polemics continued and grew even worse at times when the Jewish community was very weak or even totally absent. What was operative in the anti-Jewish tradition was the convergence of several pathological trends connected with the exercise of religion. First, Christianity was the daughter religion dependent on and yet struggling against its parent religion, caught in a curious love-hate relationship; the Church desired the humiliation and even the death of Israel, and at the same time it could not forget Israel. Israel became the necessary parent that had to be put down in every generation. Second, the Jewish people became "the shadow" of the Christian Church, if I may use this Jungian expression; they were the people on which the Church projected its own repressed destructive side. Calling itself holy and regarding itself as the messianic community, the Church became unable to look at itself realistically; the Church then denied the ambiguity of its religion, its infidelities, its betrayals, its legalism, its hypocrisy and its blindness, and projected these onto the Jewish people. Hatred and contempt for the Jews serve as the Christians' defence against self-knowledge. Third, since the Christian people found it difficult to lose their own resentment against a strict religion and the negative feelings they entertained against God and Jesus Christ, they shifted these hostile feelings onto the Jewish people, who had brought Jesus Christ to them. Hating Jews was the sublimation of hatred for God and Jesus. Fourth, we must recall that the Platonic trend in Christianity made people understand the spirit in opposition to the bodily dimension of life, especially sexuality, and this collective repression created the image of a carnal people, the Jews, which embodied the disguised underside of the Christian community. Finally, we call to mind the social pathology that makes society inflict wounds on a conquered people and then, ironically, regard these wounds as justification for renewed contempt for the conquered. Thus the marginalization of the Jews pushed them into certain sectors of social life, for which they were later despised; the Christians hated the Jews for bearing some features of the caricature that Christians had created and transferred on them. The Church's myth that the Jews were a reprobated people mystified these pathological trends and often prevented Christian people from opposing injustices inflicted on Jews by secular forces.

Auschwitz was a turning point for Christian self-understanding.[55] It revealed to us the power of social and religious pathologies. It brought to light the terrible consequences of the destructive trends in religion. *Corruptio optimi pessima* [the corruption of the best is the worst]. What Christians were summoned to do – and this is part of the purpose of this book – is to confront the structures of oppression and the symbols legitimating injustices within the Christian tradition. This means not only radically confronting the anti-Jewish trends in Christian preaching and teaching, but also wrestling against the patriarchal domination and the suppression of women mediated by the Christian tradition. It includes overcoming the church-centred understanding of world history, which served as the legitimation of the white man's hegemony in the world, and painfully confronting all the ideological elements in the Christian religion.

5

The Ambiguity of Religion:
A Social Science Account

I n the first three chapters, we examined different theories relating religion and alienation. While we were unable to follow the one-sidedness of these theories, we saw that they contained a great deal of truth. The young Hegel presented religion as source of human alienation. The young Marx saw in religion the symptoms of the alienation inflicted on people by economic institutions. Toennies, speaking for a wide group of sociologists, regarded religion as the celebration of the common values and ideals grounding traditional society, and hence foretold that the individualism and utilitarianism of modern life would undermine the common social bond and eventually destroy religion altogether. There is no reason why these different theories could not all be true at the same time. Religion is a highly complex, many-levelled, ambivalent phenomenon; even if these theories offer mutually exclusive explanations, they may well refer to diverse layers and trends in religion, each with different characteristics and different social effects. In the last chapter we saw that the Scriptures present religion as an ambiguous reality. In the present chapter we shall turn to the social critics of modern times to study in greater detail the ambiguity of religion. We want to examine the distinction between religion and magic introduced by Émile Durkheim and Max Weber, the distinction between authoritarian and humanistic religion made by Erich Fromm in reliance on Sigmund Freud, and the distinction between ideological and utopian religion derived from Karl Mannheim's sociology of knowledge.

Christian theologians should be interested in the ambiguity of religion. Since they embrace the ideal of genuine religion derived from the Scriptures, they should have examined existing religious practices to distinguish in them the expression of authentic religion and the manifestations of its inauthentic trends. It is, in a certain sense, surprising that the distinction between the various forms of religious life was made by philosophers and social scientists who were often agnostics or atheists. We saw that the young Hegel distinguished between good and bad religion, and Tocqueville between religion in aristocratic societies and religion in egalitarian societies. Marx and Toennies regarded religion as a much less differentiated social phenomenon, yet subsequent social thinkers, making use of the ideas of Marx and Toennies, detected in the phenomenon of religion divergent trends, some of which alienated people from their human potential and other which helped people to develop their human potential.

* * *

Durkheim and Weber made a clearly defined, ideal-typical distinction between religion and magic. While they recognized that the religions studied by social scientists, including the monotheistic religions, were never totally free of magical trends, they regarded the distinction as useful precisely because it enabled them to gain a more nuanced and critical understanding of religious practice and its effect on social life.

According to Durkheim, society generated religion. He argued against the anthropologists of his day who regarded magic as primary and religion as a later development derived from magic. In his famous study, *The Elementary Form of Religious Life*,[56] Durkheim tried to demonstrate that religion was the symbolic celebration of the values, ideals and hopes that bound a society together. This, we recall, corresponds to the sociological intuition of Ferdinand Toennies. Religion is society becoming conscious of itself: "For a society to become conscious of itself and maintain at the necessary degree of intensity the sentiments which it thus attains, it must assemble and concentrate itself.... A society can neither create itself nor recreate itself without at the same time creating an ideal."[57] Religion is the encounter of society with the ideal on which it is based. For Durkheim, then, religion is at one and the same time created by, and creating, society, even though he does not sufficiently clarify this dialectical interrelation. Religion is created by the community as the symbolic self-manifestation of its own depth; and in turn religion creates the community, that is, religion confirms the members in the common values, initiates the new generation into the living tradition, and confronts the entire community with the highest ideals present in its history and thus acts as an impetus for renewal and social change. For Durkheim, religion is connatural to social life. While he himself was an atheist, and while he observed the decline of religion in modern society, at least among the urban population of France, he argued that if modern society survives, it will inevitably generate a new worship expressing its social bond in symbolic form. For Durkheim, "there is something eternal in religion."[58]

Religion, then, is primary. Arguing against James Frazer,[59] who thought that religion had developed from magic and that there was really no difference between the two, Durkheim insisted that religion was a foundational dimension of the earliest human communities and the source of their social and mental life, and that magical rites, found everywhere in and through religion, were expressions of the decline or the decay of religion.[60] There is an inner antagonism between religion and magic.

Religion, according to Durkheim, is always and inevitably associated with a community. The priest serves within a community, and the sacred rites create a social bond between the people and their priest as well as among the people themselves. Religion expresses itself in a worship that constitutes the many into a single church – Durkheim used this word in regard to all religions![61] Religion is always social, serves the common good, saves humans from egotistical preoccupations, and nourishes in them the power to love others and to surrender themselves to the social reality that embraces and transcends them. From this point of view, magic is the decay of religion. For while the magician may use the same rites as the priest and relate himself to the same gods and spirits, his magic does not create a bond between himself and his clients nor among the clients themselves. Magic does not create a church. Magicians do not belong to a community; they simply have a clientele. Magical rites, therefore, are not social, do not serve the common good, and do not facilitate surrender to the transcendent. On the contrary, magical rites seek power over the gods to make them serve the personal interest and advantage of the petitioner. Magic makes the petitioner selfish and undermines his religious dedication. While magic is never wholly absent from the historical religions, and may sometimes even be practiced by priests, it is intrinsically opposed to the true nature of religion.

Max Weber's approach to the study of religion was quite different from Durkheim's, but he, too, made a clear distinction between religion and magic.[62] Weber did not follow Durkheim's holistic, social understanding of religion; he studied religious phenomena from a more evolutionary perspective and hence shared the view of the anthropologists who claimed that religion developed out of magic. But Weber thought that the transition from magic to religion had an important social meaning.

Magical rites – here, Weber agreed with Durkheim – seek power over the gods to make them solve the problems of the people who invoke them. Magic is concerned with particular, localized problems. In his account of Weber's sociology of religion, Talcott Parsons says that magic deals with "ad hoc interests and tensions."[63] By contrast, religion does not seek to exercise power over divine forces; religion expresses itself in ordered worship and surrender to the gods. Religion is a principle that creates a believing community, while magic, concerned with particulars, is basically irreligious. Max Weber contrasts the priest with the magician. The priest as guardian of religion speaks in the name of the community; the magician speaks in his own name and is a man of great personal power. People trust the priest because they believe in the divine power residing in the community; people trust the magician because of his personal, inexplicable power.

What is important for Weber is that the passage from magic to religion is due to the application of "reason" to the social life of people living in community. Since the human being, according to Weber, is a meaning-creating animal, he holds that significant changes take place in culture and society when humans achieve greater unification of the various aspects of their lives, combine more successfully personal needs with the needs of the community, and acquire a more unified world view. This trend – which Weber called "rationalization"[64] – is a principle of social evolution. The religious breakthrough, overcoming the inherited magical trends, is part of a movement that creates a more complex, ordered, differentiated society that demands the transcendence of private wishes and family interests for the sake of a wider common good. In this perspective, religion is a principle of socialization. It detaches people from the fulfillment of their personal needs and, by investing with sacred importance the destiny of the entire community, in this world or in the next, religion generates what magic is unable to do: a selfless, sacrificial, communal way of life.

Weber clarified the contrast between magic and religion in his distinction between taboos and religious ethics.[65] Taboos correspond to magic: they regulate behaviour according to purely ritual demands, they have only particular applications, they cannot be generalized, they appear arbitrary from the viewpoint of the totality of people's needs and purposes. Religious ethics, on the other hand, corresponds to religion. Religious ethics operates at a higher level of generalization; it is concerned with the well-being of the community and provides norms of behaviour that enable people to participate in building the common life. Weber realizes, of course, that present in priestly religion are many elements of taboo; nonetheless, he thought that the ideal-typical distinction between magic (or taboo) and religion was useful for a clearer understanding of existing religions.

For Max Weber, the evolution from magician to priest, due to a wider application of "reason," continued to a third type of religious leader: the prophet.[66] The prophet is someone invested with extraordinary power who utters a special message or recalls a forgotten teaching. Prophets resemble magicians because, like them, prophets act out of a power that resides in themselves, but differ from magicians inasmuch as their prophetic task is to announce a message that has meaning for the entire community. Both priests and prophets, then, are concerned with the community and its well-being, but the priest acts as a member of a priestly caste, exercises a power that resides in the community, and hence speaks largely as the protector of the existing social order, while the prophet speaks at a distance from the religious institution and traditional society. In Weber's view, the prophet is the important agent of "rationalization." We shall examine this sociological theory further on in connection with the creativity of religion.

We note in passing that Durkheim also recognized the role of prophets in the history of religions. But for him it was religion, as the primary reality, that generated prophecy. For even the most critical prophet condemns the practices and institutions of the religious community in the light of truths and values received from this very community. The prophet criticizes the present state of the community in the light of its highest ideals.[67] Thus a prophet, exiled or even executed by the community, may in a deeper sense embody, more than any other person, the spirit of that community. What is involved in prophecy, then, is not the application of "reason" to religion but an act of fidelity to the genius of the inherited religion. Socrates was more faithful to the genius of the Athenian republic than the judges who condemned him, and Jesus embodied the highest ideal of Israel's prophetic tradition, which was ignored by the temple hierarchy that opposed him. Yet this difference between Weber and Durkheim is more apparent than real, since for Durkheim a certain society-building rationale is part and parcel of religion, thus making religion the source of logic and critique.

Both Durkheim and Weber, we conclude, despite their differences, distinguish in the historical religions disparate tendencies, which they call magic and religion, with different social and personal effects. Since the magical trend goes against the wider common good, it separates people from the full human potential that is present in the community. This is certainly Durkheim's view. Magical trends alienate people from the religious community and the development of their full human stature; religion, on the other hand, integrates people into social life and brings them in touch with the sources of creativity. Weber uses a more value-free language, but he also regards magic as a principle of separation and an expression of ad hoc concerns, while religion produces a more comprehensive vision of life, reconciling personal interests and aspirations with the destiny of a whole community.

It is worth mentioning in this context that under the influence of the sociological theory called functionalism,[68] the distinction between magic and religion has tended to disappear in sociological research.[69] For functionalists, all elements of social life are understood in terms of the contributions they make to the stability of the whole. Functionalists regard as given the equilibrium of the existing social order, and all phenomena within this order are looked upon as contributing agents. Research carried out from this point of view has shown that magical rites, even though on the surface mainly concerned with private interests and tensions, have nonetheless a social function in protecting the well-being and equilibrium of society. Magic has a "latent" social function – one that is hidden from the practitioners. In some cases, magical rites dispel the fears in a certain section of the population and hence make them more peaceful workers; in other cases, magic causes anxieties in people and hence generates energy for special tasks in society. In this perspective, magic and religion become indistinguishable.

The distinction between magic and religion, made by Émile Durkheim, is a sign that he may not be regarded as the father of functionalism as it is sometimes supposed.[70] Durkheim did not look upon society as the stable equilibrium of social forces; he had a great sense of the vitality, the creative dynamism of society and its historical evolution. He did not try to find in the anti-social trends of magical religion latent functions, unknown to the practitioners, that made significant contributions to the maintenance of the social system. Despite his attempt to produce objective science, he did not hesitate to speak of "pathological religion" – that is, of religion that works against the common good of the community, destroys dedication and concern, and is the bearer of magical trends.

* * *

We now turn to a second distinction, found in social studies, between divergent trends in religion. In his book *Psychoanalysis and Religion*, [71] Erich Fromm distinguishes between authoritarian and humanistic religion. Fromm, we note, does not speak as a believer. He regards himself as an atheist, but his study of religion arrives at the conclusion that the negative critique offered by Freud, while true and valid, does not exhaust the reality of religion, and that in addition to sick-making or pathogenic trends of religion exist therapeutic and humanizing ones. Fromm acknowledges the epochal breakthrough of Freud's negative critique of religion. Freud, as we shall see, extended the kind of thinking we encountered in the young Hegel's account of alienating religion. As a projection born out of the inability to be fully human, religion has the power to lock people more tightly into their impotence and intensify their estrangement from their human environment and their human resources. Yet – Fromm here follows the young Hegel – other religious trends sustain and nourish the ability to be more fully human.

Let me summarize two central Freudian critiques exposing religion as projection. The first is expressed in a little book, *The Future of an Illusion*, written late in Freud's life, which reaffirms the general orientation of his psychoanalytical research. Here religion is understood as a compulsively extended infantilism, religion as "baby-trip" – if I may use this colloquial expression. Little children enjoy the protection of the parents who appear all-powerful and wise to them, the embodiment of warmth and care. As the children grow up to face a complex and hostile world, fear is engendered, a fear of the threats and burdens confronting them, a fear that makes them cling to their childhood memories. If they remain passive, if they refuse to grow up, they may, instead of breaking the desire for security and parental warmth, project the parental figure onto the cosmos, believe in a god with paternal or maternal features, and then experience the warmth and care they were afraid to lose. This, according to Freud, is the illusion of religion: it is a projection founded on wishful thinking. Once the parental figure has been successfully located in the sky, it becomes a dangerous obstacle to growth and freedom. For this parent, invoked in prayer, now prevents the believers from leaving their childhood behind. Religion makes people dependent, it encourages their passive trends; it makes them uncritical, gullible and immature; it nourishes their need for protection. People kept immature by a successful religious projection feel safe only in social, political and ecclesiastical institutions where few decisions are demanded of them, where they are led by strong authority figures, and where they can fit themselves into a rigid structure of law and order. Authority and obedience, which define the believer's relationship to the divinity, also determine the forms of his or her participation in church and society. What emerges is authoritarian religion.

This theme is further developed by applying to this religious projection the Freudian discovery of the Oedipal complex. If the projected divinity is father, as it is in biblical religion, then the dependence on and veneration of this father figure are accompanied, at least unconsciously, by hostility against him, by a desire to remove him from his place, by a revolt against religion as such. Authoritarian religion, then, is not simply the promotion of a harmless infantilism; it also evokes in religious people strange and unaccountable feelings of anger, hatred and revolt. Because these feelings cannot be given public expression or even be inwardly acknowledged, they are shifted away from the divine object to another and find expression in a hidden self-hatred, or in hostility towards people who do not accept the same religion, or both. Authoritarian religion, twisted through the unresolved Oedipal complex, becomes the source of self-punishing behaviour and of collective hatred towards outsiders and non-conformists. This pathological development explains the extraordinary cruelty that authoritarian religion has produced in human history.

Let me add that theologians too readily pass off the organized expressions of cruelty as sins of individuals and unfortunate accidents, related to the inherited religion in a purely extrinsic way. Yet this is too easy. We have to ask ourselves what is in the religious tradition that has prompted hatred for outsiders and dissidents and justified violent actions against them. An advantage of the Freudian critique is that it offers an explanation for why religions that give love and mercy central roles in their preaching become the sources of organized and rationally planned cruelty towards non-believers and non-conformists.

A second critique of religion, supplementing the first, is found in another of Freud's small books, *Civilization and Its Discontents*, which combines somewhat vague sociological speculations with the major themes drawn from his psychoanalytical studies. Here, religion is understood as a projection induced by guilt feelings – religion as "guilt-trip." In his conservative and pessimistic little book, Freud describes the pressures that modern, industrialized society exerts on individuals by increasing the demands made on them in terms of hard work, conformity, achievement and obedience. The more complex the organization of society, the less the personal freedom of the individual. While individual people still dream of happiness, free self-expression and the satisfaction of the instincts, they are made to feel guilty about their dreams by the imperious demands of industrial society. Modern civilization accuses people in a strong voice: You are guilty because of your deep wishes and desires. Freud believed that contemporary society drives people into neurotic guilt-feelings, with devastating consequences for their personal lives.

In this book, Freud reveals his lack of sociological sophistication. The great psychologist always saw people as individuals standing over against an impersonal and even hostile society. By contrast, sociologists recognize that individual persons come to be by participating in a social process. Society is thus never purely external to them, but enters into the very constitution of their consciousness. If we follow Toennies's analysis, Freud's turn towards critical introspection was not simply a personal choice; it was also a cultural product of modern, Gesellschaft-type society. That Freud experienced this society as hostile may be related to his experience as a Jewish doctor in an anti-Semitic environment.

Society, according to Freud, makes people feel guilty. But who are the mediators of society's negative judgments? According to Freud's more basic psychoanalytical research, the parents are the ones who communicate to the child the harsh demands of society. It is the voice of parents, internalized as the so-called superego or infantile conscience, that exercises the rule over the children, covers them with guilt, and executes society's harsh judgment on them. Morality, in this Freudian perspective, is nothing else than the voice of superego. Created through the internalization of the parents' demands, superego becomes the organ for receiving orders from teachers in school, priests in church, and authoritative persons in society. Our own rational sense of what is right and good remains weak and ineffectual before the voice of superego. Thus we are easily overwhelmed with guilt feelings without having a clear sense that we have done something wrong. Neurotic guilt feelings of this kind lead to many forms of irrational behaviour. One of them is religion.

Overwhelming guilt feelings may give rise to a religious projection of a divine lawgiver as lord of history. The accusation and condemnation addressed to us by our infantile conscience are so powerful that we cannot attribute them to mother and father nor to the social order to which we belong; they must come from a transcendent lord in whose debt we shall always be and before whom we can be at ease only if he is merciful and does not count our transgressions against us. If this projection is successful, people will remain in their guilt prison, punish themselves except for occasional experiences of release, mistrust their own deep wishes, and lose confidence in their own powers.

Yet there are in religion significant moments of relief and forgiveness, as Freud readily acknowledged. Since the scientific spirit inevitably undermines religion – Freud follows here Comte's positivistic thesis – people in the modern society are deprived of the occasional ecstatic release from guilt feelings, formerly offered by religion. As a result, the strict demands of modern society drive people into severe guilt feelings of an intensity unknown in a previous, more religious age. In today's world, religion as a collective neurosis may well be able to heal people from the debilitating symptoms of their private neuroses. For Freud, then, unrelieved guilt is the typical illness of the modern age.

The religion created by guilt projections is complicated by the unresolved Oedipal complex operative in it. For the superego is often linked to the image of the father, whose power is the source of anger and resentment. While on the conscious level people are eager to obey, on the unconscious level they resent his authority and yearn for independence. We know from our own experience how easily this superego can be projected on authority figures of various kinds, on police officers or superiors, with the result that we feel restless in their presence, have strong feelings of resentment against them, entertain compulsive fantasies about them, and are unable to find the inner freedom to carry on an adult conversation with them. Such a projection makes people both servile and touchy; they seek the superior's approval with a smile and yet resent his or her very acts of kindness. By the same sort of unconscious process, the superego with Oedipal charge can be projected onto the Church and its priests, and even onto the divinity.

This is the perspective from which Freud read the entire biblical story. God appeared to him like a supreme yet arbitrary ruler, handing his people a set of laws, punishing them for their transgressions and demanding worship and loyalty. Read from this perspective, the Christian story leads this development to its climax, for here the divine father, displeased with his disobedient children, demands harsh punishment and derives great satisfaction from the crucifixion of his favoured son. Once his justice and honour have been restored, he bestows his forgiveness on the rest of humanity. In Christianity – interpreted from this perspective – the believer approaches the divine father by invoking the sacrificial death of his son on the cross. Authoritarian religion creates an imagination of law and punishment, offence and satisfaction, bloody sacrifice and cruel retribution.

Freud was so pleased with his analysis of religion in terms of guilt and repentance that he created his own imaginative myth, countering the biblical story, according to which belief in God originated in the Oedipal murder of the powerful father. Here the men in early tribal community, in an Oedipal frenzy, murdered the father who had access to all the women; and since these men were unable to forget the father in their guilt, they projected him as the heavenly avenger of their crime and the supreme guardian of law and order in the community. We recall here the young Hegel's analysis of bad religion. Following this line of thought, God becomes the symbol of everything people hate.

Erich Fromm accepted this radical, twofold critique of religion as a significant breakthrough on the way to human liberation. Yet he did not believe that the Freudian critique exhausted the reality of religion. Fromm was convinced that there also existed religious movements that supported human growth. He combined a perceptive reading of Freud with a sympathetic understanding of the world religions. First, Fromm did not interpret Freud purely and simply as an enemy of religion. He recognized that Freud himself was dedicated to human development defined in terms of knowledge, brotherly love, reduction of human suffering, independence and responsibility, and Fromm saw in this dedication "the ethic core of all great religions."[72] Freud did not explicitly recognize this humanizing trend in the world religions, but at least, so Fromm thought, the Freudian critique of religion in no way undermines and invalidates the religious dedication to human growth. "The statement that Freud is against 'religion' therefore is misleading unless we define sharply what religion or what aspects of religion he is critical of and what aspects he speaks for."[73] It is at this point that Erich Fromm introduced his distinction between authoritarian and humanistic religion. Freud's critique revealed the alienating nature of authoritarian religion, but left room for another kind of religious orientation, one that promotes human self-discovery and self-expression.

Fromm understands religion as any style of thought and action, shared by a group, which gives the individual a frame of orientation and an object of devotion.[74] From his study of the world religions he comes to the conclusion – I have called this his sympathetic reading of religion – that all of them contain elements that further human development and the unfolding of the specifically human powers, even if they also contain elements that paralyze these powers. Religion is ambiguous: it is both alienating and life-giving. Fromm's account of the humanistic trend of religion remains somewhat vague, yet he makes one remark that moves his reflection into the field of theology and enables us to clarify his underlying thought. He writes, "Inasmuch as humanistic religions are theistic, God is a symbol of man's own power which he tries to realize in his own life, and is not a symbol of force and domination having power over man."[75] This sentence can be read as a formal definition of how humanistic religion differs from authoritarian religion: the former conceives of the divine in terms of participation and communion and the latter in terms of power and domination. There exists then, in the eyes of Erich Fromm, within human history a vast movement towards freedom, development and the transformation of life, which unites religious and non-religious people, which cuts right through the existing religions and communities of other kinds, be they political, scientific, or whatever, a movement that allows believers and atheists to work together for human liberation and resist together the forces that enslave men and inhibit human life.

How does a theologian evaluate Fromm's distinction between authoritarian and humanistic religion? Since Fromm remains vague in regard to his understanding of humanistic religion and tends to restrict it to purely ethical aspects, one possible interpretation is to deny that what Fromm calls humanistic religion is religion in any true sense. At the same time, another possible interpretation is to fill out the vagueness of Fromm's description and then relate his concept of humanistic religion to the religious and theological developments going on in the churches at this time. Since Fromm himself repeatedly mentions that contemporary theologians have given a humanistic understanding of religion, it is quite likely that his own thought has been influenced by the religious development in the churches. In particular, his sentence that in humanistic religion "God is not a symbol of power over man but of man's power"[76] recalls the effort of Protestant and Catholic theologians in the 20th century to interpret God not as a supreme being over and above the world, but as the mystery of life in and through human existence, delivering humans from their brokenness and orienting them towards a redeemed future. For these theologians – we referred to them in the first chapter – God is not the symbol of power over humankind but rather a symbol of power in and through humankind: that is, the symbol of the release of humankind's own power and its orientation towards growth and liberation.

Since, in a previous paragraph, we have presented a reading of the biblical and Christian story from the perspective of authoritarian religion, we must at least mention, however briefly, how this story is read from the viewpoint of humanizing or redemptive religion. Here God is not the supreme ruler or master. What the Scriptures call God is the Truth, the Love and the Life, operative in human history as its deepest dimension, hidden from human eyes, especially because of humanity's sins. This divine mystery, hidden from the beginning, has manifested itself in significant events, in the history of Israel, in the history of other peoples, and in a special way in the life, death and resurrection of Jesus Christ. It is possible to formulate the Church's traditional christology in this way.[77] The Church holds that in Jesus is made manifest the divine truth or logos that is working in a hidden way in all of history. In Jesus, the Christian encounters the living God. In Jesus is revealed and communicated the triune mystery of God, as truth or logos addressing people everywhere, as spirit empowering people wherever they are to follow the call of truth, and as love defining the ground out of which people come and the horizon towards which they move. It has been the effort of contemporary theologians to proclaim the Christian creed as the revelation of God's presence in the humanization and liberation of humankind.

We conclude, then, with Erich Fromm that religion is both pathogenic and therapeutic. This includes the Christian religion. We are now able to appreciate the new sensitivity Sigmund Freud's work has created among us. Theologians should no longer reflect on the teaching and practice of the Christian religion without asking themselves to what extent the inherited symbols initiate people into dependencies, guilt and blindness, and to what extent these same symbols, read out of different presuppositions, deliver people from dependencies, guilt and blindness. In a book called *Man Becoming*, published in 1972, I tried to show that the Gospel is in fact a healing message, and that to remain faithful to this Gospel it is necessary to submit the teaching and the practice of the Christian Church to an ongoing therapeutic critique. There are indeed ways of speaking about God and praying to God that alienate people from their depth and their destiny; and yet there are others that reconcile people with life and free them for a new future.

* * *

We now come to a third distinction between contrasting trends in religion. Following the sociology of Karl Mannheim, especially the articles collected in his *Ideology and Utopia*, I wish to distinguish between ideological and utopian religion. Mannheim extended and modified the Marxian concept of ideology. We recall that for Marx, religion was always and inevitably ideological, in the sense that it was an expression of false consciousness, legitimating the power of the dominant class and hence defending the existing order of society. We noted that Marx had also spoken of religion as "the sigh of the oppressed creature," and acknowledged that religion may record the dreams of an oppressed group convinced that human destiny transcended the present state of misery. Later Marxist thinkers made use of this idea to interpret certain trends in Christian history – in particular, the rise of early Christianity and the Anabaptist movement of the sixteenth century. Under certain political circumstances and the influence of revolutionary leaders, the religion of the oppressed may spell out a judgment on the powerful in society, summon people to a realistic awareness of their misery, and mobilize forces among the people that lead to radical social change.

The careful study of religion made it increasingly difficult for sociologists to look upon religion purely and simply as the sacred legitimation of the existing social order. Max Weber himself, in a series of three brilliant articles published in English in *The Sociology of Religion*, examined the relation between religion and various classes in society.[78] He studied the religious trends among peasants, warrior nobles, the aristocracy, merchants, craftsmen, the dispossessed groups, and finally the various strata of intellectuals – and found that the kind of religion practised by each of these groups was related to their concrete interests in society. At the same time, prophecy or critical religion was not confined to any one group or class. Weber concluded that the most oppressed classes have never been the bearers of new religious impulses. Innovative religion is found in those sections of society for which a rational ethics is of great importance, such as craftspeople, merchants and skilled workers. Needless to say, Weber did not deny the phenomenon of ideological religion, which serves the dominant class as a defence of its privileges and consoles the dominated classes with promises of heavenly rewards. Yet the conclusion of his essays was that an easy generalization of the relation between class and religion is not possible; in every case the concrete, historical situation must be studied.

Karl Mannheim, building on the sociologists who preceded him, extended and modified the Marxian notion of ideology and integrated it into sociological theory. For Marx, the concept of ideology had been a weapon for wrestling against bourgeois science and bourgeois ideals; he tried to defeat the arguments of the liberal philosophers by showing that their positions served the interests of the middle class. But Marx did not apply the ideological critique to the ideas of revolutionary movements. The most oppressed classes, Marx held, were not vulnerable to ideology, or at least, by becoming aware of their actual situation, they would acquire true consciousness. Consequently, the Marxists themselves did not examine how their own movement made ideas serve revolutionary interests and hence to what extent it produced distortions of the truth. Karl Mannheim insisted that all groups, in virtue of their concrete place in society, look upon reality from a certain angle and entertain certain political aspirations; they consequently acquire a definite mindset or mental horizon that defines the framework of their thought, their cultural life and their religion.

The study of these mindsets became a central concern of Mannheim's sociology of knowledge. Each mindset is associated with a particular group of people – a social carrier (*Träger*), in Mannheim's terminology – and is dependent on the socio-political situation of this group in society. One of Mannheim's most important contributions to sociology was the discovery that the ideas and ideals of people develop as the group to which these people belong undergoes significant social changes. The development of ideas, of art and of religion cannot be understood apart from the mindset to which they belong and apart from the socio-political changes taking place in their social carrier (*Träger*). Ideas, in Mannheim's terminology, are *seinsgebunden*[79] – they are grounded in social reality. This sociological principle has far-reaching implications for the study of religion.

Religious ideas are socially grounded; their meaning and power cannot be understood without taking into consideration the historical situation of the believing community. Applying this to Christianity we have to say that creeds have different meanings depending on the mental horizon with which they are associated and on the historical situation of the community in which this mindset resides.

That the meaning of religious statements is *seinsgebunden* is not foreign to contemporary theology. From the study of hermeneutics it has become clear to many theologians that the meaning of a religious statement is not only dependent on the social context in which it was uttered, but also on the presuppositions brought to it by the interpreter, presuppositions that depend on the historical experience of the community to which the interpreter belongs. The Christian Gospel thus gives rise to many meanings. What counts today is to find an interpretation of the Gospel that is appropriate to the Church's present historical experience.

While surprising at first, the emergence of the same insight in various disciplines can be explained by the very sociology of knowledge we are here discussing. Mannheim himself often made the point that the emergence of the sociology of knowledge and the awareness of several mindsets or mental horizons became possible and inevitable after the breakdown of the homogeneous character of society. What happened in modern society was the intermingling of people with diverse cultural backgrounds and social interests, as well as changes in social structures that led some people to convert from one mental horizon to another.[80] Only in modern times, especially after World War I, has it been possible for people to compare and contrast various mindsets, either because they have passed from one mindset to another in their personal history, or because they associate daily with people who belong to different mental universes. It was thus the new social conditions that led to the discovery of the socio-historical nature of truth in several academic disciplines.

In this context, Karl Mannheim examined what he called the utopian mindset and related it to the study of religion. I wish to use his reflections clearly to distinguish between utopian and ideological religion. Let me define ideological religion first. Religion (or any symbolic language) is ideological if it legitimates the existing social order, defends the dominant values, enhances the authority of the dominant class, and creates an imagination suggesting that society is stable and perdures. By contrast, religion is utopian if it reveals the ills of the present social order, inverts the dominant values of society, undermines the authority of the ruling elites, and makes people expect the downfall of the present system. Mannheim, let me add, did not always follow this strict definition of utopia. He often uses "utopia" in a wider sense as referring to visions of a new society that evokes criticism of the present order and releases energy for social change, without necessarily subverting the existing order. Utopias may be reformist or revolutionary.

A certain ambivalence in the definition of utopia pervades Mannheim's entire book. At first he offers a radical definition of the utopian imagination and presents it as a mindset that, like ideology, distorts the perception of reality and leads to false and dangerous political judgments. However, in the course of his book he modifies his understanding of utopia. He begins to recognize that without an utopian imagination, a culture is unable to generate new thoughts and inspire new actions. Mannheim examines the various forms of utopian consciousness that have been important in Western history, and while he identifies himself with none of these, he comes to the conclusion that the disappearance of utopias leads to a static society and the reification of human life.[81]

At another place in his book, Mannheim sets out to prove that a vision of the future is operative in sociological and historical research, obliging him to abandon as illusory the idea of objective or value-neutral social scientific research.[82] Truth is not available from any standpoint whatever. Mannheim searches for a new definition of objectivity that includes the scholars' commitment to totality and social transformation. Yet in trying to define this commitment, the German sociologist remains rather vague: he speaks of a commitment to "an ethical position," "a political elan" and "a total view," which expresses the willingness or readiness to regard their perspectives as partial, to situate themselves in ever wider spheres of reference, to remain open to other people's perception of reality, and to reach out for a conception of humanity and the historical process that leads to ever greater human liberation.[83] Through research carried out from such an orientation, scholars are able to overcome the distortions of ideology and utopia in a new objectivity, and yet – and here is the ambivalence – it is only through a commitment to a certain utopia that historical truth becomes available.

Historical religion, to return to our topic, can be both ideological and utopian, depending on the historical age, the political situation of the religious community, and the form of people's religious experience. Looked upon from this viewpoint, religious symbols inevitably have a hidden political meaning. Religion may not be reduced to its political implications – such reductionism must be rejected – yet it cannot be denied that religion, even if highly private, has a certain political meaning. Religion is never socially neutral. We conclude that Mannheim's distinction between ideological and utopian religion has opened up a new field of research for the student of religion.

Theologians engaged in inquiries of this kind are surprised to find that Christian spiritualities that are God-centred and that recommend the contempt of the world may in fact be subtle legitimations of worldly powers. Even the great saints were often so identified with their culture that without knowing it, and despite their other-worldliness, they unconsciously sanctioned the injustices of their society. Reading the letters of Thérèse of Lisieux and Père Charles de Foucault, both remarkable religious figures and prophetic in the context of the ecclesiastical tradition, we discover that they provided religious legitimation for the colonial expansion of France and its claim of cultural superiority. Karl Mannheim's sociological approach has shown that a religious attitude that encourages contempt for the world may go hand in hand with an uncritical identification with this world and its power structures.

Since the word "utopia" is used by Mannheim in a special sense, distinct from ordinary usage, it is important to point out that not every dream of a perfect future is, in Mannheim's terms, utopian. Hopes of future happiness that are based on the prolongation of present values and strengthen the dominant institutions are in fact ideological. The perfect world painted in television advertising, where beautiful people living in beautiful houses solve their daily problems by buying appropriate commodities, is produced by a highly ideological imagination, for it is nothing but the extension into unreality of the values and institutions basic to the present consumer society. Was the picture of the future painted in *The Greening of America*,[84] a book widely read in the 1960s, a utopian or an ideological imagination? Did it shake people loose from the inherited values, make them critical and summon them to action? Or did it persuade them that a new culture was in the process of creating itself, blind them to the real holders of power, and thus encourage a political passivity that left the established order without challengers? These questions are not always easy to answer. In a later chapter we shall see that the Christian preaching of future hope, the coming of God's kingdom, and the creation of a new heaven and a new earth bears within it the same ambiguity.

Many scholars simply ignore that religion can ever be utopian. Marx himself was blind on this issue. Yet, later Marxists, as we mentioned earlier, were aware of the radical character of the apocalyptic elements in early Christianity and recognized the theory and practice of revolution in the sixteenth-century Anabaptist movements. In his *Ideology and Utopia*, Mannheim devotes a section to the study of "chiliastic religion"[85] – that is, the radical religious movements of the late Middle Ages, which expected the coming of the new age of the Spirit, an ecstatic age in which the contradictions of life, largely imposed by government and institution, would be overcome. These movements created great unrest among the population; sometimes they encouraged people to revolt. Because of their utopian orientation, these groups suffered persecution and death at the hands of the established authorities, secular and religious. In her book *The Radical Kingdom*, Rosemary Ruether has shown that the revolutionary mindset had its origin in Jewish apocalypticism in the centuries preceding the Christian era, and that it was mediated to Western culture through the apocalyptical passages in New Testament literature.[86]

The radical consciousness of Jewish apocalypticism emerged among faithful believers who read the ancient messianic promises made to Israel under the pressure of political occupation and cultural oppression. Since the prolonged occupation of Israel threatened the survival of Jewish independence and the cosmopolitan culture of the Empire undermined the traditional faith, at least among the upper classes, some Jews began to form resistance groups. Some of them found refuge in the mountains. These groups regarded themselves as enemies of the Empire and sometimes even repudiated the official Judaism. Their precarious existence was nourished by the hope that the messianic promises were about to be fulfilled. The injustices of the present order cried to heaven for vengeance. God would not remain silent. These radical groups created a new kind of religious literature that revealed that God's judgment was upon the present order, that the seats of power were about to be overthrown, that God's victory was near, and that he, the Lord, was about to create a new society where his faithful people would live in justice and peace. Some of the apocalypticists acted as erratic freedom fighters. This apocalyptical mood lasted into the first century of the Christian era. We mentioned before that Jesus preached his Gospel in this environment and occasionally even adopted apocalyptic themes, even if he never identified himself with the radicals. The early Christian communities caught the apocalyptic fever, and many of them expected the arrival of God's victory in their own generation (cf. Mt 10:23; 16:28; 24:34). Some of them even produced their own apocalyptical literature, best known among which is the last book of the New Testament. The Gospel was not identical with these apocalyptical trends, yet these trends were so closely associated with it that Christian preaching has repeatedly, under certain social and political conditions, created a radical mindset.

How can we define this apocalyptical consciousness? First, it regarded society as evil. Human sin and oppression had penetrated to the very fibres of the institutions so that social reform had become impossible. Second, society must be destroyed. In fact, this destruction was already beginning; the evil operative in it was already tearing it apart. God's judgment on it was definitive. Third, a new society was about to be created, free from the injustices of the old. This new order would be God's work, and for this reason no one knew exactly what it would be like. It would embody the divine promises of love, justice and peace, but it could be spoken of only in figurative and symbolic language. According to Mannheim, this consciousness, mediated through the apocalyptical biblical passages and the radical Christian groups, is the source of the Western revolutionary tradition: political radicalism to this day has the identical threefold structure. The radicals hold that their society is so rotten that it cannot be reformed; they hold that the society must be destroyed, and since its inner contradictions are already tearing it apart, its future is doomed; and, finally, they hold that the new society to be created after the destruction of the old will be qualitatively different from it, cannot be described in detail by people caught in pre-revolutionary consciousness, and must be spoken of, for the time being, in the symbolic language of justice and peace.

In *Ideology and Utopia*, Karl Mannheim does not explore the connection of the chiliastic-utopian consciousness with ancient Jewish apocalypticism. What interested him more was the need to distinguish the chiliastic-utopian consciousness present in the early socialist movements from the more deterministic and scientific form of consciousness that emerged in the Marxist movement following the Enlightenment and found expression in official Marxist doctrine. Yet critical Marxist thinkers of the 20th century and the social critics of the New Left have recovered some of the chiliastic elements and regard their political movement as bearer of utopia.

Revolution is not the only form of utopia. Karl Mannheim presented other forms of utopian consciousness that have been effective in Western history. Unfortunately, since he was not primarily interested in religion, he did not link the other utopias to religious ideas and developments as he did in the case of revolution and chiliasm. But the close connection between the radical tradition of Western society and expressions of biblical religion is sufficient evidence to repudiate the idea that religion is always and inevitably ideological. Religion is ambiguous; it is the bearer of diverse and sometimes contradictory trends; it is both the creator of ideologies and the bearer of utopias. A weakness of the functionalist approach to the study of religion – we referred to this previously[87] – is the one-sided emphasis on those elements of religion that contribute to the creation and maintenance of the social equilibrium and hence the insufficient recognition of the utopian religious trends. Peter Berger and Thomas Luckmann are no functionalists – far from it; society for them is not a self-stabilizing system but a precarious creation ever in need of props and defences. And yet they understand religion in largely functionalist terms as the sacred canopy or ultimate sacred legitimation of the social reality and man's ever-threatened self-definition. True, in his *The Sacred Canopy*, Peter Berger acknowledges that religion, especially biblical religion, has often played a world-shaking role and questioned the taken-for-granted character of the inherited institutions. He concludes that "religion appears in history as both a world-maintaining and a world-shaking force."[88] Still, by adopting a systematic sociological approach that defines religion in terms of its world-constructing and world-maintaining function, he does not leave adequate room for exploring the aspects of religion that go counter to his principal definition.

We find the same functionalist trend in Berger and Luckmann's understanding of science, including sociological science. In their famous book, *The Social Construction of Reality*, they classify science with theology and philosophy as "a conceptual machinery of universe-maintenance."[89] Science, the two authors argue, produces a symbolic universe legitimating the precarious social reality. While science, including social science, undermines the inherited sacred symbolic universes and thus removes universe-maintaining knowledge from the person in the street – thus making social science appear radical and critical – science, including social science, in fact fulfills the task of world-maintenance. But if this is so, then what else is Berger and Luckmann's famous book but a legitimation of the precarious social order! True, in other books Peter Berger has defined the task of sociology as "debunking" or the removal of mystification,[90] but by defining science so exclusively in terms of world-maintenance, he leaves little room for this critical dimension. The functionalist trend, when uncorrected, tends to underestimate the creativity of sociology, making it a symbolic discourse legitimating the social system.

What is the reason that we find this extraordinary stress on legitimation and symbolic world-maintenance in the sociology of Peter Berger? The answer to this question is quite clear. For Peter Berger, all social life is essentially precarious. Society is created by people acting together and for that reason remains at all times threatened by possible dissolution. What if people stopped acting together? Society would simply fall apart. Berger has no Durkheimian trust in the inner coherence of the societal forces. Berger follows the Weberian suspicion that people form a society because there is an authority with a big stick that makes them do it. This authority is, for Berger, mainly symbolic. To keep social action going and make the social reality stable, we need symbols that make us believe that society is the way it is meant to be. We need world-maintaining symbols or a world-maintaining myth. We must become partially blind or else live with the nagging fear that the precarious construction of society may fall apart tomorrow.

Society, in the perspective of Peter Berger, is in need of alienation to survive. For him, alienation is the illusion that the societal processes are fixed and unchangeable realities; alienation is the repression of the truth that society is simply people doing things together and hence is basically fragile and unstable. Whenever we repress from consciousness that the social order is simply manmade, we experience society as a compelling force making us act in this or that way, even if this does not correspond to our wishes. We experience alienation because society forces us to act against our will. If we all did what we really liked, Berger holds, we would find ourselves very quickly in social chaos. Some alienation is necessary for the protection of society. A few people may be lucky enough to be able to "do their thing," but unless there were vast numbers who feel compelled to conform, to work and bear the burden, the social reality would dissolve and, with it, the possibility for personal life. Alienation is anthropologically necessary.

We need many symbols of legitimation, Berger continues. Among all of these, the most efficient alienating force is religion. Religion casts a spell of sacredness on the structures of society and makes us forget that they are merely manmade conventions. Religion produces the sacred compulsion that is necessary to keep this mad world going. This sociological theory, we note, does not differ very much from Marx and Freud, who also thought that religion was an alienating sacred canopy, except that Karl Marx believed – an accountable theological a priori! – that humanity was destined to overcome alienation and be free. Peter Berger does not share this conviction. Contrary to Marx and Freud, however, Berger does recognize world-shaking religion. In particular, he holds that the basic inspiration of Hebrew religion, expressed in its origins, its prophetic tradition and in the person of Jesus, is critical, de-alienating religion; but he thinks, if I understand him correctly, that this inspiration inevitably leads to secularization and the waning of religion, leaving the world without sacred norms. This, for Berger, is the present situation. In a secular society, the world-maintaining symbols must be supplied by non-religious legitimating systems, possibly even by scientific theories. Yet without religion society remains unstable. If I read Peter Berger correctly, religion is for him essentially a legitimating factor in society, and to the extent to which it becomes innovative and liberating, it prepares its own demise.

In this chapter we have come to a different conclusion. Religion, we have seen, is a complex, ambiguous reality with many trends, some of which may even be contradictory. Because of this complexity, religion is able to blind some people and make others see; it produces sickness in some and leads to health in others; it acts as legitimation for the status quo and as catalyst for social change. It appears that religion is capable of generating its own critique.

I have, moreover, great difficulties with Berger's view of alienation. I do not wish to look at life from a perspective that makes alienation appear as anthropologically necessary. It is of course quite true that life in society demands many services and sacrifices and, in this sense, prevents us from doing what we like and diminishes our freedom, but there is no reason to suppose that these limits will always be imposed on us against our will. Marx, we recall, clearly distinguished between imposed labour and creative work. In Marx's view, people were essentially builders, co-operative builders. Prior to Marx, Hegel himself in his mature thought distinguished between two kinds of alienation:[91] there was the alienation (*Entfremdung*) that was inflicted on people and diminished their humanity; and there was the alienation (*Entäusserung*) that was freely chosen, grounded in love, and made people more truly human. Hegel held that people who discover themselves and assume self-possession are thereby rendered capable of forgetting themselves, identifying with society and freely assuming the burden of social responsibility. Hegel adopted this anthropology, I suppose, because he believed that operative in personal life is a transcending Spirit. The very word Entäusserung was taken from the biblical message that Jesus "emptied himself." But then, there is no anthropological theory that does not begin with an a priori. Since the concepts we devise and the social analyses we propose affect our imagination and eventually influence our very perception, I object to Peter Berger's theory of alienation. I do not wish to encourage an imagination that regards alienation as anthropologically necessary. I prefer to analyze the social process from the viewpoint that freedom is humankind's promised destiny.

6

The Discovery of the Symbolic: Freud and Durkheim

The dominant intellectual trend in the industrialized societies of the nineteenth century was scientific positivism. Even in Germany, in the second half of that century, scientific positivism replaced the previous Romantic rejection of the rational Enlightenment. According to the sociologists we have studied, this scientific mindset corresponded to the rational and atomistic nature of associative society (Gesellschaft), with its contractual and hence external bond between people. The extraordinary achievements of science and technology, moreover, persuaded scientists and philosophers that the scientific method was the only valid method of inquiry and scientific knowledge was the only reliable access to truth. These thinkers looked upon reality, including human society, as a complex mechanism, as material particles interacting according to a set of mathematical laws. Reality was, for them, a universe defined by quantity, and hence they thought that all qualities could eventually be translated into quantities. Scientific positivism was based on a naive epistemology, according to which the observing subject gained knowledge of the observed object by gathering quantitative information about it and then constructing a verifiable theory explaining its behaviour. This knowledge was regarded as objective and valid universally. Positivism engendered the hope that eventually, with the advance of science, scientists would be able to solve all the problems of society.

At the end of the nineteenth century, sociologists and other social thinkers, while adopting a moderate form of positivism themselves, made the startling discovery that human culture and society, whether ancient or modern, could not be accounted for without paying attention to the symbolic dimension.[92] The human world was not simply an aggregate of quantities. It became clear to these thinkers that people did not define themselves in purely rational terms, that their interrelationship was not purely contractual, that their behaviour was not simply analyzable in quantitative terms. Operative in the production of culture and society is the symbolic self-understanding of human beings. The symbolic structure of the mind affects the creation of society, and this in turn determines people's own self-constitution.

In this chapter, I wish to present the discovery of the symbolic by two great thinkers at the turn of the 20th century: Sigmund Freud and Émile Durkheim.

Sigmund Freud was brought up in an intellectual climate determined by positivism, and in his psychological books and essays, especially in the early ones, he adopted a highly scientific and in fact mechanistic terminology for dealing with psychic phenomena. As a theorist, he never went beyond the positivism he had inherited. Yet his great discovery, that dreams have meaning and reveal in symbolic language aspects of personal life hidden from consciousness, was a turning point in the Western intellectual tradition. Dreams could not be fully explained, Freud held, as remnants of the brain's waking function; they were not uncontrolled reflexes produced by external stimuli or inner organic causes; they could not be accounted for in purely quantitative terms. Dreams had meaning. It is hard for us today to imagine how shocking Freud's theory appeared to the community of scientists at the beginning of the 20th century. They were looking for hard, quantitative data to come to a better understanding of the human mind. To attach so much importance to the fleeting images that skipped through the mind during sleep seemed to go against the scientific understanding of human life. Even though Freud thought of himself as a scientist and presented his theory of dreams as scientifically demonstrable, he was not followed by the scientific world of his day. Only poets believed him at first.

Freud's famous book, *The Interpretation of Dreams*, written at the beginning of his psychoanalytical career, is dedicated to the theory – demonstrable, he thought – that dreams reveal the hidden and unconscious depths of the human mind.[93] In significant night dreams, our unacknowledged wishes express themselves in symbolic language. Dreams are symbolic wish fulfillment. Dreams manifest people's deep inclinations and their great frustrations. While the meaning of the dream usually escapes the dreamers, dreaming it offers them a certain amount of psychic release. Freud's controversial discovery was that people's significant dreams were related to a psychic drama at the core of their personality. Freud upheld – and he was supported in this by all representatives of depth psychology – that there are psychic processes in us of which we are not aware and which nonetheless have a great influence on our action and well-being. These psychic processes can even make us sick. While we have no direct access to our own unconscious, Freud argued that these hidden psychic forces express themselves in moments of spontaneity, such as laughter, free associations, or slips in speech or action, but more especially in the symbolic language of dreams. The dream is the royal road to the unconscious. It is a revelation of the hidden truth about oneself.

We note that the revelation of the deep takes place in symbolic language. The symbol is here not the second-best, an imprecise approximation of the truth, eventually to be displaced by a clearly defined concept. The symbol is the proper mode of a person's self-manifestation, and it is the encounter with this symbol that may lead to self-knowledge and eventual psychic transformation. Healing is not due to the content of the dream analyzed by the psychotherapist and presented to the dreamer in conceptual form; healing may come about as persons discover for themselves, with the help of a therapist, that the dream discloses a hidden truth about their personal existence. Patients in quest of healing will not be helped by assimilating intellectually the interpretation offered by the therapist; what counts, rather, is that the patients stay with their dream and use the interpretation worked out in collaboration with the therapist to make the symbolic language of the dream meaningful and powerful. Symbols, for Freud, were not only revelations of the unconscious; they also had power to transform the unconscious. It is true that Freud tended to confine the meaning of the dream to the fulfillment of hidden wishes and tried to interpret anxiety dreams in terms of repressed desires, but the psychotherapeutic practice, inspired by Freud, has widened the understanding of dreams as manifestations of a person's unconscious life, including his or her deep wishes. The various schools of depth psychology look upon dreams as the symbolic language revealing a person's hidden life, in a form that enables people to encounter their own depth, listen to its hidden message and, by responding to it in a creative way, initiate significant transformation of their personal lives. The symbol is here both revelation and power.

It is also true that Freud tended to regard the content of the unconscious as made up of material repressed from consciousness, as if there existed no unconscious process in the mind that had not previously been conscious. He emphasized this aspect of the unconscious because it was the most important one in the psychotherapeutic process. In his more theoretical work, however, he recognized the existence of primary psychic processes that never reach the conscious mind. He even seems to have acknowledged a collective memory in the unconscious, handed on in largely hidden ways, that affects people's imagination and creativity.[94] Freud did not object in principle to the "collective unconscious," to which Carl Jung attached so much importance.[95] What Freud objected to in Jung's theory was the idea that the inherited symbolism was trans-historical, that it related people in every culture to the identical symbolic reality. For Freud, this collective unconscious was strictly historical: it was produced by the significant experiences of a people in their evolutionary past. Freud objected to the use of the collective unconscious in psycho-therapeutic practice, at least until the personal unconscious had been dealt with adequately. He feared that a hasty turning to a collective symbolism would serve only as defence against, or disguise for, the unresolved personal conflicts repressed in one's own past, especially in infancy. Taking these restrictive remarks into account, we may conclude that Freud's understanding of the unconscious, operative in people's lives, included not only the repressed material that had previously been conscious, but also hidden memories transcending personal history that may become sources of creativity or burdens that wound the soul. Symbols exercise power in the self-constitution of human existence.

Freud's theory was challenged by his contemporaries. In the highly rational culture, scientists and educated people in general tend to regard symbols as approximate formulations of a reality that could be expressed with greater precision in conceptual terms. Symbols are often seen as appeals made to the emotions rather than to a person's mind. Symbols are here regarded as decorations in a room that is essentially complete; they do not enter the very making of the room. Freud's theory of dreams and unconscious processes was thus repudiated by the scientific community of his time. Many laypeople listened to him, especially artists and poets. It was only gradually that psychoanalysis affected the self-understanding of Western culture.

Even theologians began to listen to Freud, despite his negative evaluation of religion as collective neurosis. For if i) the symbol is the revelation of the deep and in fact the only way in which the deep can manifest itself, if ii) the symbol can never be replaced by a concept or a clear and distinct idea, and if iii) the symbol enables persons to confront the hidden dimension of their lives and in doing so be significantly changed, then it should be possible to use this notion of symbol for a better understanding of divine revelation. Since contemporary theology, as we have repeatedly mentioned, tends to speak of God as a presence in human life, as matrix, vector and horizon of human history, it is possible to affirm the divine mystery as the deepest dimension of human existence that reveals itself in symbol forms. These symbols in turn enable believers to encounter the divine operative in their lives and in doing so to enter into a significant transformation of their personal and social existence. The encounter with God's self-revelation in these symbols is a saving event. We may even present Jesus Christ as the ultimate symbol in which the divine ground of the human and cosmic reality reveals itself: by encountering him and believing in him, people come to know their own depth, their own humanity as well as the divine mystery that sustains them.

Freud himself did not engage in philosophical reflection on the role of symbols in man's making of man. But in his therapeutic practice he did make use of symbols, of one symbol in particular, in a way that reminds theologians of the role played by symbols in biblical religion. Sam Keen, in his public conversations, has often referred to psychotherapy as a process whereby people are taught to tell their story in a new way, and, by doing so, to experience deliverance from their psychic blocks and inhibitions. Telling one's story is never easy. When we do decide to tell the story of our private life as far back into infancy as possible, we inevitably do so under the guidance of the symbol we have adopted for our own self-understanding. This symbol determines what we remember of the past and what we forget, and selects from the wealth of material the details we regard as worthy to be reported. If I think of myself as the one who always gets the short end of the stick, then I will tell of my past by recalling the incidents, beginning in earliest childhood, that show how I have been disfavoured. I will find that I remember in detail the incidents when I have been cheated, when others have been preferred to me, when I did not get the love or appreciation I thought I deserved. The rest of my childhood I have largely forgotten. It is in these painful disappointments that my true self appears. Or if I think of myself as the one who always wins, then I will tell my story by relating those events of my past that reveal my own superiority. I will be able to recall from my earliest childhood the moments of triumph and the incidents where people praised me, found me gifted or handsome, and regarded me as a special kind of person. The other incidents I will have forgotten. The telling of my own story, then, is always mediated by a particular self-symbolization. People who approach a therapist to be healed from symptoms of various kinds will tell their personal story through a symbolic self-understanding closely related to their illness. They may have no self-knowledge at all. They may have repressed from memory the incidents of their lives that had the most formative influence on them. Even if the events told by them in their story are true, they may still be ignorant of their past and in no way suspect the origin of their present turmoil. Now it is the claim of Sigmund Freud – and here, for many, he leaves the realm of science – that there is one single model story, one Story with a capital S, that applies to all individuals wherever they may live; and if people learn to tell their own story in dialogue with the normative story, then they will remember the significant events they have forgotten, they will come to understand their own dreams, they will acquire a realistic understanding of their own past and eventually experience the deliverance of the symptoms that made them suffer. What is this normative story? According to Freud, it is the story of King Oedipus, who killed his father and married his mother.

The Oedipal story is the salvation myth in Freudian therapy. If people are taught how to tell their own story in the light of the normative story, they will eventually get in touch with their unresolved psychic conflicts and be empowered to transcend them. People in dialogue with the Oedipal story will begin to understand their own dreams, remember long-forgotten childhood experiences that reveal their desperate attachment to their mother and their hostility and fear of their father, and even recall many incidents in later life when the unresolved Oedipal feelings of childhood have manifested themselves in their relationship to men and women. Freud held that by learning to tell their story in a new way, through a new self-symbolization, they would be able to face the repressed material – and here dreams play an important role, come to greater self-knowledge, re-solve the hidden conflicts of childhood and adolescence, and experience a new freedom in creating their own future.

How could Freud, the scientist, make the extraordinary claim that a legend belonging to Greek mythology is the one normative story revealing the central psychological complex of every single individual? This claim seems to move beyond the realm of science. In the past, only religions have spoken of normative stories. However, Freud based the universality of the Oedipal complex not on metaphysics, but on the biology of the family: he thought that being born of woman and being nourished and protected by this woman and the man to whom she belonged would

inevitably introduce the male child into the Oedipal constellation. What
Freud overlooked was how much the structure of the family and hence
the experience of infancy and childhood depended on cultural factors and
the social order.[96] Freud's theory, which proved so useful in the therapy
of his own patients, reflects the middle-class environment characteristic
of European society at the turn of the last century. Freud did not realize that by making Oedipus Rex the normative myth of human life, he
excluded women from his essential imagination; for him, the typical
human being was male. It may well be that for great numbers of people
in Western culture, the Oedipal story is still a central model for arriving
at self-knowledge and personal deliverance; yet by investing this story
with universal validity, orthodox Freudian psychoanalysis has become
an ideology that subjects people to a preconceived image and possibly
imprisons them in a false imagination.

Theologians read Freud with amazement. Freud's idea that a normative story can become a guide leading people to personal transformation
may help theologians to understand how the biblical stories of salvation
mediate the re-creation of human life. The Exodus is a normative story,
for it not only reveals God's mercy in redeeming Israel from slavery, but
also manifests the hidden divine will in regard to all peoples burdened
by oppression. In contemporary liberation theology, this model story has
acquired central significance. Oppressed societies and classes are here
trying to understand themselves and their histories through the revealed
model of Exodus and thus open themselves to the divine power capable
of rescuing them.

Even more central in Christianity is the story of Jesus Christ, crucified
and risen, which offers the model of God's saving grace acting in human
life, personal and social. How does this story affect the believing community? Let me adapt the Freudian use of the normative story. Christian
believers, I propose, try to see their lives and tell their own stories in
conversation with the life, death and resurrection of Jesus, and in doing so
they are enabled to discover the sinful and destructive trends threatening
their lives from within and from without, and discover – with surprise – a
gracious power present in their lives, saving them from these trends and
strengthening them to overcome the obstacles to love and surrender.
Jesus here becomes the key to people's personal life. In him, believers
discover their true selves. In other conversations, Jesus becomes the one
who reveals the truth about life in society. Jesus reveals to us who we are
meant to be as a community, a church and a society. He initiates us into a

self-symbolization through which we come to understand ourselves as a sinful and redeemed people, as a people with a destiny, called to hope in the future promises. This symbolization, we note, is not imposed upon us from without, for if God is the deepest transcendent dimension of human life as matrix, vector and horizon, then Jesus as God's Word reveals to us not an extrinsic truth to which we must submit, but our own unexplored depth. In him, we encounter God and our true selves.

Perhaps it is necessary to add that in making Jesus the normative story, we do not propose him as the model for psychological transformation or social change. His story reveals the divine mystery that works itself out in and through human growth and the various transformations of personal and social life. Jesus is a theological model. In him salvation is offered to us. Making his story normative in their lives, Christians do not invalidate model stories of psychological healing and social reconstruction. Christians believe, rather, that through the various ways in which people are humanized and liberated, psychically and socially, they are carried forward by a mystery that transcends them and that has revealed its features in Jesus Christ.

Let me add at this point that in the story of Oedipus Rex, the maleness of the hero is of central importance, for it determines his relation to mother and father. In the story of Jesus, on the other hand, maleness in no way enters into his redemptive role. The story presents Jesus as open to the mystery of God; he heard the voice and followed it; he saw himself as the bearer of the divine; he believed in the coming kingdom and his own role in initiating it; he saw through the false consciousness of his society; and, because he revealed to the people the falsifying structures of empire and religious hierarchy, he undermined the prestige of the authorities and was duly hated by them, persecuted and eventually nailed to the Roman cross. Yet his death was not the end. Triumphing over the powers of darkness, God had the last word: God raised Jesus from among the dead. In this entire story, there is nothing specifically male. The redemptive task could have equally been performed by a female. This deserves to be noted since there are theologians who oppose the ordination of women to the priesthood by referring to the maleness of Jesus.[97] I think they are wrong: the normative story of Christianity is not sexist.

Do Christians claim that this Jesus is the symbol of salvation for all mankind? Does this symbol have universal application? For practical and urgent reasons, to overcome enmity and foster peace, contemporary theologians try to reconcile the Christian Gospel with religious pluralism. Christ's universal vocation does not necessarily mean that there is no room before God for other religions and other wisdom traditions. At Vatican Council II, the Catholic Church tried to relativize the symbol of Christ in a theologically responsible way by recognizing God's redemptive presence, fully revealed in Jesus, in the whole of human history, including the world religions.[98] After the Holocaust and the Church's painful recognition of its ancient anti-Jewish rhetoric, the Church reread the New Testament, especially Romans 11, affirmed the ongoing validity of the Mosaic covenant, and acknowledged an honoured place of Jewish religion before God.[99]

After this theological digression, let us return for a moment to Sigmund Freud. Since he was so closely identified with the positivistic intellectual climate of his day, Freud was unable to reflect on the methodological implications of his own discovery. He was a brilliant psychotherapist and an original thinker who broke new ground in the understanding of human life; yet even though his discovery of the symbolic had in principle overcome his positivistic presuppositions, he was unable to critically re-examine his own starting point. Freud's discovery made such a re-evaluation necessary. Why? Because if our self-symbolization determines the telling of our story, then it also will determine the perspective in which we look upon the human world in general. What follows from this is that scientists studying human behaviour can no longer take for granted that they stand on wholly neutral ground, observing the human world with objectivity. The human world studied by social scientists is not a given reality confronting them as an object; it is rather mediated to the understanding by the symbolic structure of their mind. The claim to objectivity made by positivistic scholars disguises from them their own symbolic self-understanding and hence makes them blind to the ideological dimension of their research. We have in Freud, then, the seed for the overcoming of positivism and the beginning of a new approach to social science, one that takes into account the presuppositions of the observer.

* * *

The discovery of the symbolic took place in a dramatic way in the sociological work of the great French thinker, Émile Durkheim. As we shall see, Durkheim changed his mind in mid-career. Like Freud, he was closely identified with the positivistic intellectual climate. He took for granted the scientific method as the one valid approach to research and repudiated metaphysical reflection on the meaning of human life. Yet coming from the more rational positivism of the French tradition, in contrast with the more empirical positivism that influenced Freud, Durkheim was convinced that the scientific method could discover the structure of the social reality, including the values on which it was based, and thus define the moral ideals that people must embrace to assure the well-being and development of their society. Here, science included ethics. Durkheim held that scientists, especially social scientists, were engaged in research and reflection out of moral commitment. Social science, he argued, discerns the structure and the values of the social order, thus enabling society to become more faithful to its destiny. It was during Durkheim's scientific effort to understand the society to which he belonged that he made the discovery of the symbolic.

In his early work, *The Division of Labor in Society*, published in 1893, Durkheim distinguished between two types of society, traditional and modern, in terms that have become familiar to us. We recall that Toennies's distinction between Gemeinschaft and Gesellschaft expressed a certain consensus among social thinkers, even if they did not necessarily agree in their evaluation. Durkheim was focused especially on the social bond operative in these two types of society. Traditional society, Durkheim argued, was made up of self-contained units adjacent to one another, such as families, clans or village communities – units that were largely self-sufficient, able to produce their own means of subsistence, and thus essentially independent from one another. What, then, kept traditional society together? Durkheim replied that the social bond that united people in traditional societies was a common symbol system. In these societies, social solidarity was created through sharing the same rites, values, dreams and myths.

By contrast, modern society, according to Durkheim's analysis, was held together by a complex division of labour. The units of modern society were interdependent, each in need of the others for the means of subsistence and the expansion of life. Durkheim tried to show that modern society – Gesellschaft – was not simply produced by rational and contractual elements, but also – contrary to Toennies – by the organic interdependence of all citizens in their social, economic and political existence. The social bond of modern, industrial and democratic society, then, was not weak, as was supposed by most social philosophers; it was in fact very strong, grounded in the complex division of labour. Despite the individualism of modern life, Durkheim argued, there does exist a profound social bond among people, a bond that serves as the foundation on which contracts are made and kept. Contracts do not create the social bond; they presuppose it. What Durkheim tried to do in *The Division of Labor in Society* was to clarify the moral foundations of modern society. While many sociologists supposed that Gesellschaft inevitably undermined morality and promoted selfishness, Durkheim tried to demonstrate that the social laws operative in modern society actually create a profound social bond and establish new values, values that enable people to transcend egotism and commit themselves to the common good.

While traditional society was held together by common symbols and rites, modern society, held together by the complex division of labour, was no longer in need of a symbol system to remain united and grounded in common values. In modern society, Durkheim argued, religion would disappear. While he disagreed with sociologists in the evaluation of Gesellschaft, he agreed with them in their theory of secularization. With the ongoing complexification of the division of labour, religion will eventually wither away: it will no longer have a social function in modern society. "That is not to say," Durkheim insists, "that the common conscience is threatened with a total disappearance." Something new will be emerging. The common conscience

> increasingly comes to consist of a very general and very indeterminate way of thinking and feeling, which leaves an open place for a growing multitude of individual differences. There is even a place where it is strengthened and made precise; that is the way in which it regards the individual. As all the other beliefs and all the other practices take on a character less and less religious, the individual becomes the object of a sort of religion. We erect a cult in behalf of personal dignity which, as a very strong cult, already has its superstitions.[100]

Durkheim hoped that his own sociology, by laying bare the moral foundations of modern society, would help to make people more conscious of the social bond that unites them and thus overcome the isolation from the social matrix that threatens individuals in times of change.

A few years later, Durkheim made a study of suicide. To demonstrate the power of sociological analysis, he tried to show his contemporaries that even phenomena as irrational and unpredictable as suicide, on the surface the most private and least social of all actions, could be understood more clearly through a sociological analysis. In his book *Suicide*, published in 1897, Durkheim distinguished between various forms of suicide. There were the selfless suicides, by which individuals in traditional societies executed the judgment of the community on a fault they had committed. Disgraced in the eyes of the community, they were willing to put an end to their lives. In modern society, however, most suicides take place because persons had been pushed to the margin of the social order or because the values on which they had built their lives were undermined by significant social change. Durkheim spoke of egoistic and anomic suicides. On the basis of empirical information provided by statistics available in various parts of Europe, Durkheim came to the conclusion that the rate of these suicides remained constant in a given area as long as the social order remained unchanged. Suicide was thus related to social conditions. With the advance of modernity, i.e., with the growth of industrialization and the spread of individualism, the rate of suicide increased. There were more suicides in cities than in the country, more among men than among women, more in Protestant than in Catholic areas, more among the individualistic middle class than among the more communally minded lower strata of society. Since suicide is unplanned and unpredictable, how can there be social laws governing its frequency? Durkheim could explain the constant rate of suicide in traditional society; here he could invoke the symbol system that created the social bond and affected the minds of the people. The tensions in society were transmitted to people through this symbol system and could be thought of as pushing a constant number of individuals into suicide. But Durkheim was unable to explain why in modern society the suicide rate was constant as long as social conditions remained unchanged. Since he had denied in his earlier book that a symbolic system was operative in Gesellschaft, he was now unable to explain how social conditions could impress themselves on the consciousness of individual citizens and with growing tensions push some of them, at a constant rate, into suicidal action.

This was Durkheim's dilemma. How could he account for the social law he observed? Here are some of the reflections that led him to resolve his difficulty.

> Victims of suicide are in an infinite minority, which is widely dispersed; each of them performs his act separately, without knowing that others are doing the same; and yet, so long as society remains unchanged, the number of suicides remains the same.... There must then be some force in their common environment inclining them all in the same direction, whose greater and lesser strength causes the greater or lesser number of suicides. ... This force then must be collective. Each people has collectively an inclination of its own to suicide, on which the size of its

contribution to voluntary death depends. ... These tendencies are forces *sui generis* which dominate the consciousness of single individuals. ... They have an existence of their own: they are as real as cosmic forces, though of another sort.[101]

Durkheim, then, changed his mind. To account for the empirical evidence, he postulated a position he had previously denied: namely, that modern society expresses itself in a symbol system that has an objective facticity, and at the same time creates the consciousness of the individual citizens.

At the end of his *Suicide*, he speaks of *la conscience collective*, the collective consciousness, which was to become the central topic of his later book on religion.[102] Modern society, then, as much as the traditional one, is bound together by a common symbol system. The individualistic and scientific mindset characteristic of modern life is itself generated by a symbol system reflecting the social order that creates a common bond between people, despite their greater personal freedom and their relative independence from traditional values. In modern society, symbols remain constitutive of personal consciousness and of society.

With this discovery of the symbolic, Durkheim acknowledged that it was impossible to account for the social evolution of human life and consciousness purely and simply in terms of the material factors that enter into it. His discovery overcame both scientific positivism, which sought to reduce the human reality to measurable quantity, and rigid historical materialism, which tried to account for the evolution of consciousness in terms of the evolving means of production. The creation of consciousness and society could not be understood apart from the symbolic dimension. Yet Durkheim was unable to clarify the dialectical relationship between society and symbol. Sometimes he said that society expresses itself in symbols and at other times he claimed that symbols enter into the very constitution of society. He failed to say that these two contrary positions must be affirmed simultaneously and then develop a dialectical understanding, according to which social institutions create the symbolic structure of the mind, and conversely, at certain critical periods, the symbols of self-understanding affect the life and structure of society.

While Durkheim's sociological approach had nothing in common with Freud's psychological analysis, both thinkers came to similar conclusions: people's self-symbolization enters into the creation of their history, their culture and their society. Even if the two scholars were atheists by personal conviction and adopted reductionist approaches to the study of religion, they helped nonetheless to create a new openness to religion in modern culture. They made room in the social sciences for the symbolic dimension of human existence.

Durkheim's discovery of the symbolic did not make him re-examine the positivistic assumptions implicit in his scientific approach. He continued to think of himself as an objective observer of the social reality which he tried to understand by means of the scientific method. Durkheim, we recall, thought that this method enabled him to grasp the moral foundations of society, and in this he differed substantially from the dominant empirical positivism. In fact, measured by the value-neutrality characteristic of contemporary sociology, Durkheim's moral tone makes him a radical. Yet he failed to recognize that if consciousness is created by symbols mediated through the social order, then this is also true of the mindset of scientists. Scientists, then, are not objective observers. What scientists must do, in fidelity to truth, is to become aware of their own symbolic presuppositions and their relationship to the social object they studied. While Durkheim's discovery of the symbolic overcame positivism in principle, he did not transcend it in a theoretical way. Durkheim continued to defend the purely objective character of social science.

At the end of *Suicide*, as we mentioned above, Durkheim moved from the affirmation of a collective consciousness to the concept of religion.[103] He here anticipated a theme that he was to examine several years later in his famous *The Primitive Forms of Religious Life* (1912). Already in his earlier book, Durkheim felt that his discovery of the symbolic dimension enabled him to gain a better understanding of religion. He rejected the various theories of religion that ascribed its origin to purely personal experiences, feelings, needs or frustrations, whether these theories were proposed by believing philosophers eager to defend religion or by atheistic thinkers bent on undermining it. Religion, Durkheim insisted, is never found apart from a collectivity. Religion unifies people; it links them to their common history and strengthens them in their common task. Religion is the source of social identification. Why is religion able to do all this? Because it is the symbolic representation of the vision and the values immanent in society. In religion, society gives expression to its highest ideals and deepest aspirations. Only a sociological definition of religion does justice to its total reality.

For Durkheim, we note, society does not remain purely external to the people who constitute it. He vehemently repudiated the individualism of his day and the utilitarian concept of society based on social contract. Since people's entry into personal consciousness takes place through participation in language, culture, institutions, and eventually the whole structure of society, this society becomes a constitutive element of their self-definition as persons. Because of this process of socialization – Durkheim did not yet use this expression – each person encounters society as a dimension of his or her own consciousness. All of us encounter within ourselves a reality that transcends us, to which we belong, and that exists beyond our death.[104] For Durkheim, it is the encounter of people with the transcendent element in their own consciousness that creates morality: people experience within themselves that they are called to serve society. Biological and instinctual egotism is overcome by a more powerful, spontaneous dedication to the common good. People experience that they exist through society and their participation in it. Morality leads in the direction of self-sacrifice. The encounter with the transcendent in personal consciousness eventually gives rise to devotion, to worship, to religious experience. Our social matrix, present in consciousness, summons us to awe and surrender.

Religion, then, is people's encounter with the depth and the height of their society. The gods are simply "the hypostatic form of society,"[105] Durkheim writes. Through these gods – that is, through the symbolic representations – a society discovers its hidden potentialities, its richest resources, and its most daring dreams. Durkheim writes: "Religion is in a word the system of symbols by which society becomes conscious of itself, it is the characteristic way of thinking of collective existence."[106] Durkheim, the atheist, found himself pushed to the conclusion that every society will create its own religion. Every society in the process of living up to its highest ideals will generate the worship of its symbolic self-representation. In *The Primitive Forms of Religious Life*, after having examined in detail Australian totemic religion, Durkheim concludes, "There is something eternal in religion which is destined to survive all the particular symbols in which religious thought has successively enveloped itself. There can be no society which does not feel the need of upholding and reaffirming at regular intervals the collective sentiments and the collective ideas which make its unity and personality."[107] The symbols generated by society ultimately lead to religion; they communicate the experience of the sacred and involve people in the worship of the principles out of which they become alive.

While Durkheim believed that the traditional religions of the West, Judaism and Christianity, were unable to survive the critical spirit of

Enlightenment, his sociological theory made him expect new forms of religious life in modern society. These forms had not yet emerged, since society was still in transition and turmoil: "The old gods are growing old and already dead, and others are not yet born."[108] Yet he repudiated Comte's conscious effort to produce a humanistic religion suited to the conditions of modern life. Religions, Durkheim clearly saw, cannot be rationally constructed. Religion happens; it is created through the experience of the sacred by which people are brought in touch with the deepest dimension of their social existence.

Sociologists have often regarded Durkheim's view of religion as purely ideological. Religion, they understand Durkheim to say, is the sacred power legitimating the existing social order. Religion creates social stability and provides a symbolic system that protects society from the forces that seek to undermine it or modify its structure. Some sociologists go so far as to suggest that for Durkheim, religion was the worship of society. This, I think, is an inadequate reading of Durkheim's sociology of religion. For the great French sociologist again and again insisted that religion celebrates the deepest values operative in the social order, commemorates the moments in the history of society when its nature found the highest expression, and draws a symbolic image of what the society is meant to be in the future. "A society can neither create itself nor recreate itself without at the same time creating an ideal. This creation is not a sort of work of supererogation for it, by which it would complete itself, being already formed; it is the act by which it is periodically made and remade.... The ideal society is not outside the real society, it is part of it."[109] Religion, then, as the celebration of the highest aspirations of society, grounded in the significant moments of history, is able to generate a critique of the existing social order and create strong impulses to change it. "The society that reality bids us desire is not the society as it appears to itself, but the society as it is or is really becoming."[110] While at certain times religion may well serve as protector of the social order, at other times it judges the present social conditions by the ideal of society and produces movements of reform. The values in terms of which the existing society is found wanting are themselves generated by a deeper level of the same society.

Durkheim rejected Marx's view of religion as the inverted image of society. Religion was not simply the mirror of society that made sacred the existing power relations in the social order. While Durkheim believed that Christianity (as well as Judaism) had largely become an ideological symbol system protecting the *ancien régime* or other outdated social orders, he did not wish to define the essence of religion in terms of this particular historical development. Religion for Durkheim was not simply a dependent variable. His sociological research convinced him that culture and society were constituted by a process in which both the social infrastructure and the symbolic superstructure exercised a creative role. For Durkheim, the passionate ideals that enabled a prophet such as Marx to condemn the existing social order were themselves generated by the best of the society and its tradition. He wrote, "Socrates expressed, more clearly than his judges, the morality suited to his time. It would be easy to show that, as the result of the transformation of the old society based on the *gens* and the consequent disturbance of religious beliefs, a new morality and religious faith had become necessary in Athens…. It is in this sense that Socrates was ahead of his time while at the same time expressing its spirit."[111] Religion, for Durkheim, we conclude, cannot be equated with a sacred canopy protecting the existing society; at its best, it produces a crisis period in history where society recreates and reconstitutes itself according to its own highest aspirations. Religion again and again turns out to be utopian.

* * *

Durkheim's theory that every society eventually generates a form of religion has led to an important contemporary controversy on civil religion in America. In a now famous essay,[112] Robert Bellah finds evidence in the foundational documents of the American republic, the ceremonies of handing on public office, and the public holidays commemorating the important events of American history that there exists in America a civil religion with its worship, its rites and its divinity. The structure of this religion, Bellah tries to show, is the fusion of two symbolic legacies bequeathed on the republic: the Enlightenment heritage of trust in the laws of nature and nature's God, and the biblical heritage of faith in the high destiny of the chosen people in their promised land. This civil religion, Bellah holds, can be distinguished from the historic religions of the churches and synagogues. The traditional biblical religions may be linked in some way to civil religion, but they retain their independence and autonomy, and in fact their relationship to civil religion varies greatly over the years from warm welcome to critical distance.

What is the role and function of civil religion? Readers have differed greatly in the understanding of Bellah's article.[113] Some regarded Bellah's civil religion as pure ideology legitimating the American way of life; others

took an even more negative view of civil religion, seeing in it a dangerous idolatry whereby a nation worships its own success and motivates an
aggressive foreign policy. In a subsequent article, Bellah explained that
neither of these interpretations corresponds to his own view.[114] While
he admitted that civil religion could deteriorate and become ideological
pretense or, worse, idolatrous worship, civil religion according to its own
nature was the celebration of the greatest values of the nation and its highest ideals – Durkheimian religion – and provided transcendent norms for
criticizing its actual collective life and its governmental practices. Civil
religion was "the subordination of the nation to ethical principles that
transcend it and in terms of which it should be judged."[115] For Bellah,
civil religion was not devoid of utopian elements.

Another famous study on religion in America, written in the 1950s,
had presented a very different picture of the religious situation. In his
Protestant, Catholic, Jew,[116] Will Herberg examined the faith of Americans
in churches and synagogues and found little evidence for critical utopian
trends. He came to the conclusion that while the churches among themselves and the churches together vis-à-vis the synagogues differed greatly
in terms of doctrine and ritual, they preached and promoted the identical
religious ethos. A superficial look at churches and synagogues suggests
great diversity of religion in America, yet a more careful study reveals that
Americans have a common religion. "A realistic appraisal of the values,
ideas and behavior of the American people leads to the conclusion that
Americans, by and large, do have their 'common religion' and that that
religion is the system familiarly known as the American Way of Life."[117]
Will Herberg presented a detailed study of this religion. He sums up the
American religion in the single word "democracy" – which includes law
and order, free enterprise, optimism and the middle-class values that
dominated American life in the 1950s and made this period one of universal conformity. Civil religion, or what Herberg calls "the operative faith
of the American people,"[118] is here a vast ideological system, subsuming
the inherited biblical religion, that sacralizes the dreams and aspirations
of the American middle class, persuades the lower classes to imitate as
much as possible the middle-class style, blinds people to the exclusion
of whole sections of the population from the American consensus, breeds
intolerance with public criticism, and fosters political aggression against
nations that have repudiated the American values.

There is no reason to suppose that the studies of Herberg and Bellah are
contradictory.[119] Herberg wrote his book in the 1950s, an age of conformity

characterized by an absence of public criticism. Even the churches and synagogues had become silent. In his study, Herberg wanted to confront the religious institutions with what they had become. Bellah wrote his article in the 1960s, when criticism abounded. He wanted to convince the young critics of American civic life and foreign policy that they stood not against but within the tradition of American civil religion. The inherited symbols of the American republic provided norms that condemned the injustices and the racism of American life and the aggressive posture of American foreign policy. The radical self-criticism of the '60s was not anti-American; it was rather an exercise of the American civil religion.

In a more recent article,[120] Bellah tries to show that the original American ideals even generate a criticism of present-day corporate capitalism. The free enterprise policy of the young republic recommended the family farm and the family business as the defence of personal freedom, and implied a criticism of the large corporations that were being formed in England at that time. American civil religion could become the bearer of utopia.

Civil religion, then, according to Darrol Bryant's analysis,[121] fulfills a threefold function: it serves as an intentional horizon projecting an image of the nation's destiny, as an integrating myth permitting all sections of the nation to be equally members of society even if they perpetuate diverse cultural traditions, and as a public court protecting social values and keeping people critical of the existing social conditions. Looked upon from this point of view, civil religion becomes ideological only if it collapses the ideal with the actual. In Bellah's perspective, only a corrupt civil religion sanctifies the present social order and fosters political trends towards national self-aggrandizement. If this corruption proceeds, the civil religion may eventually lead the self-worship of the nation and an idolatrous over-evaluation of its role in history and become an advocate of right-wing reactionary politics. Civil religion, we conclude, is ambiguous: it thrives in ideological and utopian forms.

At the end of this chapter, let me add that it is not always easy, and it is sometimes even impossible, to distinguish between utopian and ideological trends in religion. Religion always promotes a certain behaviour and legitimates certain values. But to know whether a Durkheimian analysis of a particular religious phenomenon, which sees in it society's *élan* towards its highest ideal, is appropriate, or whether a Marxist analysis, which sees in it a legitimation of the status quo, is preferable, is often difficult . There may well be situations where this question is resolved by social scientists in accordance with their political standpoint and their vision of the future. If we suppose, for instance, that limit to growth has become the only intelligent and humane politics of survival, then a religious movement that fosters diligence and makes laziness a sin would be an ideological defence of the inherited system, while a religious trend that stresses contemplation and does not invest time with a sense of urgency could in fact exercise a utopian function. If, on the other hand, the policy of minimal growth is seen as unrealistic, of benefit to the wealthy nations and of harm to the poor, then the evaluation of these religious trends would be the opposite. Yet there is no neutral ground on which sociologists can take refuge. Sometimes only the actual course of history will enable us to discern the true nature of the ideas and values that have contributed to it. It is a principle of hermeneutical sociology that the analytical understanding of critical issues depends on the scholar's vision of the ideal society and represents, in some way or other, an active attempt to create this historical reality. We here touch upon a subject that will occupy us further on: the power exerted by the symbolic structure of the imagination in the making of culture and society.

7

The Secularization Debate

In the preceding chapter, we examined the discovery of the symbolic by two great thinkers, Freud and Durkheim, and suggested that this breakthrough led to a greater appreciation of religion on the part of the social sciences. Did this new sensitivity simply prepare a greater openness of sociology to the study of religion? Or did it also represent a new cultural trend favourable to the practice of religion? On this question sociologists are divided. A good number of sociologists, while appreciating the role of symbols in people's social existence, believe that modern industrial society inevitably leads to the disappearance of religion. This is the famous theory of secularization. Other sociologists do not think that this theory has ever been demonstrated. In this chapter we shall examine the arguments in favour of the theory of secularization as the starting point for the study of contemporary religion.

We recall that the nineteenth century witnessed several theories of secularization, even if the term "secularization" has been used in sociology only fairly recently.[122] In the preceding chapters, we encountered three versions of this theory. There was, first of all, the Comtean theory, endorsed in one way or another by a great number of scientists and Enlightenment philosophers, according to which the advance of rationality and the scientific spirit would inevitably undermine the religious heritage; religious myths would give way to scientific explanations. This theory of secularization was linked to a philosophy of progress based on science, technology and liberal democracy. A second theory of secularization we found in social thinkers who regarded religion as a symptom of human alienation and who anticipated the disappearance of religion as people were able to overcome the deprivations and frustrations inflicted on them by society. The views of Marx and Freud belong to this category – even if the latter also helped to overcome scientific positivism and create a new sensitivity to symbols. Finally, there was the theory of secularization proposed by sociologists, many of whom were Germans, who regarded the transition from traditional to modern industrialized society as a decline of culture and predicted the waning of religion with regret. The empirical evidence to which these social thinkers appealed was the dramatic transition of European society from an old order, in which religion was a taken-for-granted dimension of social, cultural, political and personal life, to a new, as yet undefined order, where religion was losing its social, cultural and political importance and where even its significance for personal life was being increasingly questioned. But was it reasonable and scientific to make the description of this particular European experience into a sociological law of universal application and predict that modernity would necessarily lead to the disappearance of religion?

To this day, sociologists are divided in regard to the theory of secularization. Some still claim that the advance of industrialization and individualism inevitably leads to the disappearance of religion, while others insist that this theory is by no means demonstrated and that there is no fixed sociological law relating religion and modern society. The present state of the controversy is well brought out in two books published in England in the 1960s, Bryan Wilson's *Religion in Secular Society*,[123] which makes a persuasive case for the theory of secularization, and David Martin's *The Religious and the Secular*,[124] which tries to show that the concept of secularization has introduced confusion in the study of religion and hence ought to be banished from the sociological vocabulary. In this chapter I wish to discuss the three arguments proposed by Bryan Wilson and make them the starting point for reflections on religion in North America today.

Bryan Wilson's first argument is taken from empirical studies. He presents an impressive amount of statistical evidence to show that the Church of England has lost power and influence over the last hundred years. A comparative study of the number of baptisms, confirmations, enrollments in parishes, children in Sunday school, Sunday school teachers and Easter communicants shows beyond a doubt that the power the Church of England holds over the imagination of the people is steadily declining. This conclusion is confirmed by studying the steady increase of secular over religious marriages. Similar evidence, one may add here, could be given for other European countries. At one time, religion was fully established in European culture in the sense that religious symbols and religious institutions were part of the basic social structures that defined society; today religion has become a set of convictions that certain families cherish and hand on to their children, or something that people freely choose. This is the sociological process called secularization. On the basis of empirical research, then, Bryan Wilson tries to establish the law that the more closely people are involved in industrial production, the less religious they become. Thus, people in the city are less religious than those in the country, men are less religious than women, men and women of working age are less religious than children and the aged, the highly industrialized countries in Europe are less religious than the less industrialized ones, and so forth.

The great exception to the European pattern is the American experience. A study of church membership in the United States over 80 years reveals the opposite trend. In 1880, only 20 per cent of Americans were church members; in 1960, they represented 63 per cent of the population. Some sociologists think that because of the great mobility of the population, church members may have been counted more than once. Yet Wilson accepts the high figures as reliable; they are moreover confirmed by Gallup Poll data. At the same time, he is seriously puzzled by the contrasting pattern in America.

Andrew Greeley, in several important studies,[125] has examined the empirical data on religion in America and presented the contrasting pattern as an argument against the theory of secularization. The available information reveals a certain cycle of slightly higher and slightly lower church attendance and membership, for which it is difficult to find a sociological explanation, but there is no evidence whatever for the theory that increasing industrialization and individualism lead to a weakening of religion. The American experience, then, should offer enough evidence to show the inadequacy of the theory of secularization, at least in the Comtean and Weberian versions. One of the obvious reasons for this alternative pattern is the fact that in America religion had not been "established" and that consequently the starting point of its religious development was quite different from that of Europe. The American experience shows that the impact of industrialization on religion in Europe cannot be made into a universal law.

How does Bryan Wilson deal with the counter-evidence of the American experience? He attributes little weight to it, because religion in America seems to him rather superficial. He writes, "The travelers of the past who commented on the apparent extensiveness of the church membership, rarely omitted to say that they found religion in America to be very superficial."[126] In regard to the more recent period, he himself concludes, "Thus, though religious practice has increased, the vacuous-ness of popular religious ideas has also increased."[127] The evidence does not count because American religion is not of the right kind. The same curious inconsistency is found in the sociological studies of Peter Berger, another proponent of the theory of secularization. He writes, "The situation is different in America, where the churches still occupy a more central symbolic position, but it may be argued they have succeeded in keeping this position only by becoming highly secularized themselves, so that the European and American cases represent two variations on the same underlying theme of global secularization."[128] Again, American religion is not the right kind to constitute counter-evidence to the theory of secularization. It is apparent that both Wilson and Berger here engage in faulty reasoning. If the theory of secularization intends to express a law relating religion and secular society, then it is inadmissible to introduce qualifications that exclude some forms of religion from being admitted as evidence. American religion is undoubtedly different from religion in Europe. In his important study on American religion, *Protestant, Catholic, Jew,* [129] published in the 1950s and mentioned above, American sociologist Will Herberg tried to account for the extraordinary success of organized religion in the United States. He observed that churches and synagogues, despite the enormous differences in religious beliefs and rituals, stand for the same ethos, the same virtues and the same social vision. They are all equally the embodiment of the American Way of Life. Commitment to religious belief and membership in a religious organization have become visible signs of being a true American, that is, of being identified with America's social and economic ethic. Despite its diversity, religion is an integrating factor in America. It enables the people of this vast land, coming from different ethnic, racial, religious and linguistic backgrounds, to be united in the same way of life, to live truly American lives, and at the same time to remain faithful to an important aspect of their past. Herberg showed that the second generation of immigrants tended to reject their ethnic heritage in an effort to become complete Americans and that the third generation, now fully Americanized, in the search for social identity in a highly mobile population, tried to return to the ethnicity of their grandparents. Yet since they had forgotten the language and hence could not participate in their cultural heritage, they joined at least their grandparents' religion. Writing in the 1950s, Herberg interprets organized religion in America as a legitimation of the American Way of Life, as conservative and ideological. According to Herberg, this religion did not generate a critique of the American ethos; it was almost completely identified with the dominant cultural trends. This, I suppose, was the kind of phenomenon Wilson and Berger had in mind when they spoke of American religion as superficial and secularized. Let me add, however, that it is by no means clear that other-worldly religion built around the worship of the sacred is for that reason necessarily less ideological.

It would be a mistake to make Herberg's study of religion in the 1950s normative for the understanding of American religion. We recall our discussion, in the last chapter, of Robert Bellah's important article on civil religion, which brought out the complexity of religion in America. First, civil religion is itself ambiguous. At certain times it upholds ideals for the collective life of the nation that judge the present political practice, and at others it may partially collapse into a religious legitimation of the actual political powers. Second, Bellah had indicated that the relation of civil religion to the historic religion of Judaism and Christianity may vary greatly; at certain times the churches and synagogues express their religious ethos interwoven with the ideals of civil religion, and at others these historic religions define themselves over against the civil religion of the day. Religion in America has been both conformist and critical. In its adaptation to North American life, religion has shown considerable creativity. Herberg has described but a single phase. It is my contention that sociologists who defend the theory of secularization do not make themselves sufficiently sensitive to the creative and critical aspects of religious life.

Religion changes as culture and society change. Yet how does it change? Does it adapt itself to the new social conditions in a conformist way, or does it respond to the challenges produced by the new conditions in a creative way? When Alexis de Tocqueville visited the United States in the 1830s, he observed that important changes had taken place in the Christian religion, changes that he interpreted, at least in part, as creative responses to new social needs.[130] Tocqueville, the original social thinker before the word "sociology" was invented, analyzed egalitarian democracy in America and contrasted it with traditional aristocratic society in Europe, in terms that anticipated the later sociological distinction between Gesellschaft and Gemeinschaft. While Tocqueville appreciated the civil liberties of men and women in the new society, he was keenly aware that the political and economic institutions that upheld these liberties were producing a new individualism, eagerness for personal advancement, a highly utilitarian ethics, and the domination of culture by business values.

Here people were exposed to problems and anxieties hardly known in traditional society. Tocqueville recognized the threats to human well-being posed by these developments and, in response to this, the new social role played by religion. The visitor from France observed that in the individualistic, egalitarian society of America, the new task of religion was to curb people's selfish desires and create communities in which people could find friendship and solidarity. Religion now enabled people to overcome their social isolation. In a highly competitive society, religion was becoming a school, educating people in selflessness and social concern. The diversity of religion in America and the ongoing multiplication of denominations, which the French observer found troubling, exercised an important humanizing function in American society and in fact produced a greater sense of unity among the people.

According to Tocqueville, religion fulfilled another new and unexpected role in America. In his view, the great danger of egalitarian society was the power it bestows on public opinion. A society according equal honour to all citizens tends to undermine people's respect for the great men of wisdom and the authoritative traditions of the past; instead, people begin to invest with great authority the opinions and attitudes upon which the majority of citizens are agreed. People become victims of public opinion. In such a social situation, Tocqueville held, religion protects people's personal freedom and delivers them from the pressure of commonly held ideas and prejudices. Religious faith links people to a great wisdom tradition, grounds them in values that transcend the immediate needs and purposes of society, and hence enables them to hold out against the ever changing, superficial and often tyrannical public opinion. Tocqueville was convinced that in America, the Christian religion had responded creatively to the social needs of people.

Tocqueville tried to describe the changes that would take place in religion in an egalitarian society and that had already been partially realized in the United States. Religion would become less hierarchical, more democratic in its organization, less ascetic and world-denying, and more oriented towards work and action. Religion wants to temper, not deny, people's quest for well-being, comfort and success. Tocqueville foresaw that religious worship would eventually resemble less and less an assembly at court; it would become more like an assembly of equals. Since the main function of religion is exercised in the local congregation, religion in an egalitarian society will not have a public and political presence, except through the religious sentiment of the citizens; but this, Tocqueville thought – anticipating here Talcott Parsons – is not a negligible quantity. All of this the French social critic saw happening not as a weak adaptation of religion to the existing social conditions, but as an original response of religion, revealing its power to save and protect human life in new social circumstances.

Tocqueville testified that even the Roman Catholic Church in the United States had been profoundly affected by the egalitarian society and acquired a simplicity unknown on the European continent.[131] What he could not foresee, of course, was that thanks to the interference of the papacy and the condemnation of Americanism and Modernism at the end of the nineteenth century, the democratic temper of Roman Catholicism in the United States would be replaced by a highly authoritarian spirit and organizational style. In a very shrewd paragraph, Tocqueville goes so far as to suggest that people whose consciousness is formed by egalitarian social institutions will have increasing difficulties with acknowledging God as Lord of the universe; their piety will tend to identify God with the community.[132] Personally, Tocqueville regarded such a development as pantheistic and harmful to the genius of Christianity. Still, he here anticipated the shift in modern theology that looks upon God as ground of being and matrix of humanity. Tocqueville recognized – as Hegel had done before him and many sociologists did after him – that there is a close relationship between the social institutions in which people live, the consciousness which is theirs, and the form which religion assumes in their minds.

If religion is a creative factor in society, should one not expect it to help overcome some of the alienation inflicted by the conditions of modern life in Europe? Émile Durkheim eagerly looked for institutions capable of overcoming the isolation and anguish produced by industrial society. How, he asked, can people be saved from the anomie that threatens them? Durkheim did not believe that traditional religion (Christianity and Judaism) had sufficient vitality to be of any help. He had never studied the role of religion in America. What he advocated, therefore, was the creation of "intermediary societies"[133] that would provide social matrices for the personal well-being of the participants. Durkheim somewhat naively believed that professional associations were able to fulfill this task. What Durkheim was doing, unintentionally to be sure, was describing the role religious communities could play in the humanization of modern industrial society.

Theologians who study Durkheim find in his work the foundation of a new ecclesiology. This was done, for instance, by Andrew Greeley.[134] In traditional society, the churches either regarded themselves as the exclusive bearers of the symbolic life of society, and hence identified themselves with culture and nation, or else they understood themselves as marginal communities rejecting the symbols of society and living in critical distance from the dominant culture. Sociologists have called these two types of communities "churches" and "sects." Yet if religious communities assume the function ascribed by Durkheim to "intermediary societies," they will transcend the distinction between church and sect and play a new and original role in society. Such a development has actually taken place in America.

The originality of American religion is developed in Andrew Greeley's interesting book *The Denominational Society*. The author shows that the sociological study of religion in America must operate with categories of its own. In particular, the distinction between church and sect, helpful in studying European religion, has confused sociologists when study-ing religion in a country that has never known, except very early, an established church. Religion in America is constituted in denominations. Denominational religion communicates a sense of belonging to its fol-lowers – the Durkheimian perspective – and inspires them with a sense of meaning or purpose in life – the Weberian perspective, as we shall see. Greeley writes,

> in the disorganization, personal and social, that occurs as part of the pilgrimage from the peasant communalism to the industrial city, man attempted and still attempts to compensate for the deprivation he en-dured and for the absence of the social support and the intimacy of the village by evolving quasi-Gemeinschaft institutions – the nationality groups, the lower-class religious sects, the radical political party and, in the United States and Canada, the denomination.[135]

The religious denomination is different from church or sect. The denomination is pluralistic; it takes for granted that it is surrounded by others, and in this it differs from the church. At the same time, it is open to culture and society, and in this it differs from the sect. The denomination is an intermediary society that introduces people to social cohesion in a highly mobile and atomizing society. The great number of denominations in America are not obstacles to the unity of the population. For despite the conflicts and tensions that occasionally arise from the competing interests of the denominations, they do not provide alternate definitions of reality.

They provide a sense of community to their members and a meaning of life besides the daily struggle for existence, and hence promote the unity of the people. The divergence of doctrine need not necessarily have divergent social effects. Andrew Greeley shows that sociologically speaking, even the self-understanding of the Catholic Church in the United States has become denominational. It is this original American development, and not the supposedly superficial or secularized character of American religion, that accounts for the differing pattern of church attendance and membership. Religion has flourished in America because it has created an institutional and cultural form that serves the people well.

Is American religion as analyzed by Greeley necessarily ideological? Must it always be a defence of the American Way of Life? The answer is that American religion, like all religion, is ambiguous. It can exist – like American civil religion – in both ideological and utopian form. In particular, since denominational religion is pluralistic and hence need not be identified with the symbol system undergirding the national life, denominational religion often communicates a sense of personal freedom to its members. Already Tocqueville made a reference to this.[136] Religion enables people to define themselves in terms of a transcendent identity. While the structure of society makes people define their identity in terms of the roles they play, as citizens, as workers, as mothers or fathers, etc., religion offers them a self-definition in terms that transcend these roles: in religion people share the vision and purpose of a wider community, movement or church. Thanks to these wider identities, people are able to stand over against their roles in society. They are more than citizens, workers, or mother and father; they are capable of being critical of the roles they play, and this gives them a sense of personal freedom. American religion has often been ideological, but it has also been the bearer of utopia.

* * *

Bryan Wilson's first argument in favour of the theory of secularization, drawn from statistical evidence of the decline of the Church of England, led us to a more careful analysis of religion in America. His second argument was taken from the close relationship between pluralism and secularization. Wilson thinks that pluralism in religion, and mutual tolerance and recognition, inevitably weaken the hold of religion on people's minds. Pluralism implies a certain relativism and hence tends to undermine the unconditional surrender to truth at the heart of every religion. Peter Berger has proposed the same argument: religious pluralism inevitably leads to secularization.[137] If there are several religions, all of which are regarded as valid, it is possible to choose between them and adopt the one that seems best suited to one's life; in this way religion becomes a private affair, a spiritual hobby, as it were, and loses its nature as the ultimate grounding of reality. Pluralism transmutes religion beyond recognition and ushers in its total demise.

After our analysis of denominational religion in America, this argument is no longer convincing. It may well be true that churches and sects, understood according to their sociological definition, cannot survive in a pluralistic society, for both of these types of religion understand themselves in exclusivist terms. Denominational religion, however, is pluralistic. It takes for granted the existence of diverse religious communities. There is no reason, moreover, to suppose that an absolute surrender to the divine mystery in one's own religion cannot go hand in hand with a willingness to recognize the validity of other religions or other versions of one's own. Especially under the impact of the ecumenical movement, contemporary Christians in quest of unreserved fidelity to the Absolute are usually quite unwilling to regard their own religious organization as an expression of this Absolute. Religion is here indeed due to personal choice, but the important social function of denominational religion shows that it is by no means a purely private affair. Sociologists who hold that pluralism undermines religion and ushers in its disappearance underestimate religion's own proper creativity.

Bryan Wilson refines his second argument by proposing and defending the idea that the movement towards an ever more secular society is implicit in Protestantism itself. Wilson follows here the famous thesis of Max Weber, which in some form or other has been adopted by many sociologists. According to this thesis, the worldly asceticism of Calvinist-Puritan Christianity has i) enabled the spirit of capitalism and entrepreneurship to spread rapidly among the class of manufacturers and merchants, ii) supplied an inwardness to the lower classes enabling them to break away from traditional bonds and rise to greater social power, and iii) encouraged a work ethos that helped to create the modern, industrialized world, unique among all previous civilizations. Since some readers present this thesis in an exaggerated way, I wish to insist that Weber did not claim that Protestantism has produced the modern, rational world! Weber did not overlook the effects that the development of science and technology, the expansion of commercial enterprises, and the creation of new means of production had on the creation of the modern world. His thesis was

more modest. He asked himself the question why the beginnings of capitalism, which were found in many cultures and which were present in
sections of European society prior to the Reformation, led to extraordinary
growth and development in Western Europe and generated the modern,
rational culture, unique in human history. Weber showed that it was the
new Protestant asceticism, the new sense of divine calling, that removed
the traditional religious obstacles to the spread of the secular orientation
and provided a religious impetus for a new, worldly dedication. Obedience to God's call now meant hard work, limited pleasure, appreciation
of personal achievements, and a critique of government based on a new
sense of individualism and free enterprise.

Wilson accepted the Weberian thesis not only for the period studied
by Weber himself; he demonstrated that the various Protestant movements,
including early Methodism and the Adventist and Millenarian movements
of the later period, continued to create among their followers a spirit of
worldly dedication that promoted the advance of secular society. He writes,
"Christianity's genius was in the adaptability to new classes throughout
the process of social change."[138] Each new wave of Protestant revival and
renewal was able to supply a rising class with new self-confidence and
religious discipline that enabled its members to rise in the existing social
and economic order. This thesis is reaffirmed in Richard Niebuhr's *The
Social Sources of Denominationalism* [139] for the United States and in S.D.
Clark's *Church and Sect in Canada* [140] for British North America. More recent
research has shown that new Christian sects, such as the Pentecostals,
still perform the same social function.[141] They supply people of the lower
classes, devoid of formal education, with new spiritual self-confidence,
transform them into disciplined, hard-working and reliable persons, and
thus enable them to do well as industrial workers, to become successful businessmen and -women in a competitive world, and to rise on the
social scale. These sects still teach people to be frugal, save their money
and invest it wisely. Research in Pentecostalism and other Christian sects
in Latin America, the West Indies and Africa has shown that there, too,
these religious movements enable people, torn from their tribe or village
and culturally destroyed in the big city, to find self-respect, lay hold of
themselves, become hard workers and rise in the economic order. Even the
ecstasy of revivalist religion is not the symbol of world negation, for these
ecstasies, circumscribed in the worshipping community, enable people
to express their frustrations, become quiet and reconciled, and return to
their rational, confined existence in the social and economic order.

Protestantism, according to Wilson's analysis, leads people to a more worldly life, weakens the mystical and sacramental elements of the Christian tradition, directs people's attention to secular aims and purposes, and thus prepares its own disappearance. After the rise in the social and economic system, people lose interest in their religion and drift into a vague agnosticism. Protestantism initiates its own undoing. The worldly asceticism, Max Weber's "Protestant ethic," is handed on and communicated in Western secular society by cultural and economic institutions; the Protestant ethic has become independent of its religious source. The claim is proved by the fact that in the United States the Protestant ethic is found as much among Catholics and Jews as among Protestants.[142] The Protestant work ethic expresses the spirit of the culture we have inherited.

There is much truth in Wilson's thesis. Ernst Troeltsch, contemporary and friend of Max Weber, often expressed his fear that Protestantism was creating the conditions of its own demise. The glory of Protestantism was also its weak point. Yet this persuasive thesis is not in itself a proof for the theory of secularization. Wilson studied mainly the English experience. In America, Protestantism has remained strong precisely because it is, in a certain sense, the "established" religion; it articulates the spirit that makes American democracy and the economic system work, and for this reason vast numbers of Americans continue to find themselves in the symbolism of their churches. It is in part the ideological nature of Protestantism in America that has made it a thriving religion. Wilson's thesis can be turned around as an argument against the theory of secularization. For it was Protestantism, in its various movements and denominations, that enabled the aspiring classes in the English-speaking world to acquire greater social power and thus prevented not only the violent social change of the French revolution but also the vehement anti-clericalism and aggressive atheism associated with radical social reformers in Catholic countries. Wilson himself writes, "Whereas in continental countries, and especially in Catholic countries, secularisation was expressed in the development of secularist and anti-clerical movements, in the Anglo-Saxon countries it found less direct and more subtle expression."[143] If these observations are correct, then Protestantism is not only a secularizing influence but also, paradoxically, a factor that prevents the disappearance of religion.

One more remark on this topic. While it is true, from one point of view, that Protestant Christianity is the established religion of the Western capitalist and democratic society, it is equally true that Protestantism is much greater than that. Protestantism has generated new utopias. Religions, as I hope to show, move, change and produce their own self-criticism. Protestantism has brought forth many forms of Christian socialism with its negative judgment on the capitalist system and its critique of the work ethic.

Wilson's thesis of the secularization implicit in Protestantism has been placed into an even wider context by a number of social philosophers and theologians. The claim has been made that biblical religion itself, from the very outset, aimed at the secularization of culture and that the social process by which different spheres of social life in modern society have made themselves independent of religion was in keeping with biblical religion and the spirit of Protestantism. Some theologians think that this development ought to be welcomed by the Christian churches. We find this theory in the work of Friedrich Gogarten in Germany[144] and Harvey Cox's *The Secular City* in the United States.[145] It is claimed that Old Testament faith made a radical break with the cosmic religions of Egypt and Mesopotamia. God revealed himself as the totally other, the creator of heaven and earth, beyond the cosmos and in no way identified with it. Old Testament faith de-divinized or secularized the earth. Nature is therefore not divine; it is not the locus of God's presence; the world is only world, and it is humankind's calling to live in this world, assume responsibility for it, and transform it into a garden. Peter Berger, following a few hints of Max Weber and the extensive studies of Eric Voegelin, expresses much sympathy for this theory.[146] According to this theory, then, the central inspiration of scriptural religion is a movement towards secularization. The New Testament records the struggle of Jesus against inherited taboos, sacred laws and the domination of life by religious authorities. In Catholicism, according to this theory, the central inspiration of biblical religion has been suppressed in favour of sacramental and divinizing religious trends. The Reformation recovered the original inspiration of the Bible and became a bridge, with Renaissance humanism, to the secular culture of our own day. The secularization implicit in Protestantism (Wilson's thesis) is here presented as part of a wider historical movement.

Since Wilson's thesis did not appear to us as conclusive evidence for the theory of secularization, we need not concern ourselves with the wider historical interpretation. Yet I do wish to raise the question whether the interpretation of Old Testament religion here proposed is not based on a peculiarly Protestant reading that projects a problematic of modernity onto an ancient culture. It is not clear at all whether the radical separation between God and nature is actually found in books of the Old Testament. In the Bible God remains creator of the world; he is the ground and protector of nature, and he reveals himself in the dramas of the natural universe. The earth remains the locus of God's presence. While he is a redeemer God, he is not any less the God of the universe. In the New Testament in particular – as Rosemary Ruether has pointed out in many lectures – we are far away from a secular understanding of the world. The world appears either as possessed by demons or inhabited by the Spirit; it is either demonic or sacramental; it is either an obstacle to God or a means of God's self-communication. The great secularization theory of Gogarten and Cox may turn out to be a specifically Protestant reading of the evidence, supported by scholars identified with cultural Protestantism (as Weber himself was), at a time when secularization seemed the dominant cultural trend.

* * *

Wilson's third argument in support of the theory of secularization follows the social analysis of Toennies and Weber, according to which the passage from Gemeinschaft to Gesellschaft undermines traditional values, applies rational thinking to an increasing range of social processes, and thus removes the religious dimension from the different spheres of social life. Religion here loses its social base; it no longer exercises a social function. Society becomes dominated by utilitarian and pragmatic purposes. Wilson does not describe this process in the tragic tones of the German sociologists; he does not lament, as they do, the decline of culture in modern society. Wilson simply affirms that the spread of industrialization leads to the waning of religion. Who can deny that this is a powerful argument? It certainly describes a certain European experience.

Still, there are sociologists who have interpreted the process of modernization differently, and it is not surprising that the different reading of the identical data has come from America. In a famous essay, "Christianity and Modern Industrial Society,"[147] Talcott Parsons tried to demonstrate that modernization is not so much a process of secularization as it is of differentiation. What does this mean? Differentiation is a central concept in Parsons' sociology. According to him, the application of reason to various social processes and the growing complexification of society leads to increasing specialization of the various functions exercised in society and increasing co-ordination among them. The various tasks performed by society tend to be separated out and exercised by distinct institutions, interrelated among themselves. This sort of differentiation is observable in government, industry, business, education – in short, in all sections of society. This differentiation also leads to the detachment of the religious component from the non-religious spheres of social life. This theory enables Parsons to acknowledge the gradual disappearance of religion from public life and yet interpret the evidence in a new way. What takes place, he argues, is not secularization but simply the differentiation of religion as a distinct sphere. Religion becomes more separated, independent and personal, and yet remains related to society. The process of differentiation allows religion to reveal its true nature and power, which is to create personal commitment and, through this, to influence the choices and decisions people make. While the various spheres of social life are no longer linked to religious institutions and religious symbols, Parsons thinks that they remain dependent on a personal ethos of responsibility, a highly developed and critical ethics, which is grounded in the inherited religion, Christianity and Judaism. Religion, he argues, has by no means lost its social function, even if its point of insertion in the social process is simply the human person. Parsons holds that the survival of the social order still depends on the spiritual link of people's willing and responsible co-operation – on a certain inwardness, in other words – that is mediated for the majority of people by traditional religion. This highly personal religion is institutionalized in the concrete churches and synagogues. This Parsonian perspective has been partially incorporated in Andrew Greeley's analysis of American religion – as we saw above – as exercising the people-sustaining meaning and belonging functions in society. The process of differentiation, associated with the modernization of society, has made religion a highly specialized sphere of life, embodied in specifically religious organizations that are independent of other public institutions and yet make an essential contribution to the well-being of modern industrial society.

In the 1960s, a number of theologians, following Gogarten and Cox, enthusiastically endorsed what they regarded as the movement towards secularization in society. Basing themselves on a particular reading of the Scriptures, they understood this secularization as the promised destiny of humankind. These theologians were at the same time deeply committed to the Christian faith. They believed that God's summons recorded in Scripture called people to maturity and reconciliation and commissioned them to transform society according to God's will. This faith, the theologians argued, is being nourished and kept alive in the churches that announce and celebrate the biblical message. Despite the movement

towards secularization, these theologians continued to assign an important function to the churches. We recognize, therefore, that what these
Christian authors were enthusiastic about was not – as they thought – the
theory of secularization, but rather the counter-proposal, the Parsonian
theory of differentiation. The use of the word "secularization" in theology
has been very confusing!

The Parsonian theory of differentiation has a strong ideological dimension: it presupposes that the American system is the perfect system
towards which all previous societies have moved and that it is the task of
biblical religion to make this system operate efficiently. Yet the theories
of secularization, refuted by Parsons, are also tainted by ideology: they,
too, defend a particular world view, they are not the result of value-free
or objective research. This was one of the arguments proposed in David
Martin's *The Religious and the Secular*.[148] In this book, Martin demonstrates
that all theories of secularization have been ideological: they have all
intended to justify a particular philosophy of life. Martin gives several
examples. He points to the optimistic, rational positivism of Auguste
Comte and the more modest forms of empirical positivism, both of which
understood religion as a cluster of superstition. Martin also points to the
world views of Marx and Freud, both of which left no room for religion
in a liberated society. Martin could also have mentioned the more pessimistic world views of Toennies, Weber and other German intellectuals
who associated industrialization with the decline of culture. This ideology
of decline, analyzed by us in a previous chapter, presupposed a radical
conflict between modernity and the ethical life, including religion. This
ideology inspired Oswald Spengler's notorious book, *The Decline of the
West*.[149] Martin could also have given as examples of ideology various
cyclical theories of culture, such as Pitirim Sorokin's,[150] which predicted
the breakdown of civilizations through the loss of the spiritual dimension. Because of the ideological themes operative in the various theories
of secularization (and the theory of differentiation), I prefer to conclude
that there is no fixed law relating modernization and religion.

There are sociologists who look upon religion as an abiding dimension
of social life. In the writings of Émile Durkheim and the social thinkers
influenced by him, we read that religion may appear with greater or less
intensity in society, that it may even disappear altogether for a certain
period, but that as society finds itself and assumes a more stable form,
people will come to express their encounter with the ultimate in religious
symbols and rites. This view is based neither on philosophical theories

nor on psychological analysis; it is, properly speaking, a sociological theory. Society generates its own religion in the same process in which it constitutes itself as a strong and self-confident community. Sociologists who, from this perspective, study a society in which the inherited religion is breaking down will immediately look for new religious manifestations or various substitutes of religion. David Martin remarks that the sociologists who defend the theory of secularization tend to identify religion with organized religion and do not make themselves sensitive to other religious manifestations. Here again, the studies of Robert Bellah[151] and Andrew Greeley,[152] following Durkheim's lead, have brought out the variety of religious manifestations in contemporary industrial society.

I do not wish to close this chapter on the theory of secularization without mentioning the great German social philosopher Max Scheler, who has written an important sociological study to refute the Comtean theory of the three stages.[153] While Scheler followed Toennies and Weber in the evaluation of Gesellschaft and feared that the rise of the commercial and industrial bourgeoisie would lead to the decline of culture, he was passionately convinced that religion was a dimension of human life as inescapable as sexuality, love, wisdom and morality. Scheler adopted this viewpoint from personal and philosophical convictions. Yet to refute the theory of secularization, which he despised, he decided to become a sociologist. He created a sociology of knowledge that explored the relationship between the ideas of philosophers and scientists and their social location in society. He tried to show that the theory of secularization formulated by Comte, endorsed by scientific positivism and followed by the owning classes, the bourgeoisie, corresponded to the materialistic and pedestrian preoccupation of this sector of society. The theory of secularization, Scheler argued, was a creation of bourgeois resentment! The bourgeoisie, imprisoned in its petty concerns, was jealous of the flights of spirit and the ecstasies experienced by religious people. Inverting Nietzsche's famous formula, Scheler made resentment the source of hostility to religion. The theory of secularization, he argued, was nothing but the disguise of the human poverty and spiritual emptiness of the middle class. Scientific positivism was the ideology of the class dedicated to making money. Scheler's brilliance and passion made him the original creator of the systematic sociology of knowledge, but his analysis of the role of religion in society was a curious combination of conservative sentiment, elitist prejudice and radical social thought. We recall that Marx also thought that Enlightenment atheism was the ideology of the bourgeoisie. Yet should we take Max Scheler's theory seriously? His claim that modern secularizing trends are the products of resentment is based on an overly polemical view of the bourgeoisie and an inadequate analysis of the social role played by traditional religion. As a great accuser of modernity, Scheler was not sufficiently sensitive to the ambiguity of religion.

8

Creative Religion:
Max Weber's Perspective

Can religion be an independent, creative, original force in human life? In the preceding chapters we met sociological thinkers who stressed the dependence of religion on society. Religion here appeared as a faithful or distorted (inverted) reflection of the social and economic infrastructure. Yet we also encountered authors who recognized in religion an independent variable. The young Hegel regarded "bad" religion as source of personal and social alienation, yet conceded that there was another kind of religion that promoted movements of de-alienation. We saw that Durkheim recognized religion as creative; for him, religion, though dependent on society, generated values for social reform. We mentioned Weber's view of religion as breakthrough overcoming magic; we spoke of Erich Fromm, who recognized, in addition to the compulsive religion described by Freud, trends of humanistic religion that exercise a creative role; and we introduced Mannheim's concept of utopian religion as the source of a new political imagination. Religion, though ambiguous, does have a life-giving, creative side.

Is there good sociological evidence for the power of innovative religion? Are we quite sure that, after the application of various ideological critiques, there will be anything left of the world religions? After all, it has happened that believing Christians who opened themselves to the negative critiques in the hope of purifying their own religious tradition found to their dismay that these critiques affected all aspects of their religion, left nothing intact, and ultimately dissolved their faith in the Christian message. Is there good sociological evidence, I ask, for creative religion?

As a Christian theologian, I trust that the mystery of God operative in human life again and again produces creative religion – and as a Christian believer, I understand my own personal inwardness not simply as a reflection of the human context in which I live, but also as an encounter with a mystery that radically transcends this context. But I do not wish to raise this theological issue at the beginning of this chapter. What I want to ask instead is whether sociologists, relying on their sociological research, have presented strong evidence for creative, innovative religion.

The great sociological witness for creative religion is Max Weber. While Durkheim concentrated on the forces that held society together, Weber was more interested in the forces that carried society forward and modified the conditions of culture. One of the principal issues that preoccupied his mind was the origin of modern, rational culture, unique in the history of civilizations. His early empirical studies had acquainted him with the problems of work and employment in Eastern Germany where German (Protestant) employers and Polish (Catholic) labourers were set over against one another. When the owners of industries, in the hope of speeding up production, offered the Catholic workers more money for piecework, they were disappointed. Instead of working harder to make more money, the workers quit work early in the afternoon since they had earned enough money for the day. This study revealed to Weber that involved in problems affecting labour were not only material interests, but also different symbolic world views. He pursued his intuition that religion had something to do with the creation of culture. In his famous book, *The Protestant Ethic and the Spirit of Capitalism* – mentioned in the previous chapter – he studied the origin of the modern, hard-working, capitalistic world at the end of the Middle Ages and concluded that Protestant worldly asceticism had something to do with its rapid spread and unequalled success. Weber's book determined the direction of his subsequent research, but it also produced one of the most important controversies in the intellectual community of the 20th century, a controversy that continues.[154] What is the creative role of religion in the making of culture?

Let me repeat that Weber formulated his thesis in a modest way. He did not claim that Reformed Christianity was the cause of modern capitalism. He realized, of course, that the beginnings of capitalistic enterprises were present in pre-Reformation Europe as they had been in other cultures, and he was keenly aware that the new technologies affecting production and transportation were essential factors in the development of modern capitalism. But why was the new economy accompanied by a cultural development that favoured its rapid spread in certain parts of Europe? This development, according to Weber's thesis, was made possible by a new spirituality. Weber did not deny that this new inwardness was, in part at least, an adjustment to the growing commercialism and entrepreneurship present in these parts of Europe, but it was not simply a concession to social pressures. Weber argued that an original, creative, religious break-through took place in Calvinistic Christianity where the divine summons was experienced as a secular calling. Christians experienced the meaning and power of the Gospel in their dedication to hard work and personal enterprise, and they regarded the success of their undertakings as God's approval and blessing. This new spirituality removed the religious obstacles to capitalistic expansion. In the Middle Ages, Weber reminds his readers, the Church had not only regarded as gravely sinful the taking of interest on money loaned, but had also held up contemplation, otherworldliness, patience in one's providential position, and even elected poverty as the ide-als to be followed by the most dedicated Christians. The worldly asceticism fostered by Reformed Christianity supplied strong religious motivation for the secular effort to build a society that would reflect the new freedoms of the burgher and allow for his free enterprise in industry and commerce. Thanks to this new ethos, rational principles were gradually applied not only to the expansion of trade and production, bookkeeping and invest-ment policies, but to all institutions in society, including the government. The Protestant ethic was eventually handed on to subsequent generations by secular social institutions – the home, the school, the trade; it became detached from its religious origin and in the long run undermined the traditional values. This was the ethos that had created and, at least in Weber's day, was still creating the modern world.

Weber's thesis offers a certain corrective of the Marxist understand-ing of social evolution, and hence it has lent itself to many ideological uses. Needless to say, Weber himself was not an idealist who neglected the economic factor in the creation of culture. But he studied this factor along with others – social, political and even symbolic – that affect per-sonal and social consciousness. Weber did not deny that under certain historical circumstances, the economic factor may be the dominant one and provide the key for the understanding of cultural and social change, but there are other historical circumstances, according to him, where this is not true. One difference between Weber and Marx was that the latter believed his sociological concepts – such as social class or class conflict – were representations of the existing social realities, while the former understood his sociological concepts as "ideal-types" applicable more or less to a given society. We discussed the meaning of ideal-types in the chapter on Toennies.[155] Weber's study of the relation between religion and class arrived at the conclusion that there are periods of history when the same religion serves the upper classes as ideology and the lower classes as otherworldly consolation, periods for which the Marxist analysis holds true. But studying history over a much longer period reveals that the relation between religion and class has been varied and does not lend itself to easy generalizations. In history, religion has played both a legitimating and an innovative role.

According to Weber's thesis, the new ethic, having become the inner logic of the economic system, increasingly applied greater rationality to all institutional processes of society. Weber calls this "rationalization."[156] In his writings dealing with the modern world, rationalization refers to the application of technical, quantified reason to society, inevitably leading to the ongoing specialization of institutions and a corresponding complexification of their interaction. The modern ethos, moreover, creates personal lives that are almost wholly dominated by the needs of this rational society. Occasionally, Weber gives the impression that rationalization is a principle of evolution; yet when we read his writings more carefully, we learn that he regards the ongoing application of technical reason as a tragic principle of social change that will eventually reduce the true dimensions of human life and transform society into an iron cage. We referred to his famous sentences earlier in the book.[157] Reason, in this context, means instrumental or functional reason, having to do exclusively with means, not with ends or values.

However, in *The Sociology of Religion*,[158] Weber seems to speak of the application of reason in a different way. Let us look at his theory of religious evolution. We recall Weber's distinction between magic, priestly religion and prophecy. Magic refers to a turning to the gods for the sake of solving private problems; it is inspired by the intention to make the gods do the will of the client. By contrast, priestly religion is a turning to the gods for the sake of wider, communal concerns. Religion transcends magic. It is inspired by the surrender to the divine that orders and enlivens the community. Religion appears here as breakthrough. It results from the application of reason to magic, but in this case, reason is mainly substantial, concerned not simply with means but with the end. Reason here changes the orientation of personal life and reveals the place of the person in the wider community. A similar breakthrough takes place in the passage from priestly religion to prophecy. Operative in the religious development is rationalization. For through the prophetic message the community is brought to greater self-knowledge and gains a clearer understanding of its own ideals. Again the reason spoken of is substantial, for through prophecy people acquire a greater sense of responsibility for their future. In the early chapters of his sociology of religion, then, Weber introduces a notion of reason that differs from the instrumental reason at work in the institutional changes of capitalist society.

It is possible – though probably misleading – to read Weber's sociology of religion as an evolutionary theory. This is the way in which Talcott Parsons presents it in his famous introduction to the English translation of Weber's book, published in 1964.[159] Parsons shows that Weber creates categories for the understanding of religion by abstracting from the total social process sets of two alternative social structure (for instance, magic/religion or religion/prophecy), where one reinforces the traditional order of society and the other creates a breakthrough and becomes a source of evolutionary change. Magic is conservative, and the breakthrough to priestly religion leads to social change; at a later historical moment, priestly religion legitimates the existing social order, and prophetic religion becomes a factor in the evolution of society. Weber tried to detect in religion the moments of breakthrough. Parsons writes, "Weber's primary interest is in religion as a source of the dynamics of social change, not religion as reinforcement of the stability of society."[160]

It is indeed possible to read the opening chapters of Weber's sociology of religion as presenting the categories of an evolutionary scheme, if one forgets that his categories are simply ideal-types. They do not propose a theory of inevitable evolutionary progress; they are simply useful tools for detecting the significant breakthroughs in the creation of consciousness and society. Weber did not believe in evolution – he did not think that scholars had enough evidence to speak scientifically of a necessary direction implicit in the historical process. Hence he did not regard religion as the breakthrough agent that continues to apply reason to social processes, moving history in a progressive direction and eventually producing the modern Protestant critical consciousness characteristic of the Great Society – even if there are tones in Parsons' introduction that suggest this. Weber was personally convinced that present in the human world were many diverse and, in fact, irreconcilable values, all deserving of loyalty and admiration, which could never be brought together in a single synthesis. Every development in one direction, faithful to a certain ideal, will inevitably neglect other values, irreconcilable with it, and hence ultimately produce a reaction, a new movement, possibly mediated by religious breakthrough, that would seek to recover some of the neglected values. Polytheism, Weber felt, was the only realistic religion.[161]

Weber was fascinated by the idea of change and non-conformity. He made "charism," a word derived from the Pauline epistles, the starting point for his study of religion as well as the key concept for his theory of social change.[162] Charism is a mysterious power attached to an individual that attracts and fascinates people and makes them obedient to this individual's will. The charismatic person is experienced as a human with superior powers, out of the ordinary and not subject to the laws of daily reality. Sometimes, the charismatic person is regarded as having divine powers. This situation, Weber believed, was the origin of religion. The charismatic leader creates a community and begins a movement of people who accept his word and submit to his authority. To make this charism available to people living at a distance from the leader or to hand it on to subsequent generations, the original charism is institutionalized in rites, symbols or sacred writings and ritually communicated to a group of chosen disciples and their successors. This institutionalization of charism – which we find especially in the world religions – always implies a certain weakening or cooling of the original charism: the fervour of the beginning is lost in the second generation. In Weber's terminology, the charismatic power of the founder is eventually transformed into traditional authority invested in the religious institutions. What happens again and again, according to Weber, is the outburst of new charisms: new leaders emerge who attract people and exercise power over them. Sometimes these new charismatic movements aim at restoring or reforming the religious tradition, and at other times they break away from the institutionalized religion or are forcibly excluded by it. In the history of religion, these kind of charisms have never disappeared.

At the beginning of this chapter, we posed the question whether religion could ever be original and innovative. According to Weber, religion always begins in an innovative movement; it becomes tamed only through its institutionalization, but it continues to remain the locus of new charisms.

We must not overlook that Weber used the term "charism" in a value-free way. Its meaning is not confined to the religious context. Charism may refer to the superior power some persons have over groups of people and hence apply to good and wicked leaders alike. Charism is present in the magician as well as in the prophet; charism is present in Hitler as well as in Pope John XXIII. Because of the value-free use of the term, Weber was able to make charism central in his theory of social change.

There are, according to Weber's ideal-typical analysis, three basic kinds of authority that constitute social life.[163] Authority is here defined as the power to make people obey. There is, first, *traditional* authority, associated with the rules and customs of inherited cultural systems, including their religious and political elements. Since these systems are venerated by their members and looked upon as almost sacred realities, people obey this authority without questioning it. This authority is seen by people as part of the order of things; it belongs to their cosmos. Yet because of new problems or changed circumstances, the tradition is eventually challenged. Some people desire to make the social order more rational. They ask questions regarding the social usefulness of the laws, and when they find them no longer serving the conscious purposes of the population or sections of the population, they advocate change. What takes place then is the transition from traditional to *legal* authority. In this reformed social order, people obey because the laws have been made on rational grounds by men and women who were legally appointed to legislate. The passage from traditional to legal authority is not usually a smooth transition. The struggle for change is often released by those with *charismatic* authority. They exercise personal power, organize people in a reform movement, introduce more rational social processes and in this way modify the traditional structures. No society, we note, is wholly constituted by legal authority; it always retains some traditional elements.

Even if society were completely dominated by legal authority, it could not for that reason be assured of stability. Since even a rational society inevitably suppresses certain human values and neglects certain aspects of human life, radical persons wielding charismatic authority are likely to emerge who break with the fundamental assumptions of the social order. What may take place is a much more radical questioning of society than the passage from traditional to legal authority. A critical countervailing movement may peter out if it is based on irrational impulses or false presuppositions; it may be crushed by those who exercise legal authority in society; or its special insights may be used by the leaders of society and integrated, in modified form, into the dominant social system. But what can also happen is that the countervailing movement receives growing support, gains influence among the people, affects the consciousness of the majority, and eventually produces a radical cultural transformation, or, by reaching a powerful group in society, produces radical political upheaval and reconstitutes the social order according to new principles. If the charismatic element is very strong in the countervailing movement, it may even give rise to a new sacred tradition, and the new society, after the revolution, will exercise power demanding obedience in the name of traditional authority. And so history moves forward.

For Max Weber, charismatic authority is the dynamic element in the history of institutions. Curiously enough, he does not say very much about what this authority is. He speaks of extraordinary, inexplicable power attached to some people as a special talent. Charism is not a religious concept, even though Weber derived it from his study of religion. How is the charism related to the social order? As a sociologist, Weber could not suppose that it drops from the sky, for even the extraordinary is socially grounded. He suggests in his writings on religion that the charismatic person has power over people because he or she touches them where they suffer. The charismatic person is intuitively aware of what disturbs, wounds and exasperates people in their society. This is true of magicians as of prophets; this is true of demagogues who seduce people to follow them on a futile political journey as of radical reformers who inspire people to recreate the order in society. Those gifted with charism can put into words the hidden oppression from which people suffer; as they speak, people verify the words through their own experiences. Charism cannot be acquired by intelligence and effort; it is a gift that allows certain people to intuit what goes on in others behind their social façade. Charismatic persons give voice to the common suffering; *they articulate the alienation of the community*; they speak with an authority ultimately derived from the misery or unredemption of the many.

Charismatic persons sense the hurts of people and *propose a new imagination* by which this harm can be overcome. It is here that charismatics are distinguished from one another. Demagogues draw people with them along a road that leads to destruction; mystagogues use tricks to blind people and manipulate them for their own purposes; prophets summon people to greater self-knowledge, release new energy in them, and inspire them to recreate society according to higher ideals of justice and equality. Weber often speaks of charism as the breakthrough that applies reason to the social processes. This is operative, according to him, in the evolution leading from magic to priestly religion and prophecy. This sort of charism has also been at work in some of the significant social changes in Western history. In this sense, Weber saw the Protestant ethic as a charismatic breakthrough phenomenon. It produced a new imagination that enabled people to transcend the limitations of the past and enter upon a new way of life.

To understand charismatic authority as the dynamic element of history, we must look at the role of the imagination in the creation of the future. This theme has been greatly developed by social thinkers such as Karl Mannheim and Ernst Bloch. We mentioned above that Mannheim distinguished between ideological and utopian consciousness.[164] A utopian imagination makes people sensitive to the breaking points of the present system and nourishes in them a longing for a new kind of society, and as such exercises a significant role in a movement for social change. Mannheim thought that the disappearance of utopia would bring about a static state of affairs in which people become increasingly like objects and behave according to the fixed laws of the social system. In ordinary language, the word "utopia" is often used in a pejorative sense; it then refers to unrealistic dreams of the future that lead to passivity and despair. We mentioned that Mannheim regarded such an imagination as ideological rather than utopian, for dreams that lead to inaction simply reinforce the present social order. Ernst Bloch called such unrealistic dreams of the future "abstract utopias" and distinguished them from "concrete utopias," which provide an imagination that influences people's thoughts and actions.[165] Concrete utopias are images of the future that are grounded in reliable intuitions of the contradictions present in society; they negate the oppressive elements of this society, offer a vision of an alternative social order, summon forth new thought and prompt new ways of acting that could lead to radical social transformation. According to Mannheim and Bloch, the imagination of the future exercises great power in directing people's engagement in the world. For if this imagination comes to govern people's hearts and minds, it will guide their perception of society, create a keen awareness of the existing injustices and inequalities, nourish a yearning for the liberation from these oppressive conditions and provide guidance for the reconstruction of the social order. If I read Weber correctly, it is through the exercise of charism that a utopian imagination spreads among the people and becomes the guide for the transformation of culture and society.

Weber looked upon the Puritan dream as the last utopia. He did not expect any more charisms in the age of industrial society, dominated as it was by techno-scientific rationality. Weber's extensive study of modern of bureaucracy convinced him that society on all its levels – government, corporations, educational institutions, etc. – would become increasingly rationalized, that is, controlled in its exercise by instrumental reason, without ethical reflection and attention to its impact on human well-being. All subsequent utopias, he thought, would be levelled down by techno-scientific rationality. He foresaw that the Marxist movement, if victorious, would produce not the dictatorship of the proletariat, but the dictatorship of the bureaucrat. Weber predicted Herbert Marcuse's analysis in *One-Dimensional Man.*[166] The bureaucratization of society, Weber argued, would lead to the decline of culture, the loss of values, the waning of religion, "the disenchantment of the world."[167] The fully administrated society would become "a iron cage,"[168] a tedious society without beauty and passion, painted grey upon grey.

Let me add a few more comments on Max Weber's remarkable theory of social change. When Weber looks upon society and culture, he sees both a dominant trend, a trend imposed by the major institutions, and countervailing trends, sparked by personalities with charismatic gifts of varying strength. Durkheim, we recall, and with him a great many sociologists, looked upon society principally as a unity; they concentrated on the equilibrium of the social system and understood the conflicting trends as so many factors that, in their own way, contributed to the ongoing balance of the social order. For Weber, on the other hand, the unity of the social system is imposed by authority (*Herrschaft*, as he called it); unity is produced by the dominant forces in society, the government and the ruling classes. At the same time, Weber expected the existence of countervailing movements in society, challenging the established order. Weber's special insight was that these critical movements were sustained by powers and by an imagination that were related to the dominant forces and their contradictions. If the above analysis of charism is correct (and I repeat that Weber did not move far in this direction), then the countervailing forces are summoned forth by the dominant social order they seek to change. The charismatic person, we said, had power because he appealed to, and sometimes even articulated, the alienation that the dominant system imposed on people, and initiated his followers to a new imagination that was to overcome this alienation and, in some instances, actually anticipated and helped bring about the future development of society. The conflicting movements are social reactions generated by the dominant systems. In other words, the dominant system of society produces not only the dominant consciousness that keeps the system going, but it also produces, by way of critical response and passing through the creativity of certain personalities, the countervailing movements and the emergence of a new consciousness. The critical movements are generated in the womb of the old society.

Weber regarded history as undefined and open. Freedom was inserted in the historical process through the charismatic persons and the countervailing movements created by them. The bearers of the charism, in touch with the alienation of the community, produce a new imagination with varying effects; it may lead followers into blind alleys or make them agents of significant social change. The spectrum is very wide here. Each social order creates its own opposing movements, but these may vary from irrational sectarian protest groups to revolutionary movements and reformist parties, the form of the countervailing trend depending on the utopian imagination that has produced it. Weber follows Hegel and Marx in recognizing the dialectical relationship between society and consciousness, or between infrastructure and superstructure, yet unlike them, he did not believe that this dialectics would carried history forward in a clearly defined direction. For Hegel, this direction was provided by immanent reason; for Marx, it was the logic of the class struggle that moved history towards the classless society. Weber had little sympathy for theories of total world interpretation. At the same time, he had no sympathy either for the rationalism or idealism that made political scientists think they could devise rational solutions for the problems of society and impose them on the social order. If I understand Weber correctly, he thought the reform of society by social engineering would be unsuccessful, unless the new set of rules correspond to the aspirations of the disadvantaged groups.

Weber's theory of social change can be applied to social configurations of all kinds, to cultural systems, political societies and ecclesiastical organizations. It is even possible to recognize the Marxist theory of revolution as a special case in Weber's analysis of social change. For if there is a society in which the economic system is the predominant cause of alienation and oppression, so dominant that all other factors – cultural, intellectual, religious and even political – have become instruments of the economic interests of the owning class, then the countervailing movements, sparked by charismatic personalities in touch with the alienation of the people, will oppose the economic system, divide the society into two conflicting classes, and, if strong enough, overthrow the political system that protects the owners of industry. But Weber, contrary to Marx, did not suppose that economics was the exclusive determining factor in every society. As we mentioned above, Weber regarded bureaucracy and technology as such powerful institutional factors in the creation of modern culture that he was convinced that they would cause oppressive conditions and dehumanization even in countries that rejected capitalism and opted for a "rational," centralizing and industrializing communism. Even here the "iron cage" was inevitable.

Let us return to the question of Weber's pessimism. Does the bureaucratization of life inevitably lead to the crushing of all charisms and countervailing and corrective trends in society? Have we become inevitably preoccupied with functionality and lost sight of questions regarding the purpose of human life in society? Weber's gloomy theory of bureaucracy has not convinced all sociologists. Robert Merton, in particular, has shown that the movement towards increasingly controlled and rigid bureaucracies, described by Weber, actually contains dysfunctional elements that will eventually undermine the efficiency of the bureaucratic systems.[169] These dysfunctional elements can be overcome by opening up the bureaucracy to critical conversation among staff members on all administrative levels to discuss the aims of the institution and the manner in which these aims are achieved. According to Merton, the drift of bureaucracy towards greater rationality will eventually include self-corrective processes that raise questions not only in regard to means, but also concerning ends.

In a lecture given in 1919, Weber himself admitted that the drift towards growing rationalization eventually moves beyond purely functional or instrumental questions; it will eventually compel people to give an account of the ultimate meaning of their own conduct and raise the question whether the manifold values of life are hierarchically ordered and cohere under a highest value. Rationality, then, is not purely and simply confined to means.[170] Weber seems to have recognized that his cultural pessimism has not been scientifically established. Charisms then may still occur; people may still react, surprisingly and constructively, against the alienation inflicted on them by the system in which they live.

The Weberian ideology of decline is not without consequences. For to adopt a language that supposes that the future is determined, that the unexpected will no longer happen and that freedom has been removed, is to engage in a discourse that could become a self-fulfilling prophecy. This discourse extinguishes any new imagination. Christians hold that the future remains undetermined, open to human sin and divine grace. The language they want to use about history is one that protects human freedom and the occurrence of the unexpected. The new remains ever a possibility. In my book *Man Becoming*, I tried to show that to believe in God means precisely to trust that the new can happen, that tomorrow will be different from today, that the future is not wholly determined by causes operative in the present, but remains ever open to the unexpected and the marvellous.[171] I then applied this principle mainly to personal life, but it is equally valid for the historical process. Translating this theological principle into the language of Max Weber, we would have to say that charisms and countervailing movements making people transcend the alienation produced by the dominant system remain possible.

Weber's theory of social change, derived – as we have seen – from his sociology of religion, also renders an admirable account of the conflicts within the Christian Church. The medieval sects, for example, were countervailing movements opposing traditional authority, often inspired by charismatic figures who had put their finger on the ills of the established Church. Most of these movements were crushed. A few were kept by leaders within the Church – the Franciscans, for instance – as protected subcultures with rules of their own that did not apply to the Church as a whole. Charismatic leaders, living under great pressure, produced a wide spectrum of utopias from the fulfillment of biblical promises to strange and fantastic dreams. At the Reformation, a religious countervailing movement, sparked by a charismatic personality of great power, achieved its purpose in part because it was joined by countervailing political movements resisting the empire. The new churches, especially those of Calvinist inspiration, repudiated the notion of traditional authority; they introduced democracy into church life and regarded themselves to be ruled by legal authority. Yet the charismatic movements that repudiated both ecclesiastical and secular society, the so-called radical wing of the Reformation, were brutally crushed by the joining of all forces against them. It may well be that church reform can be successful only if it is carried forward by important socio-political currents in society.

Weber's theory of social change also sheds light on the changes that have taken place in the Catholic Church over the past 40 years or so. Vatican Council II had been prepared by countervailing trends of various kinds – liturgical, ecumenical, biblical, lay action, etc. – which promoted, over a considerable period of time, aspects of the Christian life that had been neglected or suppressed by the official Church. These movements had experienced the pressure of the hierarchical establishment, yet they proudly remembered the charismatic personalities, however modest, associated with their origin. It was only at Vatican Council II, through the unexpected action of Pope John XXIII, that these movements were fully recognized and allowed to influence the policy making of the hierarchy.

Through these new policies, the Catholic Church opened itself to critical scholarship, freedom of conscience, respect for human rights, theological pluralism and participation of the laity. This progressive reform movement was supported by the critical cultural trend of the 1960s, impatient with inherited authority and calling for the democratization of society.

Decades after the Council, when a certain shift to the right has come to characterize political life, the Catholic Church on the whole seems to have lost interest in the renewal. A ready identification with the dominant groups in society, as well as the unwillingness critically to examine the Church's collective life, prevents Catholic parishes, dioceses and higher ecclesiastical offices from applying the conciliar principles to their own institutions. In the contemporary Church, the critical vitality expresses itself in new countervailing movements. A minority of Catholics are involved in centres, groups and networks of various kinds, including certain schools, colleges and religious congregations – all of which promote aspects of the Gospel disregarded by the official Church, in particular those that have to do with the critical power of the Gospel in the condition of the modern world. The various groups, interrelated and supportive of one another, constitute a web of renewal that may have no institutional power at this time, but that will again, under changed circumstances, affect the Church's policy-making on a higher level. Weber's theory of social change helps Catholics to appreciate that their involvement in a countervailing movement is a realistic policy of renewal and reform in their own Church.

Weber recognized the creative and innovative elements in religion. He regarded them as so significant that he based his entire theory of social change on a model taken from his sociology of religion. Needless to say, Weber did not deny the extraordinary ambiguity of religion. He recognized the ideological trends in religion that had been brought out by the Marxist critique. He was keenly aware that the Christian religion of his own age acted as a legitimating symbol system for the traditional order of society. Yet he accepted the evidence from history that religion can also be an innovating force.

* * *

Utopian religion – we use the term in Mannheim's sense – can be both reformist and radical. Innovative religion has nourished social currents that sought to reform the existing institutions; yet in other circumstances, it has produced an imagination that looked forward to the overthrow of the existing order. Weber paid special attention to the reformist trend. So did the theologians who were taught by Weber: Ernst Troeltsch and Richard Niebuhr. It is my impression that these thinkers did not pay enough attention to the radical form of utopian consciousness.

In his famous book *Christ and Culture*,[172] Richard Niebuhr introduced a fivefold typology to categorize the various responses of Christian believers to their socio-cultural environment. Since these five types are well-known, I shall offer only the briefest description.

> Type 1: Christ against Culture – signifying the sectarian rejection of the world.

> Type 2: Christ of Culture – signifying the identification of the Gospel with the dominant cultural trends.

> Type 3: Christ above Culture – referring to the medieval natural-supernatural hierarchical cosmos.

> Type 4: Christ in Paradox with Culture – signifying the conflictive vision of the two realms: the inward realm, where believers encounter God, and the outward realm, where they must do God's will but are unable to find God.

> Type 5: Christ, Transformer of Culture – referring to Christian faith that summons believers to the transformation of the social order and to the encounter with God in the historical struggle between good and evil.

For Richard Niebuhr, writing his book in 1951, Types 1 and 2 were outside the authentic understanding of the Gospel, Type 3 represented the Roman Catholic faith, Type 4 characterized the conservative trend of contemporary Protestant religion, and Type 5 was the vision of faith that he himself wanted to promote.

In the present chapter dealing with innovative religion, we are mainly concerned with Types 1 and 5. In my opinion, Richard Niebuhr did not adequately interpret the faith of radical Christians who looked upon Jesus Christ as a judge of culture. He classified them under Type 1, at odds with authentic Christianity. He understood their faith as individualistic and world-denying and failed to detect its radical social significance. Karl Mannheim, as we have seen, recognized the political meaning of what he called chiliastic religion and saw in it the ancestor of the Western revolutionary tradition. In a previous chapter,[173] I also mentioned that in her book *The Radical Kingdom*, Rosemary Ruether brought out the revolutionary element in the Christian tradition. She showed that the apocalyptical consciousness, produced among the Jews under conditions of prolonged oppression in the centuries preceding and including the first Christian century, was mediated to subsequent generations by apocalyptical elements of the Christian religion and became the source of the Western revolutionary tradition.

Richard Niebuhr was more interested in reformist religion. What ancient Christian thinkers, according to Niebuhr, anticipated what was to become Type 5: Christ, Transformer of Culture? He mentioned the Gospel of John and the writings of St. Augustine. Yet is this fully justified? While these ancient writers acknowledged God's gracious presence in the transformation of human life, they tended to look upon this as personal transformation. They hoped that the new love created in the hearts of believers would eventually produce a new kind of society, but they did not and probably could not clarify Christ's redemptive presence in terms of social change. The transformation of the structures of society was predicted only in the apocalyptic literature that announced God's judgment on the wicked world and the arrival of God's reign. In my opinion, Niebuhr was right in finding the seeds of Type 5 in Christian thinkers of the past, yet the full-blown spirituality of Christ, Transformer of Culture, developed in the Church only after the Enlightenment. The typical figure chosen by Niebuhr is Frederick Maurice, the Anglican divine of the nineteenth century, who recognized God's gracious presence in all of humanity, discerned the movement of the Spirit towards mutuality and reconciliation in history, and advocated a social ethic which he called – in 1848 – Christian socialism.

Niebuhr recognized elements leading to Type 5 in Calvin's theology. Niebuhr appreciated the aspects of Calvinist teaching that made Christians see themselves as called to work in the world and establish God's justice on earth. Niebuhr acknowledged the revolutionary potential of this piety. At the same time, he felt that this trend was counterbalanced by a strong emphasis on the over-againstness of God. While Calvin created an action-oriented, innovative religion, he greatly stressed the dualistic character of the Christian message. "To the eternal over-againstness of God and man," Niebuhr writes, "Calvin adds the dualism of temporal and eternal existence and the other dualism of an eternal heaven and eternal hell."[174] Christ, Transformer of Culture, as described by Niebuhr, implies a more immanent understanding of the transcendent God. That God is present in the making of the social world became a religious idea only after the Enlightenment, when people realized that society is not a given, but is produced by people and can be changed by them.

It is my contention, repeatedly mentioned in this book, that over the last century and a half, a significant change has taken place in Protestant-ism and Catholicism – well symbolized by Frederick Maurice – calling for the worship of God as the gracious mystery, operative in human life and revealed in Jesus Christ, which empowers people to wrestle against the forces of darkness and restructure human society in accordance with love, justice and peace. We find this trend at first among certain Protestant and Anglican religious thinkers. In North America, the Social Gospel emphasized God's immanence in human history. Let us listen to the interpretation of two church historians. C.H. Hopkins stated,

> The Social Gospel rested upon a few dominant ideas that characterized the intellectual climate in which it grew. Its primary assumption was the immanence of God, a conception derived from the influence of sci-ence – Darwinian evolution in particular – upon Protestant theology. Belief in an indwelling God, working out his purposes in the world of men, naturally involved a solidaristic view of society which was conve-niently supplied by sociology.[175]

Richard Allen, meanwhile, said,

> The demand "save this man, now" became "save this society, now," and the slogan "the evangelization of the world in our generation" became "the Christianization of the world in our generation." The sense of an immanent God working in the movements of revival and awakening was easily transferred to social movements, and hence to the whole evolution of society…. To submit oneself to these immanent impulses of divinity was to adopt the Social Gospel and to embrace the social passion which lay at the heart of most of the movements of social reform in Canada in the period of 1890–1939.[176]

In European Protestantism, it was Hegel's influence that made Chris-tians perceive the Spirit operative in history, and in Catholicism it was Maurice Blondel who, at the end of the nineteenth century, recognized God's immanence in man's humanization. Because of the fall of German Protestant Christianity into cultural conformity, Karl Barth protested against the idea of divine immanence: God was to be worshipped as the totally other. Yet in the second half of the 20th century, when Christians wished to identify themselves not with the dominant classes but with the exploited and oppressed, the major churches moved to the theological position characterized by Type 5: Christ, Transformer of Culture. This shift is found in the documents of the World Council of Churches, even if there is still a hesitancy about divine immanence. A parallel shift is clearly present in the documents of Vatican Council II.

The conciliar document *The Church in the Modern World* is the strongest ecclesiastical document expressing faith in Christ, Transformer of Culture. We read in its Preface:

> The Council gazes upon the world which is the theatre of man's history, and carries the marks of his energies, his tragedies, and his triumphs – that world which the Christian sees as created and sustained by its Maker's love, fallen indeed into the bondage of sin, yet emancipated now by Christ. He was crucified and rose again to break the stranglehold of the evil one, so that this world might be fashioned anew according to God's design and reach its fulfilment.[177]

This passage speaks of God's victory over evil, without distinguishing between person and society or between present history and future glory, suggesting that in Christ is revealed a transformation that affects all aspects of human existence. Vatican II clearly acknowledges, in this document and in several others, the universality of divine grace. The divine call, fully revealed in Jesus, addresses people everywhere and summons them to a common task. Conscience is a sacred reality in all people, according to *The Church in the Modern World*: "Conscience is the most secret core and sanctuary of a man. There he is alone with God, whose voice echoes in his depth. In a wonderful manner, conscience reveals that law which is fulfilled by love of God and neighbour. In fidelity to conscience, Christians are joined to the rest of men in the search for truth and the genuine solution of man's social and personal problems."[178] Humankind is on the journey towards perfect reconciliation, called and enabled by God's gracious presence. At Vatican II, the Catholic Church declared itself in solidarity with the whole human family, in which God is present as matrix, summons and horizon.

How has such an extraordinary transformation of religion occurred? In the Catholic Church, this change was in continuity with very ancient doctrinal trends, acknowledging the immanence of God, the incarnation of the Logos in human life, and the divine destiny of the whole of humankind. In Protestantism, this change was in continuity with Hegel rather than with the original Reformers. I do not claim that the utopian religion, Type 5 of Niebuhr's classification, is universally accepted in the Christian churches. It is resisted by many conservative Christians. Still, this utopian religion is expressed in the ecclesiastical documents, it represents the viewpoint of a great number of Catholic and Protestant theologians, and it inspires a significant minority of believers in the Christian churches. This utopian religion exists in various forms: some inspiring a reformist, left-liberal orientation and others a more radical or even revolutionary commitment. In the mid-1970s, the faith in Christ, Transformer of Culture, was challenged by conservative circles in the churches.[179] Still, it is hard to deny that a significant shift has taken place in the churches: the interpretation of Gospel has been transformed.

Before we try to offer an explanation for this change, we want to raise the question whether faith in Christ, Transformer of Culture, simply expresses a wider endorsement of the Protestant ethic and the liberal dream. One might argue that the growing strength of the middle class in the Catholic Church, especially in Western Europe and America, has led to a wider acceptance of liberal ideals and enabled Catholicism at Vatican II to catch up with the Protestant churches. There is no doubt a grain of truth in this theory. At the same time, there are significant differences between the Protestant ethic and the utopian gospel described above. The Protestant ethic was based on a dualistic understanding of the Christian message. God was the transcendent ruler of history who commanded his faithful servants to work in the world and transform it according to his will. The Protestant ethic corresponds to what Weber has called "ethical prophecy":[180] here, ethics is obedience to God's Word uttered from on high. Here the human and the divine world are distinct and separate. It is this dualism that the transformist religion tries to overcome. Here God is seen as the transcendent mystery present in history, fully revealed in Jesus, and operative in the significant moments of human liberation, personal and social. Here we are closer to what Weber called "exemplary prophecy":[181] participation in a divine mystery incarnate in a model figure. I wish to argue that the transformist spirituality has a mystical dimension that is absent from the Protestant ethic – and from neo-orthodoxy. Human life in the world is more than faithful obedience to the divine summons; it is participation in an unmerited gift, God's self-donation, that calls and strengthens us to strive for the reconciled life. We have here the entry of contemplation in the Christian ethos of worldly orientation. The spirituality proper to the transformist faith is not a dualistic contemplation that detaches Christians from the world, but a contemplation of the divine mystery that is the source, orientation and horizon of human endeavour.

There is a second difference between the Protestant ethic and the transformist Gospel. The Protestant ethic relates believers individually to God and makes them concentrate on their personal salvation, a religious attitude that tends to foster individualism in culture, economics and society and promotes the liberal world view. The transformist faith, on the other hand, opposes individualism. It does not see a person's relationship to God as private and separated, but perceives God's grace as mediated by fellowship, by the Church and by the historical struggle for the reconciliation of humanity in God. Transformist faith fosters a movement away from individualism in personal life as well as in culture, economics and society. It tends to be critical of the free market, the profit motive and the principle of competition. The utopian faith sustains an awareness of people's collective destiny and often formulates its opposition to individualism in terms of socialism or co-operative commonwealth. For two reasons, then – support for contemplation and socialism – the transformist Gospel cannot be regarded as an extension of the Protestant ethic. It represents a critical movement in Protestantism and Catholicism, sustaining the dream of an alternative culture.

How did the transformist faith emerge in the Christian Church? Changes in religion depend on many factors, on the social and cultural conditions in which a religion exists, on the exigencies of its own institutional life, and finally on the charismatic element – charismatic in the Weberian sense – which, while unpredictable, enables a religion to respond in an innovative way to new historical circumstances. Changes in religion may strengthen the dominant ideological trend or nourish the utopian current; they may reinforce the pathogenic elements or foster the liberating trends. The question I wish to ask is simply this: What happened in Christianity, in particular in the Catholic Church, the most hierarchical, conservative and unrepentant church of the West, to generate a transformist understanding of the Christian Gospel?

To understand this shift in the interpretation of the Gospel, we must consider two distinct factors: first, the emergence of a new consciousness in Western culture, and second, the peculiar creativity of the Gospel in the face of evil. The discussion of the first factor belongs to sociological reflection; the discussion of the second factor takes us into theology.

We have already studied the creation of the Gesellschaft-type of society. The industrial and democratic revolutions at the end of the eighteenth century created an individualistic and atomistic consciousness that corresponded to the rational and scientific Enlightenment, often called the Early Enlightenment. At the same time, the new dominant institutions also produced countervailing trends. (This, incidentally, verifies Weber's theory of social change.) We mentioned that German thinkers at the turn of the nineteenth century were critical of Enlightenment culture, largely – if we follow Mannheim's sociology of knowledge – because in Germany the feudal order was still in place and there existed no large middle class. Still, their critical stance was later taken over by the sociologists, including Marx, all of whom were critical of the culture created by Gesellschaft. At the turn of the 20th century, despite the expansion of industrialization and technological development, the great critics of the rational society emerged, including Durkheim, Weber and Freud. They moved beyond positivism, discovered the symbolic dimension of human life, and often favoured a holistic rather than an atomistic understanding of society. These thinkers, including Marx, are often referred to as the Late Enlightenment. It is here that we find the trenchant critiques of rationalism, the effort to recover the emotions, a new outlook on action and social involvement, the denunciation of false consciousness, and the development of sociological theories. While the Early Enlightenment was hostile to religion, the Late Enlightenment, while often appearing non-religious, was basically open to religion. Christians could not carry on fruitful conversations with the Early Enlightenment, but there was no reason why conversation with the Late Enlightenment could not be a promising intellectual endeavour. The first scholars who attempted such a dialogue in the Catholic Church were condemned as Modernists.

The Early Enlightenment found expression in the rational and individualistic structures of Gesellschaft. We have shown above how the democratic and industrial revolutions communicated an atomistic and scientific spirit among the people. At the same time, Gesellschaft had a more latent effect on consciousness, not perceived by its early advocates. Its immediate effect was the spread of the scientific mindset, but the more remote effect was the creation of historical consciousness. How did this happen?

The expanding technological-industrial institutions and the increasing flexibility of political structures created a new awareness – first, among the intellectuals who reflected on them, and eventually among the people whose lives were involved in them – that the social and cultural world was made by humans, or at least was controlled by them, and hence could be remade to suit human needs. While at one time the human reality was looked upon as a given reality, which people tried to understand and into which they wanted to fit their lives, in the new age society was experienced by people as unfinished, as something that still had to be built, as a social process, the past of which was a given but the future of which still depended on people's choices. Thanks to the institutions in which people lived, they came to look upon reality as development, as an ongoing process involving their freedom, intelligence and dedication. As the world was unfinished, so were they. People gradually ceased to regard themselves as finished subjects looking at a world pitted as object over against them (the scientific consciousness); they began to recognize that subject and object are inseparably interrelated, that they have been produced by a common history of interaction, and that men and women, unfinished as they are, constitute themselves as subjects precisely by continuing to build the world as object. People thus began to feel responsible for their future. It was up to them as a community to build their world, and by building their world to engage in their own self-transformation. While the thinkers of the Early Enlightenment often saw this process as mechanically determined, those of the Late Enlightenment discovered in varying ways how much people's freedom, their symbols and dreams, their feelings and intentions, enter into this action. People began to experience themselves as having been produced by a historical process and being responsible for creating their future by a similar process passing through their collective decisions. This is the historical consciousness. Some people who acquired this new consciousness felt themselves as part of an evolutionary process that moved forward towards progress and the great liberal society. Others had a clearer grasp of the distortions and discrepancies operative in society and the human mind, and hence looked upon this historical process in terms of a struggle against opposing powers. Here again some of these felt that, despite these obstacles, history was destined to move forward towards the just, socialist society, while others remained unconvinced that history would inevitably lead towards the humanization and reconciliation of mankind. Yet all of these outlooks, while different in many ways, share in the same historical consciousness.

Today, the historical consciousness is no longer confined to a few intellectuals who reflect on the conditions of modern life; it is shared by a growing number of people as the unexpected, latent consequence of Gesellschaft on their consciousness. This new self-awareness may still represent a minority trend, for the scientific consciousness continues to predominate, but there are widely acknowledged signs that an increasing number of people understand themselves as responsible for their world and for their future. This development was not foreseen by Toennies and Weber, the great critics of Gesellschaft. Today, the historical consciousness is widely acknowledged. It was clearly recognized as the emerging consciousness in the documents of Vatican Council II.

> In every group or nation, there is an ever-increasing number of men and women who are conscious that they themselves are the artisans and authors of the culture of their community.... Such a development is of paramount importance for the spiritual maturity of the human race. This truth grows clearer if we consider how the world is becoming unified and how we have the duty to build a better world based on truth and justice. Thus we are witnesses of the birth of a new humanism, one in which man is defined first of all by his responsibility toward his brothers and toward history.[182]

This is the new cultural consciousness, I hold, in which Christians have experienced Jesus Christ as transformer of culture and interpreted the Gospel as a transformist faith.

* * *

In this historical consciousness, the theological imagination presenting reality as two worlds, the human world below and the divine world above, could no longer be entertained. What took place, as I briefly described in the first chapter of this book, was the rejection of what theologians called extrinsicism. Hegel was the first thinker to see this clearly, followed by important Protestant theologians. In Catholicism, theological extrinsicism was rejected by Maurice Blondel, followed by a few theologians, including Karl Rahner, and after Vatican Council II by the majority of theologians. Yet even the spiritual experience of the faithful, at least of those involved in modern institutions and situated at the Church's critical edge, no longer confirmed the traditional separation of the sacred and the profane, of the divine and the human world. Christians began to experience God not as the voice from above that called them away from this world to a higher level, but as a transcendent mystery, present in life itself, that summons people to greater self-knowledge, enables them to assume responsibility for their world, and moves them forward towards a promised future.

This takes us to the second factor responsible for the emergence of transformist religion in the Christian Church: namely, the special creativity of the Gospel in the face of evil. The Gospel of Jesus, so Christians believe, is a power unto salvation. It promises to save us from the enemies of life. It proclaims the coming of God's reign that will overcome the powers of darkness. The Gospel allows us to discern the sin in our midst and to be severed from it, and it permits us, in a limited way, to anticipate God's reign in the community of men and women touched by the Spirit. Christians believe that Jesus offers them redemption from evil.

But the face of evil changes from age to age. The forces that threaten human life depend on many cultural, political and personal factors. In every period of history, the dehumanization operative in society has a different mask. It is possible that in each age, Christians discover in the Gospel dimensions of rescue adapted to their situation, dimensions that were overlooked in the past. There is no guarantee that this will happen. The Christian religion may play an ideological role and hide the new face of evil. The churches may speak about heaven and remain silent about the aggressions and oppressions taking place on earth. Religion, as we have said repeatedly, is an ambiguous reality. Yet it may also happen – through the charisma granted to a few – that the selfsame Gospel utter a new word, reveal the present face of evil, provide a new imagination and spark a countervailing movement of innovative, utopian religion. Here Christians gain a new sense of what salvation means.

What I am proposing here is a theory of doctrinal development that takes into account the historical conditions in which the Church is located. Confronted with new manifestations of evil or simply the discovery of evil previously overlooked, charismatic persons in the Church may have new religious experiences of salvation. If these experiences stand up under the test of the Scriptures, the charismatic leaders will embrace them with confidence and communicate them to the wider community. The development of doctrine is here related to historical circumstances. Theologians dealing with this doctrinal development usually neglect the material dimension and explain this development simply in terms of logical or psychological deductions from previous doctrinal formulations. In my opinion, such explanations lose sight of the creativity of the Gospel. The sacred text read in new historical circumstances utters a message previously not heard. Responding to the Holocaust, the rereading of the Scriptures has prompted the churches to purify their teaching of the anti-Jewish rhetoric and to recognize the ongoing validity of God's ancient covenant with the Jews.

What is the face of evil in our times? This is a question that has preoccupied us in this book. We have learned from sociologists and psychologists to become aware of the alienation woven into our technological and industrial society, of the oppression and exploitation created by monopoly capitalism, of the subjugation of women, of various falsifications of consciousness, of ideological and pathological religion. We are oppressed and, simultaneously, oppressors, not only through the various institutions that dehumanize us, but also through false symbols that dominate our imagination. More than that, we are the generation after Auschwitz. We have seen the destructive power of certain myths. We have also learned that a certain church-centred understanding of Christianity has served as legitimation of the European invasion of other continents, including the Americas, and hence is related to the white man's hegemony in the modern world and his near-monopoly of many of the earth's resources. Guided by the social sciences, we have been able to discern the structures of domination in our history and to articulate the alienation inflicted on people by society. The transformist faith described above is the creative response of the Gospel to this alienation.

9

Critical Theology

The preceding chapters, for the most part, began with sociological reflections and only towards the end moved to theological considerations. This chapter deals with theology. By "theology" I here refer to its traditional definition as the reflection of believing Christians on their religious tradition. Theology is the critical task of the believing community. Theology then presupposes faith – or, more precisely, theology is an expression of faith and thus enters into the very shape that faith takes in people's lives.

And what is "faith"? Again, I here move within the traditional definition. To believe means to receive the message and be open to the gifts that accompany it. To believe means to share with others in the symbols of God and to define one's life orientation out of these. The symbols received in faith initiate the believers into a new self-understanding and relate them in a new way to the world. Faith, mediated by the biblical symbols, is the trusting acknowledgment of a divine mystery graciously operative in human history and creating a community of salvation. Coming to such an acknowledgment depends on the perspective from which we look at the world and open ourselves to the religious tradition. Over this basic approach or attitude we have no direct control. We cannot change, by willpower, the angle from which we see our lives. Faith is a gift. People are amazed and marvel when, looking at the world and listening to the inherited religious message, they discover a hidden meaning in their lives and a direction in history and are able to redefine their existence as men and women with a destiny. Theology, then, presupposes and expresses faith. Theology is the reflection of believing Christians, in conversation with the entire Church, on the world to which they belong and the religious tradition in which they participate.

It is my contention that after the Enlightenment, Christian theology assumes a new and important role in the life of the Church. Learning from the social sciences and the various critiques of religion, Christian theologians are able to discern the ideological and pathogenic trends in their own religious tradition and then, by opting for a wider meaning of the promised salvation, interpret the Christian Gospel as a message of deliverance and reconciliation. The sustained dialogue with the critical thought of the Late Enlightenment I wish to call "critical theology." Critical theology is the critical application of the various theories of alienation to the self-understanding in faith of the Christian Church. This critical method may lead theologians to discover elements of false consciousness in their perception of reality and thus produce a significant change of mind and heart.

Traditional, precritical theology studied the Christian religion in the light of its divine gifts. The Christian religion was here understood as a spiritual reality mediated by doctrine and sacraments and expressing itself in the holiness of the faithful. Traditional theologians studied the development of Christian teaching and the meaning of the Church's sacramental liturgy. According to the social thinkers, however, religious practice has a profound structural effect on people's lives far beyond the range of faith, hope and love. Religious practice, as we have seen, affects people's personal and social lives in ways that often remain hidden from them. The intended effects of the Christian religion may be quite different from the actual consequences. The early Puritans would have been surprised if they had been told that their perception of the Gospel mediated an inner dynamics to society that would eventually lead to the rationalization of economic, social and cultural life. The social sciences help us to distinguish between what religion intends to be and what it produces in people's lives: that is, between the aspirations and the consequences of religion. It is the task of critical theology to discern the structural consequences of religious practice, to evaluate them in the light of the Church's normative teaching, and to enable the Church to restructure its concrete social presence so that its social consequences approach more closely its profession of faith. What must be in keeping with the Gospel is not only the Church's teaching and practice, but also and especially the actual, concrete effects of this teaching and practice on human history. Critical theology enables the Church to assume theological responsibility for its social reality. In this preliminary sense, then, critical theology is "reflection on praxis."

We note that critical theology does not designate a particular area of theology; it does not refer to a theology of society or a theology of human life that accompanies a dogmatic theology concerned with the great moments of divine revelation. Critical theology refers rather to a mode of theological reflection that is applicable to every area of theology – moral, dogmatic, ascetical, and so forth. We have observed in the preceding chapters that the doctrine of God, while dealing with a transcendent mystery, has in fact profound, unrecognized (and sometimes alienating) structural implications for social life and personal well-being. We have observed, moreover, that the traditional formulation of christology, while dealing with God's saving act in Jesus, actually had profound, unrecognized and totally unintended structural effects: it has inferiorized the Jews and prepared their social exclusion, and it has led to a church-centred understanding of history and legitimated the white man's colonial invasion of the world. It is the task of critical theology to bring to light the hidden human consequences of doctrine, to raise the consciousness of the believing community in this regard, and to find a manner of proclaiming the Church's teaching that has structural consequences in keeping with the Gospel. In the case of Christology, this means that a way of announcing God's Word in Jesus must be found that does not devour other religions but rather makes room for the multiple manifestation of God's grace. There is not a single doctrine of the Church, nor a single aspect of spirituality, worship or church life, that may be exempted from a critique that distinguishes between its aspirations and its structural consequences and evaluates the latter in terms of the Gospel. The theological reflections in this book, I may add, have been in this critical mode. Critical theology, I insist, is not the submission of dogma to an anthropological norm as if the human were the measure of the divine; critical theology is rather the submission of the structural consequences of dogma to the revealed norm of the Gospel. Critical theology, we note, is not an exhortative theology that complains of the unwillingness of church members to live up to their moral ideals. Critical theology is not concerned with personal virtue. What is examined by critical theology are the structural consequences of doctrine or institutions – the effects on consciousness and society exerted by religious language and religious forms, quite independent of the subjective intention of the believers. The sociologists have convinced us that the symbolic structure of the imagination is able to legitimate an existing social order or, under certain conditions, to de-legitimate the present order and urge the recreation of culture and society. The structural consequences of doctrine and institution belong to the objective order. It is with these that critical theology is concerned.

In this chapter we shall discuss one application of critical theology. Since a major distortion of the Christian religion in the West has been the "privatization" of the Gospel – the excessively individualistic interpretation of the Christian message – and since this privatized religion has legitimated and promoted the atomization of the social order and an economic system of each person for him- or herself, it is the task of critical theology to de-privatize the inherited religion. Such an exercise reveals the hidden political implications of religious language and practice. That is why German theologians, following Johann Baptist Metz, refer to the deprivatization of Christianity as "political theology."[183]

The theological starting point for the following critique is the thesis, commonly accepted by students of the Bible, that the preaching of Jesus Christ had to do with repentance and the coming of God's kingdom and that it had both personal and social meaning. Christ's message was addressed to people as persons and as community. Jesus proclaimed that the kingdom of God was near, that God was about to fulfill his promises made to the ancients and recorded in Scripture, and that he himself was the special agent and servant of God's ultimate victory over the powers of evil. Jesus did not present his work as the salvation of souls; rather, he came to usher in a new age that would transform the very structures of human life. After the crucifixion and the Easter event, the disciples believed that in the Resurrection the kingdom of God had manifested itself in an irrevocable manner, that God's victory over evil and all the enemies of life was assured, and that the final coming of Jesus as the fulfiller of the divine promises was not far away. In the "between-time," Christ was looked upon as the one in whom the kingdom had been anticipated. He communicated the Spirit to the community. He was the strength, the comfort, the guide, the divine revealer enabling the community to move forward in history, impatient with the enduring power of evil yet joyful that its days were numbered. The Christian message communicates both judgment and new life, and is addressed to persons and to society. The Gospel has meaning for personal life and social history.

To reduce the Christian message to a truth about personal salvation is to suppress a basic dimension of this message and to transform it into an ideology sanctioning individualism. Critical theology counters the privatizing of the Gospel with an effort to regain its double dimension of personal-and-social.

* * *

Let us begin with the notion of sin. There can be no doubt that the notion of sin in theological teaching and religious practice has become excessively individualistic. We have looked upon sin as a personal deed, a personal violation of a divine commandment, or an act of infidelity against God, freely committed with deliberation. What we have forgotten is the social dimension of sin. In doing so we have lost the key for understanding the violence in our history and the collective evil in which we are involved.

In the Scriptures, we find a twofold language about sin. There is personal sin knowingly and freely chosen, and there is social sin accompanied by collective blindness. There is sin as deed and sin as illness. An example of personal sin is King David's adultery with Bathsheba and the premeditated murder of her husband, Uriah, in which the king acted against his better judgment and for which he did penance after the prophet's reprimand. Yet even this story had a social message, for the prophets in Israel, accustomed to a confederate structure of authority, were suspicious of the new kingship and feared the possibility of despotism. They made the story of David's sin remind the people that the king was a sinner and that they should never abandon their critical attitude towards royal authority.

Social sin is more especially the topic of the prophetic preaching. There we hear of collective blindness, group-egotism, and the pursuit of a national life that betrays the covenant and violates the divine command. Peculiar to this collective sin is that it is accompanied by so much self-delusion and self-flattery that the people involved in it are not aware of their transgression. We remind the reader of what we have said of the biblical notion of "blindness" in a previous chapter.[184] Here we have sin, understood as infidelity to God and destructive communal action, which is largely due to false consciousness. This sin is like an illness. It destroys us while we are unable to recognize its features and escape its power. While personal conversion to God's voice may make us discover the wayward direction of our collective life, we are quite unable to halt the involvement of society unless the new awareness is shared by a great number of people, and especially by the leaders.

The symbol of the purely private understanding of sin in the Catholic Church is the confessional. The confessional practice goes back to the early Middle Ages, when the Church, in an attempt to civilize the Germanic tribes, imposed detailed rules of conduct on them, regarded as sin the violation of these rules, and transformed the ancient penitential ritual into the regime of private confession. This regime created a highly private, legal and act-oriented understanding of sin. When the Reformation insisted on a more attitudinal understanding of sin, the Catholic Church defended the medieval confessional practice. This practice has created the imagination among Catholic peoples that sin is always a conscious and free decision to violate a divine commandment. To overcome this privatized understanding of sin and the problematic political consequences, many contemporary Catholic theologians[185] have recommended that the practice of private confession be replaced by a communal celebration of the sacrament of repentance in which the people, gathered in community, listen to God's word, reflect on their sins, including their objective involvement in the injustices of their institutions, repent of their past, and then receive sacramental absolution – the divine pardon and divine help to continue their struggle for the good. If Christians are in need of special counselling, and this happens occasionally in every person's life, they should have a conversation with a religious counsellor. Self-discovery, important and salvational though it be, need not be linked to the Church's public sacramental celebration of conversion and forgiveness.

In the Scriptures, sin is both personal and social, and the two aspects are closely interrelated. In our theological tradition, we have presented sin mainly as private. The biblical passages dealing with sin as illness have been too exclusively understood as referring to the inherited sin, the so-called original sin, which expresses the wounded state of human nature into which infants are born and thanks to which they share in the common inclination towards evil. At one time, theologians linked this inherited distortion to Adam's transgression in a literal sense and saw in it a quasi-ontological legacy that had no direct connection with the sins of people and the evil of their collective life. Catholics often wondered why the inherited sin, for which we are not responsible, should be called sin at all. In fact, original sin was an embarrassing doctrine for many Christians. Contemporary theologians, on the other hand, have tended to identify the inherited sin with what the Bible calls "the sin of the world" – that is, the structure of evil, built into society, which wounds people, distorts their inclinations and prompts them to do evil things.[186] The inherited sin, then, is mediated through the unresolved conflicts of parents and families as well as through the discrepancies of the institutional life into which infants are born and in which they grow up. Psychotherapists such as Freud and Laing have shown how the conflicts of parents are handed

on as distortions to their children; Marx and the sociological tradition
have demonstrated that institutions create consciousness and that the
injustices built into these institutions falsify the awareness of the children socialized into them. The contemporary understanding of original
sin brings to light the connection between personal and social sin. Seen
in this light, the ancient teaching on original sin contains an important
message for our age; it corrects the liberal misunderstanding that we are
born into a neutral environment, in which the good is available to us if
we so choose. According to the Church's teaching, the human situation
is different; we are born into a distorted environment, grow up with a
partially falsified consciousness, and the good becomes available to us
only through many conversions – only as we resist the easy inclination of
our wounded nature and follow the challenging, transcendent summons
addressed to us in life. In modern capitalism in particular, infantile nar-
cissism is reinforced by the individualism of the consumer society. Only
as we enter a counter-culture, such as the *ecclesia*, are we able to move
towards a less alienating and more reconciled experience of life.

What is social sin? This is an open theological question.[187] I wish to
reply to it by relying on the sociological considerations proposed in the
preceding chapters. Some theologians define social sin in terms of its
object; social sin, then, is an evil act of a person or persons that adversely
affects the life of society. Social sin is a deliberate act by one or several
people damaging the common good. This certainly is an aspect of social
sin, but as a definition it does not situate the sinfulness of the world at a
deep enough level. We are still in the realm of conscious and deliberate
action and hence remain very close to personal sin. I propose to define
social sin with reference to its subject. What is proper to social sin is that
its subject is a collectivity. Social sin resides in a group, a community, a
people. I am not attempting to revive here the issue of collective guilt that
occupied theologians after the war. Can a nation as a whole be guilty of
the crimes committed by its government? This is not the question I pose
here. What is proper to social sin is that it is not produced by deliberation
and free choice. It produces evil consequences but no guilt in the ordinary
sense. According to the biblical description, social sin is committed out of
blindness. People are involved in destructive action without being aware
of it. I wish to recognize several levels in social sin.

The first level of social sin is made up of the injustices and dehumanizing trends built into the different institutions – social, political, economic,
religious and others – that embody people's collective life. As people go

about doing their daily work and fulfilling their duties, the destructive trends built into their institutions will damage a growing number of persons and eventually destroy their humanity. This evil may go on without anyone being fully aware of it. For the contradictions implicit in institutions remain hidden at first; only after a long time do the negative effects appear, and when they do, they are not immediately recognized as effects of the system. It takes a long time before the discrepancies implicit in institutional life translate themselves into dehumanizing trends and are acknowledged as such.

A second level of social sin is made up of the cultural and religious symbols, operative in the imagination and fostered by society, that legitimate and reinforce the unjust institutions and thus intensify the harm done to a growing number of people. Here again we have total ignorance. We have called such symbolic systems "ideologies." Such an ideology would be the privatized notion of sin we are discussing in this chapter, for by persuading people that the source of evil is only in the human heart, we make them blind to the destructive trends built into their institutional life.

On a third level, social sin refers to the false consciousness created by these institutions and ideologies through which people involve themselves collectively in destructive action as if they were doing the right thing. This false consciousness persuades us that the evil we do is in fact a good thing in keeping with the aim and purpose of our collective well-being. Examples drawn from our own society would be the achievement-orientation of the dominant culture, its individualistic and competitive spirit, and our arrogant collective self-understanding with its implicit racism. False consciousness exists, of course, in varying degrees of intensity, from a total identification with the dominant trends of society, including all of its social effects, to a growing suspicion in regard to these trends and a gradual awakening to the injustices implicit in them. It is on this level that the wrestling against social sin begins. For here people, open to the Spirit, are able to become aware of, and turn away from, the taken-for-granted injustices built into their society. This is the level where conversion takes place.

Finally, if my analysis is correct, we have a fourth level of social sin that is made up of collective decisions, generated by the distorted consciousness, that magnify the injustices in society and intensify the power of the dehumanizing trends. These collective decisions, made by councils or boards of various kinds, appear as if they are based on free choice and deliberation, while in fact they may simply be the rational consequences of the distortions built into the institution and duplicated in consciousness. At the same time, this is the level where personal sin clearly enters into the creation and expansion of social sin. For here, out of conscious evil intention and greed, a person or a group of persons can magnify the evil done by institutional life and give a twist for the worse to human organization.

Examples of this four-levelled sin could be drawn from the preceding chapters. I wish to give a simple illustration from a pastoral letter on world hunger entitled *Sharing Daily Bread*, written by the Canadian bishops in 1974. The main cause of the impasse, according to this letter, is the free market system. No amount of generosity extended to the developing nations will significantly alleviate world hunger until the market system itself is changed. "The present market," the bishops write, "is designed primarily to make profits, not to feed people. The supply and distribution of food is determined mainly by effective demand, not by human need. Effective demand is usually defined in terms of ability to pay. Food supplies are often controlled in such a way as to drive up prices on the market." According to this pastoral letter, then, a contradiction is built into the system producing and distributing food. Human society does not plan to grow adequate food supplies for its population and then distribute them to people according to their objective requirements. Instead, the institution that regulates the production and delivery of food is defined by a principle, the profit principle, that has no direct relation to people's needs.

What do we conclude from this pastoral letter? Implicit in the free market for food is an injustice that no amount of personal generosity and goodwill shall be able to overcome (first level of social sin). What will have to change is the system. In the present society, however, the free market is legitimated by cultural and religious symbols (second level). The very raising of the question is regarded as disloyal and subversive. To indict the market system is to question a sacred element of our society. This system, which is the most pervasive in our society, has created a consciousness in us that makes us co-operate with it, look upon it as an irreplaceable element of society, and apply its principle to ever wider aspects of the social life (third level). What the pastoral letter tried to do was to raise the consciousness of Catholics in regard to the injustice built into the system. At present, the corporate decisions by which the market distributes food can become the locus of free collective sins – that is, of deliberate acts, committed by people for the sake of greater profit, that increase the injustices in the distribution of food (fourth level). As an example, the pastoral letter mentions the artificial raising of food prices. Here, personal sins give the system a twist for the worse.

It follows from the preceding that a dialectical relationship exists between personal and social sin. The alienating institutions have been created by people with inevitably limited perspective and some sinful inclinations. And the personal sins of the few can make the institutional discrepancies even worse. Personal sin may harm the neighbour or many neighbours, but it may also affect corporate life, distort the institution and magnify its destructive effects. The sin of a person in authority who uses his power and his organization for selfish ends still belongs to the category of personal sin. Even a joint decision involving several conscious agents in unjust actions is still personal sin, at least to the extent that this decision is truly deliberate. But the structures that such a corporate decision produces, and that in turn, by a logic of their own, inflict alienation on people, are bearers of social sin. These structures will eventually modify the consciousness of the people involved in them and produce an alienating self-understanding. Personal sins, then, by a dialectics that can be analyzed in each case, are translated into social sin. Human limitations and personal sins compounded have created social sins, and conversely social sins create an environment that promotes personal sins. The damaging of human life through social structures fosters attitudes that lead to personal infidelities and betrayals. The powerful in society are tempted to use their power for self-serving purposes. Economic injustices encourage greed and superficiality among the successful, which easily leads to the sins of the rich; the same injustices produce anger and despair among the disadvantaged, which easily leads to the sins of the poor. Criminals and social outcasts are the shadowy underside of an achievement-oriented society that destroys those who cannot or will not succeed and turns them into human caricatures. It is hard to think of a single personal crime that is not grounded in particular social conditions. To say this is not to belittle personal freedom or to find excuses for wicked deeds. What is asked for here is simply the need for a twofold analysis: an analysis that takes into account both the personal and the social factors.

We touch here upon the weakest side of traditional moral theology. This branch of theology has become so excessively individualistic that it concerns itself almost exclusively with the personal pole of the personal-social dialectics. Here we blame the sinner and condemn the

criminal. We leave a certain amount of room for social pressures by taking into account the gradual loss of freedom that reduces culpability. But
we do not submit the social environment to the detailed criticism that
we apply to the actor. It is true that moral theology today often includes
the study of social justice, but it does not relate this social concern to the
understanding of personal sin. Yet we have learned from the sociologists
that institutions create consciousness and that it is necessary to examine
the institutions to which people belong if we want to understand and
evaluate their personal thoughts and actions.

In traditional moral theology we look only at the actor. Most people in
society, in the climate created by the churches and the dominant culture,
evaluate the faults of people in this excessively privatized manner. We
complain that newspaper reporters love sensation and distort the news,
without analyzing that in a capitalist economy the newspaper business is
competitive, that each newspaper must struggle for survival, and that in
such a situation questionable means are easily used to attract attention
and make people buy more copies. Such a reflection does not intend to
reduce individual action to automatic responses to social conditions; what
is asked for is simply the double analysis. Our present moral impulse,
encouraged by the dominant current in culture and religion, is to find
fault exclusively with the actor. We blame the thief and the robber, but
we do not at the same time examine the social order. Since our present
system calls for the maximization of production and hence demands that
we constantly expand our markets, companies spend much money on
advertising to influence people's imagination and increase their desire for
new goods. Television advertising in particular makes us feel that unless
we have this or that commodity, we do not live up to the expectations of
society. Some people who have been successfully persuaded by society
that having things is the purpose of human life, and yet are cut off from
financial resources, may become cheaters and thieves indeed by free
choice, and then the society that has manipulated their imagination sits
in judgment over them. Christian theologians at least ought to make the
double analysis. If they omit the social analysis, they let society off the
hook, encourage the privatizing trend, and draw upon a false understanding of human life. Conversely, if they fail to make the personal analysis,
they underestimate personal freedom and in this way also distort the
image of human life.

Let me illustrate the two different approaches, the privatizing moral
theology and the insistence on double analysis, by recalling the politi-

cal events of the Canadian October Crisis of 1970, during which two public servants were kidnapped by a small circle of radical separatists, the so-called Quebec Liberation Front. When one of these men, Pierre Laporte, a minister of the Quebec government, was killed, the entire country was profoundly shocked. This had been the first political murder in Canada for over a century. A Catholic bishop of an English-speaking Canadian city made a public statement: we are horrified by the violence in our midst, he said, and may God grant Canada unity and peace. Quite unconsciously, following the privatizing trend, the bishop restricted his analysis to the violence of the extremists, and when he expressed his hope for Canada, he took for granted that God was on the side of national unity. The bishops of Quebec also made a public statement on that occasion – a joint statement, in fact. They, too, began by expressing their horror at the violence in the country. But then, in the second sentence, they asked all Canadians to reflect on the injustices in their country that made such an awful crime a possibility. The Quebec bishops chose the double analysis. They tried to derive a lesson from the cruel event that would not simply legitimate the status quo, but raise the awareness of people in regard to the real problems of their country – in this case the subordinate status of Quebeckers in an unequal national union. This contrasting response symbolizes to me a turning point in the Church's moral theology.

This brief reflection on sin as personal-and-social corresponds to the dialectical relationship between consciousness and society we have mentioned several times in the preceding chapters. The privatizing trend, overlooking the reciprocal relation between personal transgression and social contradiction, has therefore a hidden political meaning. It makes people think that the dreadful things that happen in the world are due to the evil deeds of single individuals and that there is no need critically to examine the social institutions to which they belong. The privatizing trend in the Christian religion, supported by the dominant culture, lets society off the hook – I have used this expression before – and hence protects institutional power and privilege. In other words, privatizing the Gospel is ideological.

When we listen attentively to sermons or carefully read spiritual literature, we easily detect the notion of sin held by Christian teachers and discern implicit in it a view of society and a political message. For if Christian teachers present sin as those acts and attitudes that undermine the values and the authority of the dominant groups, they make the support of the present social order a duty of religion. If they prefer obedience to disobedience, conformity to criticism, modesty to public controversy, patience to impatient longing for justice, then they make the Gospel a symbolic language for the defence of the dominant forces in society. Another kind of Christian preaching indicts as sin conformity and compliance with the world.

In this preaching, sin is the uncritical surrender to the norms of society and the authority of the inherited institutions. This critical approach is emphasized in the preaching of Jesus. As a prophet and more than a prophet, Jesus initiated his followers to a critical attitude towards the existing institutions, even including the family. "I have come to cause divisions: for henceforth in one house there will be divided father against son and son against father, mother against daughter and daughter against mother, mother-in-law against daughter-in-law and daughter-in-law against mother-in-law" (Lk 12:52-53). In his sermons, Jesus often denounced "the world" – that is, the dominant structures and the received norms – as the principle of evil. We read, "Do not love the world or the things in the world. For if anyone loves the world, the love of the Father is not in him" (1 Jn 1:15). The world as locus of sin is under the power of darkness (cf. Jn 12:31; 14:30; 16:11). At other times we are told that God loves the world and that all human beings are God's children. Yet on the whole, the preaching of Jesus offers a notion of sin that includes the personal and social dimension and raises questions in regard to the existing institutions.

We conclude that implicit in all preaching against sin is an image of society and thus, whether intended or unintended, communicates a political message. We have been blinded to this fact by the privatizing trend of our own tradition.

In the Catholic Church, the privatization of sin eventually led to the denial that the Church as church could be sinful. Since all sin was private it was unnecessary to engage in critical reflection on the Church's corporate life. Bishops and popes admitted, of course, that they were personally sinners and in need of divine mercy, but they did not acknowledge that their collective life, embodied in ecclesiastical organizations, was marked by sin and hence in need of an ongoing critique. Systematic criticism of the institution was regarded as disloyal. When people, individually or in groups, left the Church, fault was found with them: they were unfaithful; they had betrayed their heritage. What remained unexamined was to what extent the contradictions in the ecclesiastical institution had contributed to this exodus. Similarly, when priests leave in great numbers, people in the

Church tend to blame them and accuse them of infidelity, without asking the corresponding question regarding the discrepancies in the ecclesiastical institutions that have contributed to the great number of resignations. Once we discover the inseparability of the personal and social in human action, we begin to realize that a church's unwillingness to subject its corporate life to a systematic and principled critique is the great barrier that prevents it from proclaiming the Gospel with power. Some theologians defend the uncritical attitude towards the Church as organization by appealing to the divine gifts and the divine guidance bestowed upon it; they argue that trusting faith in the organization will make these gifts flourish and exert a beneficial impact on the people. But why should we think that the gifts to the Church and our trust in the Gospel would be weakened by the community's engagement in self-criticism? One could turn the argument around and ask the question whether the fear of collective self-criticism is not a sign of the lack of faith in these divine gifts. Unless we move in the direction of deprivatizing the notion of sin, we are in danger of making the Christian faith a protection of injustices in church and world and thus transforming the religion of Jesus into an ideology.

* * *

Once we deprivatize the notion of sin, we must also regain the full, personal-and-social meaning of conversion. For the sake of brevity, I shall indicate only the direction in which this theology must move. According to the biblical message, the divine reply to human sin is judgment and the promise of new life. God's gracious and critical word makes people recognize their sins, calls forth their conversion, enables them to wrestle against the structures of evil, initiates them into a new life of love and dedication, and makes them yearn for the ultimate pacification of humankind. Conversion, therefore, can no longer be understood as the repentant recognition of one's personal sins; included in conversion are the critical recognition of, and the turning away from, the social dimension of sin, present in the various collectivities to which a person belongs. The metanoia to which the Gospel summons us demands that we examine our own personal lives as well as the injustices and contradictions in the various institutions to which we belong, be they political, economic, educational, ecclesiastical or whatever. The raising of consciousness in regard to institutional life is part and parcel of the conversion away from sin.

The preaching of personal conversion to Jesus, understood in an individualistic way, as it has been done in many churches, represses one side of the Gospel and hence has strongly defensive or even reactionary political implications. For the stress on private conversion makes people blind to the structures of evil in society. People are made to think that the inequities of their society are due to personal sins and can be removed through the personal conversion of the sinners. What people who stress the conversion to Jesus as their personal saviour fail to see is that the evil in society has a twofold root, in the sinful hearts of men and in institutionalized injustices, and that this evil can only be overcome by a movement that includes social change. The stress of Jesus as personal saviour inevitably implies a defence of the political status quo. The individualistic religion of the widespread televangelism legitimates the individualism of our economic system, and while it presents its message as non-political, it has a significant political impact. The privatization of sin and conversion, fostered in Catholicism by the confessional practice, is promoted in the Protestant churches by the evangelical stress on personal conversion to Jesus. Jesus saves! Today, it is worth noting, we find critical movements not only in the major Christian churches; we also witness the emergence of a left-wing evangelicalism that seeks to recover the social meaning of sin and conversion.[188]

In critical theology it becomes imperative to deprivatize and despiritualize the notion of salvation. Again we can only point in this direction. According to biblical teaching, Jesus is not the saviour of souls. Jesus is announced as saviour of the world, as herald of a new age and servant of God's kingdom. When his message convicts people of sin and demands their conversion, this must be understood in terms of the inseparable dialectics between the personal and the social. When the Gospel promises salvation to the believing community, this must also be understood in the personal-and-social sense as the deliverance of people from all the enemies of life – their personal malice as well as the oppression and alienation inflicted on them by the structures of domination.

The effort to deprivatize the notions of sin, conversion and salvation leads to the recovery of a wider understanding of grace and holiness. For here, too, we do not want to confine the power of God in recreating human life to purely personal transformations; what the Gospel promises is that God's presence to people in grace, and their response to God in trust and obedience, introduce them to a new life of conversion and holiness whose structures anticipate in some way, despite the ongoing need of redemption, the kingdom of love and peace promised for the last days. The new life of holiness then refers to the transforming power of God in history that changes people's hearts and makes them wrestle against structural evil. The prayer of Jesus, "Thy kingdom come, thy will be done on earth as it is in heaven," does not simply refer to personal holiness nor simply to the total deliverance of people at the horizon of history, but to the ongoing personal and social conversions by which God's victorious power is anticipated in a sinful world.

Critical theology demands that the language about Jesus and his salvation reflect the two interrelated dimensions of personal-and-social. Such a language is found in the biblical tradition. Such a language is also present in the liturgy. The eucharistic worship mediates the bi-polar understanding of salvation in the Christian Church. For in the eucharist Jesus identifies himself with the believing community: Jesus enters the congregation through his word and sacrament, offers salvation to people in the community, and transforms them into a single body representing redeemed life on this earth. The Middle Ages saw the emergence of a more individualistic understanding of holy communion as a purely private divine gift to the individual, an approach to the sacrament that profoundly affected Catholic and Protestant forms of worship after the sixteenth century. The liturgical reforms of the 20th century, in the Catholic Church and some Reformation churches, have tried to overcome this privatizing trend and recover the social dimension of eucharistic worship. Liturgy is the occasion, or should be the occasion, when Christians grasp more firmly the personal-and-social meaning of divine salvation.

In some Protestant churches an unfortunate controversy has begun that creates the impression that a basic conflict exists between evangelical concern and social action.[189] Some conservative voices have opposed the social involvement on the part of the churches with a more spiritual stress on Jesus and his salvation. Other conservative voices expressed the feeling that the churches' social concern dangerously neglects the mystery of divine transcendence. These Christians complain that their church leaders have become too interested in social justice, and that this represents a loss of evangelical substance. This accusation seems unfounded to me. For what the conservative critics call social action is in fact evangelical obedience to Christ and commitment to his personal-and-social salvation. When these critics contrast secular social involvement with their more personal, more spiritual or more dogmatic religion, they suppose that their own approach.is non-political and transcends the historical order. Yet this is illusory, for the privatistic understanding of conversion and grace, implicit in their approach to religion, legitimates the individualism of the dominant political and economic institutions. The stress on evangelism is not above politics: it usually expresses an option in favour of the political status quo. In terms of Richard Niebuhr's typology, mentioned in a previous chapter,[190] the conservative critics in the Christian churches object to the transformist understanding of the Gospel (Christ, Transformer of Culture) and try to influence the churches to return to the more conformist understanding of the Gospel (Christ and Culture in Paradox), which does not apply the promises of Christ to the future of society. Critical theology insists that the salvation of Jesus Christ has a bi-polar, personal-and-social meaning, and any attempt to leave out one pole distorts the original message.

Christian advocates of social criticism and social action, reacting against the individualistic religion in which they were brought up, occasionally formulate their Christian involvement in a purely secular and moral way and fail to show that their social commitment is related to God's act in Jesus Christ. This is an understandable but unfortunate reaction. The deprivatizing of the Gospel does not intend to destroy its religious meaning; on the contrary, it seeks to recover religious roots that have been lost and to reawaken hope in the divine promises that have been forgotten. The choice that presents itself to Christians is not between a political and a non-political Gospel; every religious commitment implies a vision of human life and hence has social meaning and consequences. Today it has become the Church's task to assume conscious and critical responsibility for the political implications of its religious teaching and institutional presence.

It is not surprising that the division among Christians no longer follows the inherited, confessional boundaries but passes right through the various churches. The cultural crisis has its theological equivalent. Christians seem to be divided on whether to regard it as their religious duty to shore up the inherited social consensus and its cultural values or whether to join the critical forces in society and collaborate with them to work in making society more just and more peace-loving. The theological dialogues of official ecumenism too often have only a conservative impact. For here Christian churches concentrate on the doctrinal controversies of the past, instead of listening jointly to the signs of the times in the present cultural crisis. The new questions that confront the churches together will enable them to formulate the meaning of the Gospel in the sinful world of our time.

Christians of the nineteenth century who concentrated on the cultural mission of the Church have rightly been criticized for losing a sense of divine transcendence. In many countries of the West, Christians reflected and acted out of an identification with their country's success-oriented culture and the interests of the government and the ruling classes. Yet in the second half of the 20th century, Christians who profess the transformist Gospel and have a strong sense of their secular mission are in solidarity with the underprivileged sections of society and the hungry nations of the world. This is not a historical setting where the transcendence of the Gospel is forgotten. For the courageous Christians who walk in solidarity with the poor and oppressed often find themselves exposed to the contempt of the authorities and marginalized even in their own churches. In this setting, the cross assumes a new meaning. The lives of these Christians, marked by the cross, reveal that society punishes those who speak the truth and who hunger and thirst after justice. The critical voices in many societies are endangered. The Roman cross on which Jesus died becomes the eloquent symbol of the breakdown and the breakthrough repeatedly necessary in religious, cultural and political traditions, for the sake of the wholeness and reconciliation to which humankind is destined. The cross is not the sign standing at the end of history, proclaiming its inevitable failure; the cross is situated at the centre of history, revealing the cruel suffering inflicted on the prophets and the painful transformation of consciousness and society by all who want to enter into the newness of life. Struggling against the structures of domination, the Christian churches must transcend the controversies that seemed important to them in a previous age and move forward to a new consensus, in keeping with Scripture and their history, that responds to the face of evil in our times.

* * *

The preceding remarks on the deprivatization of sin and conversion lead us to a better understanding of the nature and task of critical theology. At the beginning of this chapter, we defined critical theology as the critical application of the various theories of alienation to the Christian self-understanding. Critical theology is reflection on the Church's praxis and enables the Church to assume theological responsibility for its social reality. Theologians engaged in this pursuit, we said, may discover elements of distorted consciousness in themselves and be led to a change of mind and heart. Theology implies metanoia. Deprivatizing the notion of sin and conversion reveals that the task of critical theology includes the critical analysis of the Church's institutional reality and of the society in which it is located. Critical theology leads to what has been called the raising of consciousness. We want to examine what this commitment means to the Christian community.

In Latin America, the critical reflection on praxis has led to the creation of liberation theology,[191] in which the raising of consciousness, or "conscientization," holds a central place. This approach was adopted by the General Conference of Latin American Bishops held at Medellín in 1968. To discover the social dimension of sin in their societies, Latin American Christians focus almost exclusively on economic oppression. The reason for this is that the Latin American countries are deeply divided between a majority and a minority, between the vast underclass of dispossessed people without access to education and the goods of life and the small class of wealthy families, owners of the land and the industries, who are linked, often as intermediaries, to the international capitalist system, and derive their power, at least in part, from the nations in which the centre of capitalism resides. In Latin American countries, there is no broad middle class as we find it in the industrialized countries of Western Europe and North America. Latin American countries are basically divided into two classes, the rich and the dispossessed, and the radical inequality between these two constitutes the overriding fact of their national existence. The blatant economic injustice determines every form of human association and distorts every expression of social and cultural life. The State becomes purely and simply the protector of the small ruling class. In these countries, then, the economic factor dominates and affects all others – the political order, the cultural trends and the ecclesiastical system. All expressions of society are reflections of the economic order. In this situation, the class domination becomes the key for understanding the misery in which people live and the form that social sin has taken. The Catholic Left in Latin America holds that the class struggle defines the reality of their countries and that conversion, in such a social context, implies solidarity with the oppressed class and its struggle for economic justice. Critical Catholics in these countries engage in the education of ordinary people to raise their consciousness in regard to their own exploitation. They want the people to understand the oppression inflicted on them by a small upper class, protected by military and police power, which acts as an instrument of a vast economic system, the centre of which lies outside their own continent. But they also want to become more aware of how this oppression has falsified their own perception of reality, how they have assimilated the ideological elements of culture and religion, and how they have unknowingly contributed to the stability of the exploitative system.

Liberation theology in Latin America is, in a wider sense, critical reflection on praxis. The praxis that is the object of reflection here includes the dominant social process in which the Church as an element of culture participates as well as the new action flowing from faith and solidarity. Liberation theology is then not a new theological system alongside other such systems; it is not a new, updated body of social teachings; it is, rather, a new mode of reflection that arises from action, modifies people's perception of their world, and thus leads to greater engagement in action. Liberation theology wants to be the theoretic component of the Church's identification with the dispossessed classes and its active involvement in the movement of liberation.

It is consistent for this Latin American theology to be critical of academic theology and the university system in the wealthy nations of the North. Theology must not be allowed to become a wisdom restricted to a privileged group, nor to reflect the structure of exclusion that characterizes academic institutions. Theology of liberation likes to present itself as the work of Christian communities rather than the achievement of professional theologians, even if such theologians occasionally become the spokespersons for these communities. The socially engaged Christians meet at regular intervals over a period of time, discuss what Jesus and his Church mean to them in the struggle for liberation, and record, with the help of a secretary, the conversations and critical reflections of the participants. After a certain period of time, the person acting as secretary rereads the remarks that have been made, gives them a more systematic form, proposes them to the group as the summary of their reflections, and, after their approval, publishes them as liberation theology.

Let me mention another characteristic of the Catholic liberation theology of Latin America. It presupposes throughout that Catholicism is a dominant cultural force on the entire continent, linking the many countries to a common tradition, and possessing a network of communication and influence without parallel.[192] It presupposes, moreover, that the dispossessed people, struggling for justice, in some way belong to the Catholic Church and that the Catholic symbols have retained a place and a power in their imagination. While the Christians of the Catholic Left work in small fellowships, they remain strongly identified with the Catholic tradition, despite their critical stance towards its institutions. They do not wish to separate themselves from the alienated and alienating religion of the illiterate people, for it is this historical Catholicism that they perceive as the organ of liberation on their continent.

Latin American liberation theology cannot be applied as such to the Christians in North America and Western Europe. To restrict the analysis of present social ills to class conflict and the economic factor is, in my view, inadequate. This does not mean that this could not be the correct analysis in Latin America! We have suggested above that the Marxist analysis of social change through the class struggle is a special case, in certain historical circumstances, of Max Weber's more general theory of social change.[193] The structures of domination in North America undoubtedly include the injustices implicit in the economic system, but they also include other factors as independent variables: institutionalized racism, the growing immobility of bureaucratic centralization, the devastation of natural resources through industrial expansion, the exclusion of women from public life, etc. These factors are interrelated. But while these factors in Latin America, according to the Catholic Left, are completely subordinated to the economic system and hence cannot be examined independently from the class struggle, in North America they have their own independent, destructive influence. In North America, it is not at all clear whether there is a single dominant form of oppression to which all others are subordinated.

The American radicals of the 1960s tried to find a single source from which all forms of exploitation were derived or a single model according to which all forms of oppression could be understood. Some focused on the dehumanizing impact of the ever expanding technocracy, and others assigned primacy to the oppression inflicted on black people in the United States.

Some young people in America were impressed by Max Weber's famous prophecy of the "iron cage." They were convinced, following Weber rather than Marx, that every institutional reform of society inevitably increases the bureaucratic apparatus and makes the system more unbending and impersonal than before, and that the reliance on technology in all spheres of life increases the power of instrumental reason over the human imagination and makes people into conformist followers of short-range pragmatic and pedestrian goals. These young people had no hope in a possible reconstruction of modern, industrialized society. For them, technocracy represented the most oppressive trend in America, the trend to which the whole of culture was subordinated. Nor could this trend be modified or weakened by a revolutionary shift from the capitalist economy to a centralizing socialism. These youths wanted to opt out of the present society, discover a new and simplified form of life, find access to a more liberated consciousness, and in this way prepare a new mode of human association that could point the way to the future. What these young people did not realize was how much their movement depended on the affluence of American society at that time. They were not worried about unemployment: they could always find enough casual work to finance their simple lifestyle.

Another radical analysis of American society focused on the oppression and marginalization of black people. The institution of slavery had created a culture of exclusion that remained intact after the emancipation of the slaves, producing the exclusion of blacks from America's political structures, social organizations and cultural institutions. The public contempt inflicted upon these people had a universal visibility painted in black and white on every institution and every community. In the 1960s, the black movement for emancipation created a discourse and provided a model that were taken up by other liberation movements in the United States. Racial oppression came to be regarded as the symbolic key to all the ills of the country. Since the American consensus excluded blacks from the definition of American institutions, black radicals created a language of liberation by inverting the inherited American symbols: America the good became Amerika the bad; the land of the free became the place of oppression; the home of the brave, the racist land; and God's own country, the Babylon of sin. Black thinkers developed a radical analysis of oppression in terms of negation and conflict that was not derived from Hegel, Marx or Weber, but from their own American experience and the biblical symbols of inversion they had learned in childhood – the first shall be last and the last first.[194] Black radicals gave new political meaning to the ancient Exodus language, which remained alive on the American continent through the Protestant dissenters who had left European persecution to find religious and civil liberty on this continent. It was the African-American struggle for effective social and political equality that taught the other liberation movements the terms in which to analyze their own oppression, including the students' protest and the women's movement. French-Canadians occasionally turned to the black people of the United States to interpret their inferior position in Canada,[195] even if they usually preferred, living in a British Dominion, to draw their images from colonialism. The racial oppression of blacks in American history has been made to typify every form of oppression in the United States.

While the model of oppressor and oppressed may be useful to analyze particular forms of injustices, it does not help to analyze the complex inter-relation between various forms of oppression, even of racial oppression, in the United States. An illustration of this complexity is the situation in some parts of the country where blacks and Mexican Americans struggle for respect, equality and access to resources, not always helping one another but sometimes standing in each other's way. The logic of capitalism has an enormous influence on the shape of racism and the exclusion of blacks and Mexican Americans from the mainstream of society, but the economic factor alone does not account for racism. The American experience has shown, rather, that however important the economic analysis may be, it alone does not suffice to understand the structures of domination of North America.

It is unrealistic, in my view, to look for a single form of oppression in the North, to which all others are subordinated. What we have is a complex intermeshing of technocratic depersonalization and immobility, economic domination and exploitation, racial exclusion and inferiorization, and other forms, including the subjugation of women. Americans will want to listen to their neighbours in the South to discover the harmful effect of American capitalism on the dependent countries and admit the devastating impact of "the international imperialism of money."[196] Still, the analysis of social sin in North American will inevitably be complex.

The commitment to justice and human emancipation, to which Christians are summoned, cannot be expressed by identification with a single movement. To shed light on the North American situation, let me turn to Max Weber's theory of social change which, as we saw above, tried to take into account the conflicts in any society. For Weber, the dominant social, political and cultural institutions inhibit the free development of certain groups of people and create historical conditions for the emergence of countervailing movements, possibly sparked by charismatic personalities, that struggle for significant social, political or cultural changes to rescue people from their alienation. The strength of the countervailing trends depends on the degree of alienation from which people suffer, on the new consciousness the emancipatory struggle creates in them, and on the rational adequacy of the new imagination that guides their action. According to Weber, the success of these movements is not guaranteed by historical necessity, nor – I would add – by divine promises. Still, it is possible that these movements affect the awareness of an ever greater number of people, reach some powerful leaders in society, create provisional institutions that express the new ethos, and ultimately, inducing crisis and polarization, produce significant social reconstruction. Yet it is also possible that these movements are crushed, or that they become unrealistic and bizarre, or that the pervasive mindset created by technocratic society does not permit them to get very far. If these countervailing movements express a quest for justice and authentic humanity, Christians will want to support them, even if their outcome is uncertain.

The raising of consciousness in the complex situation of North America means the acknowledgment of the multiple forms of exploitation, and the turning away from the social dimension of sin implies an identification with the aims of the emancipatory movements. This commitment inevitably leads Christians to the difficult question of how to relate these various movements to one another in a just and justifiable manner. This question, I believe, cannot be solved prior to the commitment to solidarity with them. To remain aloof, to seek a neutral place (which does not exist), to examine these movements simply from the outside without identification with their aims, will not provide the historical standpoint from which these movements and their interrelationship can be understood. To withhold this commitment until the question of their interrelationship has been resolved means never to be able to transcend the dominant system. Conversion away from sin, personal-and-social, implies an identification with the poor, the dispossessed, the disfavoured, and with the movements towards their emancipation, an identification that precedes the critical reflection on policy and strategy. This, I believe, is the radical demand of the Gospel. Faith precedes calculation, conversion to Christ precedes the mapping out of the converted life, solidarity with the least of Christ's brothers and sisters precedes the search for an adequate plan of joining them in their struggle.

Critical theology in North America is, therefore, different from the liberation theologies of Latin America. What is different is the combination of factors in the analysis of social evil; the form which the political commitment takes; and, as we shall see, the new imagination drawn from diverse historical experiences. At the same time, structurally these critical theologies are identical. They are reflections on faith-conversion; they are grounded in solidarity with the oppressed; they intend to raise people's consciousness; they offer guidance to social commitment; and they see themselves as the reflective or contemplative dimension of the liberating human action, in which God is redemptively present to the sinful world.

We find this approach to North American liberation theology in the work of Rosemary Ruether.[197] Since Christ identified himself with the poor, since the Gospel is a source of prophetic criticism, since the Church existed partially underground during the first centuries, since the biblical revelation of sin spells out God's judgment on the injustices of society, and since the Christian message has stirred up critical movements within the historical Church and created critical styles of the common life, Christians should feel an affinity with the emancipatory movements in society and identify themselves with the quest for liberation and authentic human existence. This identification with the multiple aims of human liberation, beginning in the United States and reaching out to join the struggle for freedom in Latin America and the world in general, has been the foundation of Rosemary Ruether's theological achievement. In Western Europe a similar approach has been adopted by Edward Schillebeeckx. He, too, demands the Church's identification with the emancipatory movements in history.[198] He, too, thinks that the Christians' solidarity with these movements provides the hermeneutical principles for understanding the Gospel and interpreting authentically the meaning of Christian doctrine. The whole of theology is here grounded in the Church's solidarity with the oppressed. Critical theology, then, cannot be exercised from any historical standpoint whatever; it cannot be produced if theologians seek a neutral place, apart from the conflictual trends in their society. Critical theology can only be created by reflecting Christians who identify with the historical movements from servitude to liberation that are taking place in their society.

It is at this point that the question arises about what the commitment to liberation means in practical, social and political terms. We saw that the Catholic Left in Latin America felt that in their societies, polarized between a tiny upper class holding all the trump cards and the great mass of dispossessed people, the Christian commitment had revolutionary consequences. In North America, with its wider distribution of classes, the oppression of people is due to several intersecting institutional trends, of which the corporate economic system, with free enterprise exercised only on the highest level, is one, though possibly the most important. We saw that there are other dehumanizing trends. Committed Christians differ here on the strategy for the reconstruction of society and culture. Some Christians have confidence that the existing critical movements will eventually succeed in modifying the political and economic order – the reformist option. Others have abandoned this hope, opt for a more radical stance, and long for the breakdown of the present system and the rebirth of a new society – the radical option. Both, it seems to me, are genuine forms of Christian commitment. The first option urges Christians to join people in the existing institutions struggling for the introduction of some public ownership into the economic system and for social change on various levels of society, while the second option makes Christians seek a more radical life, at the margin of existing social and political institutions, which expresses itself in new forms of fellowship, in simplicity and poverty, anticipating in its non-dominative style and co-operative ventures the structures that ought to define the social order of the future. In my opinion, the full Christian witness in North America needs these two options. Neither one by itself expresses the full meaning of the Gospel for our times. While these two political options may lead Christians along different paths, the two groups need one another to spell out in a living conversation the anguish and the hope that is given in Jesus Christ.

In making their political decisions, whether reformist or radical, Christians have to reflect on the history of their society: not only to detect the hidden, destructive ideologies contained in it, but also to retrieve the creative symbols of their tradition that have produced an ethical vision in the past and that could, in a new key, generate innovative ideals for a new social order. We saw that the Catholic Left, despite its criticism of the institutional Church, is profoundly attached to the Catholic tradition in the hope that the ancient religious symbols of love and unity will create, in the contemporary context, a new imagination of fellowship and promise, and supply the inwardness and the yearning for the reconstruction of the social order. From the viewpoint of sociology, it seems clear that a new political imagination can gain the confidence of people only if it recalls the great moments of their history and in some way corresponds to their ancient dreams. The political imagination of Christians always remembers the *mirabilia Dei*, the marvellous things God has done in the Exodus and the death and resurrection of Jesus.

10

The Eschatological Promises

Enlightenment critics of religion have looked upon the Christian teaching on the kingdom of God and the expectation of eternal life as important causes of human alienation. Otherworldliness, according to these critics, leads to the contempt of this world. The hope for an eternal life of happiness makes people shrug their shoulders in regard to their earthly existence and prevents them from becoming concerned enough about their situation to change the conditions of social life. The doctrine of eternal life trivializes history. A religion that promises heaven consoles people in their misery, makes them patient and meek, and protects the existing social and political orders. Otherworldly religion, according to this analysis, is inevitably ideological.

Since critical theology intends to make the Church assume theological responsibility for the unintended social consequences of its religion and free the proclamation of the Gospel from the alienating trends associated with it, contemporary theologians regard Christian eschatology as a topic of special challenge. Is it possible to understand Christ's preaching of God's coming kingdom as utopian rather than ideological religion? The critics of religion have based their negative evaluation on the ecclesiastical teaching of recent centuries with its principal emphasis on personal salvation. In the Church's preaching and the minds of the faithful, the biblical message of God's coming reign has been reduced to an assurance of personal survival after death and entry into the happiness of heaven. Hell was reserved for unrepentant sinners; and in the Catholic Church, purgatory was the realm where repentant sinners suffered painful purification preparing them for entry into eternal bliss. This understanding of the divine promises privatized the biblical message. The task of critical theology is therefore to deprivatize the Church's eschatological message.

We already mentioned that according to the New Testament, the centre of Christ's preaching was the kingdom of God. Jesus was servant and mediator of God's kingdom that was promised to Israel in the ancient days, inaugurated in his own person, and about to be made manifest in all its power. This kingdom was not an otherworldly reality; it was rather God's reign in human history, promised from the beginning, anticipated in the covenanted people and the sacramental Church, and finally coming upon the nations as judgment and new creation. This kingdom was not conceived as a realm parallel to history; it was not a heavenly dominion above the nations of the earth. The kingdom was, rather, the divine reign that revealed itself in history, rescued people from brokenness and sin, turned them into saints, and fulfilled the longing of humanity and the cosmos. God's kingdom was preached as the coming new age. It will uproot the malice in the hearts of all people and correct the injustices present in their institutions; it will heal the inequalities among peoples and give them access to the sources of life. The kingdom promised in the New Testament affects individuals as well as their society, the heart as well as the world, the body as well as the soul, present history as well as the world to come. This kingdom, we are told, will endure forever.

The New Testament records the different ways in which the early Christians understood God's promises: they expected the end of history, they looked forward to the joys of the saints in heaven, they longed for being with Christ after their death, and they hoped that the kingdom present in Christ and his Church would eventually be the source of the reconciliation of humanity as a whole.

In the patristic age, the message of eternal life remained focused on the community. Christians no longer expected that the end of history was near; their hope, based on the divine promises, focused on the redemption and the eternal destiny of the entire Church. This patristic teaching was explored in Henri de Lubac's famous book *Catholicism*, in which he demonstrated – after a critical dialogue with French Marxists – that the individualism implicit in modern Christianity distorted the ecclesial understanding of sin, grace and glory found in the writings of the church fathers.[199] The Church as God's people was the bearer of the divine promises, and it was this people that was to live eternally. The church was sign and symbol of the whole human race, the one human family, whose destiny was disclosed and made visible in the fellowship of the faithful. The doctrine of eternal life revealed first and foremost the end and purpose of history. It directed people's imagination towards God's ultimate victory over evil and the creation of a new heaven and a new earth. The question of personal survival after death was not in the foreground. The liturgy of Christian burial described the fate of the deceased in three simple words – *requies*, *lux* and *pax* [rest, light and peace]. Dominant in the Christian imagination and the Church's liturgy was the hope for the final accomplishment, the completion of history, and the resurrection of the entire people. Lubac argued that the privatization of religion has damaged the glory of Catholicism.

For the first thousand years, the Christian people looked forward to the resurrection on the last day as the fulfillment of the divine promises and showed comparatively little interest in the state of the soul after the death of the body. Eventually this spiritual attitude changed. When theologians in the fourteenth century, responding to the religion of the faithful, began to teach that after death the soul encounters the living God, undergoes the particular judgment and, if approved, is admitted to eternal bliss in the *visio beatifica*, Pope John XXII, relying on the ancient tradition, condemned this new teaching. "The soul separated from the body," he insisted, "does not enjoy the vision of God which is its total reward and will not enjoy it prior to the resurrection."[200] John XXII was the last witness of the ancient Church's collectivist imagination, which saw salvation primarily as the entry of the entire people into grace and glory. Yet the increasingly individualistic culture superseded the Pope. He himself eventually changed his mind. The next pontiff, Benedict XII, revoked the teaching of his predecessor, solemnly proposed the new teaching, and confirmed the shift of the Church's religious longing from the crowning of history in the new creation to the soul's eternal happiness after death. Until recently, this has been the common stance of modern Christianity.

In the modern period, the Church's teaching of eternal life was understood almost exclusively in terms of the fate that awaited the individual after his or her death. The eschatological framework of the Gospel was largely forgotten. Christians no longer experienced themselves as a people on pilgrimage, as a people with an historical destiny; instead they regarded society as a stable, unchanging reality and reduced the Christian adventure to the personal journey from birth to death. Society and the Church were here the unchanging scenery or background, over against which people worked out their personal salvation. The Church's liturgy retained the ancient vision and recalled that God had acted in Christ on behalf of all humankind and brought history to the new and final age, but the individualistic culture did not allow this ancient teaching to affect people's piety. Death became the end of the journey and salvation the pledge of one's own personal happiness beyond the grave.

This privatizing trend in religion corresponded to the growing individualism in secular culture, which reached its high point in modern, Gesellschaft-type society. Here the individual is wholly severed from the social matrix. At the same time, acting as impersonal agents in a rationalized society, people feel that they have lost the sense of self. The triumph and agony of individualism have made people focus on personal death as the great enemy that threatens the meaning of their lives in the present. Modern secularity imitates the Church's concentration on death. For Heidegger, the fear of death marks a person's entire life and produces a metaphysical anguish that reveals humankind's authentic nature. This concentration on personal death has even found entry into sociological reflection. Alfred Schutz integrates Heidegger's view of death into his phenomenology of the social world, and Peter Berger assigns personal death a primary role in his sociology of religion and the construction of reality.[201] The fear of death overshadows the whole of a person's life; it imbues the effort to build society and the quest for personal happiness with a peculiar anxiety. This anguish – this fear of death, the horror of chaos – is, according to Berger's sociology, the generating force that makes people seek a safe and stable world, and create sacred symbols that legitimate the present order and promise future security. Religion is created as the answer to personal death and its anxiety-producing power. Yet Berger's theory is not persuasive: it is based on a peculiarly modern psychological analysis.

It may not be surprising that the privatizing trend has entered philosophical thought, but it is curious that this perspective has affected sociology. Sociologists claim that the meaning of any event cannot be understood apart from the social context in which it takes place. This principle also applies to the event of death: mortality is not a transcendent phenomenon with meaning unrelated to the cultural world. The literature produced in certain societies that glorify the self-sacrifice of soldiers on the battlefield is a good illustration that the attitude towards one's own death depends on the social environment. Max Weber may have been only half-serious when he suggested that death has become such an absurd event only in modern competitive, achievement-oriented society because here people daily sacrifice happiness for the sake of work and economic advantage, and when they finally encounter death, they feel that after having postponed happiness all their lives, they are now cheated of their reward and their entire life is being mocked and invalidated. Weber may have thought that in other cultures people lived more wholeheartedly in the present with its joys and pains, and when death awaited them as the long sleep at the end of their lives, they were not frightened by it. Even the attitude towards death, sociologists hold, is socially grounded. To regard the anxiety over one's mortality as a primary principle of human behaviour, I conclude, corresponds not to the nature of reality, but to the privatizing trend operative in the modern world.

The attitude towards death depends on the imagination of the future, mediated in society by cultural or religious movements. In tribal society, the imagination of people projected the ongoing existence of the tribe and thus found it easy to speak of life beyond the grave. They felt embedded in a living reality that would perdure in the future. In the ages of nationalist wars, to give another example, people's imagination of the future circled around the expansion and flowering of the nation, and when they were confronted with death in this struggle, they did not fear for themselves but dreamt of their nation's future. In modern society, people's imagination of the future tends to be caught in their own personal lives. They dream of what life will be like for them in ten years, in 20 years, in 30 years. In today's consumers' society our imagination is taught to concentrate on the rising standard of living and ever greater personal well-being. Death, in such a context, seems utterly frightful. Yet even today, when a person is profoundly attached to her children and their families, her imagination will circle around their future and her own personal death will not appear as the great enemy. Herbert Marcuse, the atheist social philosopher, made a profound remark about death, a remark that one might expect to find in the great literature of religion. He wrote, "Men can die without anxiety, if they know that what they love is protected from misery and oblivion."[202] If the object of a person's love is protected from harm and assured of well-being, then the nothingness of her own tomorrow, threatened in death, is not a great source of anxiety. But if we love ourselves and if our future imagination circles around our own well-being – this is almost inevitable in a Gesellschaft-type society – then what we love is wholly unprotected, and death becomes the dreaded enemy. How does Marcuse's profound remark apply to the Christian faith? If we yearn for the kingdom of God, if we long for God's victory over evil and all the enemies of life and believe that in Christ this victory is assured, then what we love is protected and it should not be so difficult to die.

Christian teaching of eternal life, I propose, should not make believers focus on their own death and worry about what happens to them after they die; this teaching should liberate them for a greater love and make them yearn for the reconciliation and deliverance of all people. The Christian message of resurrection, understood in this deprivatizing perspective, far from making Christians concentrate on their own heaven, frees them from anxiety about their own existence and directs their hope towards the new creation. The doctrine of God's approaching kingdom summons people to forget themselves; serve this kingdom coming into the lives of men and women; and rejoice with the Christian community, gathered at worship, that in Christ God's final victory has been assured. God will have the last word. Evil will not be allowed to stand. The entry into personal salvation and future life is not prepared by concentrating on one's own life, but by trusting and loving God's coming reign. The dialect of personal-and-social, which we observed when speaking of sin and grace, must also be observed when interpreting the Christian doctrine of eternal life.

This deprivatizing trend is operative in contemporary spirituality. Perhaps one of the first signs of this reorientation was given by a remarkable woman who, in many ways, was a conventional saint: Thérèse of Lisieux. In her oft-quoted statement "I want to spend my heaven doing good on earth," she subtly criticized the individualism of traditional Catholic spirituality. She thought that she would not be able to rest with God as long as people were still suffering and the promised kingdom had not been established. This was then a startling innovation. In contemporary spiritual writers, such as Thomas Merton, Daniel Berrigan, Ernesto Cardinale and James Douglas, the passage to a more collective understanding of divine salvation has taken place. While these authors attach much importance to personal existence and one's personal union with God as the ground for a life that will never die, they understand this personal life as participation in the human community and a share in the salvation that is meant for all. Here each person is damaged by the misery inflicted on others. In this new spirituality, there is no communion with God unless mediated by Jesus – that is, by a total solidarity with humanity, especially the underprivileged and dispossessed. Here entry into eternal life is understood, following the New Testament, as repentance and identification with God's coming reign. The Christian Gospel delivers people from anxiety about their death and the preoccupation with their personal heaven. The question of personal survival after death is not the best way to approach the Christian teaching on eternal life.

The common theological approach to death and dying has also been privatized from another point of view. Usually, in sermons and books on pastoral theology, we speak of death as if people normally die peacefully in their beds. Death is here looked upon as the painful end of a person's life in a settled context of friendly faces. Yet by thinking of death in this way, we forget that endless millions of people die very differently as victims of society. A glance at statistics of people killed by wars, acts of genocide, unrelieved famines and other forms of collective violence reminds us that a peaceful death in bed is by no means the normal way for people to die in the present century. A certain highly private theology of dying, it seems to me, disguises from consciousness the cruel world to which we belong. For vast numbers of people, deprived of peace and security, death in a bed after a life well spent is the object of great hope.

In the light of the Gospel, in my view, cause of great anguish is the death of "the other"– people killed, often in their youth, as victims of war, famine, persecution or oppression. A Christian theology of death must start with the death of Jesus, the innocent youth, tortured and killed by empire and its collaborators. Christians want to be delivered from an imagination of the future that circles around their own personal lives. The Gospel promises deliverance from evil on an all-embracing scale, beginning with the victims of society, and for this reason we want to think of our personal lives as situated within this universal drama of salvation.

After reflecting on the privatization imposed on the concept of death and the Christian message of eternal life, we return to the eschatological framework of the New Testament and the emphasis of Christ's own preaching on the approaching reign of God. By a convergence of several intellectual trends this eschatological aspect of the Gospel has received sustained attention in modern Christian theology and become a focal point in the renewal of Christian teaching. At one time, liberal theologians were almost embarrassed to speak of the apocalyptical passages of the New Testament. To preach on the end of the world and the return of Christ on the clouds of heaven had become the privilege of evangelical Christians engaged in a literalistic reading of the Bible. Yet 20th-century biblical scholarship recovered the eschatological tension in the New Testament, and currents of theology influenced by process thought made the vision of the end a principle for understanding the present.[203] I suggest that dialogue with sociology enables theologians to regain an understanding of eschatology that preserves the personal-and-social dialectic and gives Christian preaching a utopian or transformist thrust.[204]

From Karl Mannheim's sociology of knowledge we have derived the distinction between ideology and utopia and learned to detect the utopian trends in the Christian religion.[205] Mannheim recognized that the doctrine of eternal life has been read in Christian history in both an ideological and utopian manner. His sociological analysis helps theologians to deprivatize the Church's teaching on eternal life.

Mannheim was not the first social philosopher who used the concept of utopia to analyze religious language and the imagination of the future. Immediately after World War I, the young Ernst Bloch published two studies on the spirit of utopia, one of which dealt with a Christian theology of God's coming kingdom. In his brilliant book, *Thomas Münzer*, with the subtitle *Theologian of Revolution*, [206] Bloch examined the relation of eschatology and politics from a (non-dogmatic) Marxist perspective and demonstrated that the Christian teaching on eternal life, in whatever form, had political meaning and, in some cases, even political effect. Bloch's *Thomas Münzer* can be compared with Weber's *The Protestant Ethic and the Spirit of Capitalism*.

Weber's book, as we saw above, tried to show that Calvinism, or a special development within Calvinism, provided religious inspiration for the rising class of merchants and entrepreneurs that made them the successful creators of a new civilization. Weber tried to demonstrate – not against Marx, but as a complement to the Marxian analysis – that present in religious commitment is a power sui generis, irreducible to other interests, that can affect our creation of culture and society. It is impossible, according to Weber, to render an account of the origin of modern, rational society without including the religious factor. Ernst Bloch offered the same kind of analysis for the revolutionary movements in Germany of the sixteenth century. He demonstrated that a political and economic analysis cannot account for the course of these events, unless it included the impact of radical religion, in particular the preaching of Thomas Münzer.

In his book, Bloch corrects earlier studies by Marxist thinkers who saw in the radical religious movements of the past only a disguised form of political protest. In his "The Peasant War in Germany,"[207] Friedrich Engels analyzed the oppression of peasants and labourers in sixteenth-century feudal society, recognized the identification of the Lutheran movement with the princes and landowners, and concluded that "the chiliastic dream-visions of early Christianity offered a very convenient starting-point"[208] to the Christian radicals for mounting a revolutionary attack on the social order. For Engels, then, the religious aspirations of

Münzer and the radicals were simply a screen or a cloak for political goals. "Although the class struggles of that day were carried on under religious shibboleths, and though the interests, requirements and demands of the various classes were concealed behind a religious screen, this changed nothing in the matter and is easily explained by the conditions of the time."[209] Engels believed that Münzer "cloaked" his revolutionary philosophy in Christian phrases to make it more acceptable to his age. Against this reductionist interpretation, Ernst Bloch shows in his book-length analysis of Münzer's life and preaching that his eschatological vision of the future produced a genuine religious passion, not a cloak for political revolution, and, furthermore, that the spreading of social unrest and the outbreak of the peasant revolt are unaccountable without taking into consideration this radical religion. Ernst Bloch, much like Weber, except with greater literary brilliance and poetic flair, demonstrated the creativity of the symbolic sphere and the world-producing power of religion. In fact, he complements the research of Weber, in line with the important work of Ernst Troeltsch, by analyzing the socio-political implications of the spiritual compromise with the world made by the Calvinist, Lutheran and Catholic church establishments. Bloch belongs to the remarkable thinkers who moved beyond the positivistic consciousness to discover the meaning and power of the symbolic.

In Münzer's personal life and public preaching, the religious imagination and the political intention were so inseparably interwoven that the attempts of his interpreters to understand him as a spiritual ecstatic who at times betrayed his vision and moved into the political arena have been unsuccessful. Münzer was neither a spiritual visionary who occasionally fanned the revolutionary fire of his listeners, nor a secular rebel who used eschatological language to condemn the men of power and privilege and stir people's hopes for a new society. Münzer is inseparably both a religious figure and a political rebel. He remained mindful of social justice when he was most concerned with God's glory, and he remained deeply religious when he gave vent to his hatred of the ruling class in church and society. Bloch recognizes that some religious leaders inspired by their religious ideals have become dedicated political actors and then, thanks to their involvement in the political sphere, lost their religious fervour and became purely secular in their concern. But this did not happen to Münzer. His was a truly utopian religion. Münzer had his odd sides, which Bloch does not deny, and yet Bloch's study arrives at the conclusion that the theologian of revolution was a great and tragic figure, not an angry fanatic crazed by his visions, but a courageous witness to a hope that does not die.[210]

Bloch shows that the entire preaching of Münzer – on sin, conversion, inwardness, asceticism, poverty and the cross of Christ – revealed his critical political consciousness and thus differed from the Catholic and Protestant preaching on the same topics that, unbeknownst to these preachers, protected the powerful and the rich. Münzer saw the world divided, beyond the inherited boundaries, into the friends of God, chosen by him, and the enemies of justice intent on their own advantage. These friends, Münzer held, were dispersed through all peoples, religions, churches and traditions. Their faith, created by God even if they never heard of Jesus, consisted – as does the Christian faith – in the conversion away from egotism, domination and the alliance with the ruling class, and in the trusting identification with the poor and oppressed, among whom God's reign will become manifest. The centre of Münzer's preaching was the impatient eschatological hope that the Lord was near, that the divine judgment has been pronounced on the sinful world, and that God was about to make known his victory in the liberation of his people from injustice and oppression. For Münzer, the biblical doctrine of eternal life became a harsh and fervent utopia, magnificent yet blind and misguided, summoning people to a struggle they were bound to lose.

The study of utopian religion in a concrete case led Bloch to the topic that remained central in his philosophical work, namely the creative role played by daydreams, poetry and religious expectations in the making of history. In Bloch's early books he writes about the power of daydreams with an almost romantic enthusiasm; in his later writings, especially in his *Prinzip der Hoffmung*,[211] he becomes more measured, contained and qualified yet retains the same basic inspiration that the new in history has its origin in the human imagination.

Reality is unfinished; it is still in the making. This is Bloch's metaphysics.[212] The future is hidden in the past, yet the future must be created out of freedom. The future is grounded in the past and yet remains undetermined. Reality is purposeful for Bloch; as a Marxian thinker he recognizes a direction of human striving. Yet the future is never created according to fixed laws; the future remains open; it is produced by a process that involves people's freedom and their imagination. Bloch distinguishes between the cold current in Marxism, which stresses the scientific, determinist aspect in the making of history, and the warm current, which recognizes the element of fantasy and human longing in the creation of tomorrow.

While these currents should remain together and stimulate and limit one another, Bloch regards it as his special task to emphasize the warm current of utopia that official Marxism has neglected. With poetic power and sociological sensitivity, Bloch writes about the unfinished world that gives birth to the future, about the process by which the hidden powers present in today's reality are projected into the future, and about the role of expectancy and hope in directing the creation of the new.

Bloch is a dialectical materialist in the Marxian sense of the word. Matter is primary. Matter is where it all comes from. Located in the dynamic potential of matter is the objective basis for the unfinished world, for not-yet-being. Bloch claims that theologians are "the Jacobs of theology, who have robbed matter of its birthright as firstborn."[213] Matter, for Bloch, is not a substratum that receives its vitality from another principle: matter is pregnant; matter possesses its own potential, its own dynamics of self-transformation. Seen from this perspective, the spirit is not "the trump card" held over matter, but "its own blood," that is, its own vitality that cannot be separated from its substrate.[214]

Bloch carries this thinking over into his anthropology. Human beings, too, are unfinished, yet alive and self-creating out of the thrust of their materiality. This basic drive is what Bloch calls hunger. We have to eat to survive; we are basically dependent on matter, and at the same time we constantly transform matter into new energies and release its hidden potentialities. Hunger, in a wider sense, reveals humankind's sense of unfulfillment, making us reach out for new life and contemplate the many possibilities of as yet untried conditions of existence. By defining humankind in terms of its hunger, it is both open to the future and directed towards it by something within itself. Hunger gives rise to dreams, to daydreams, to the longing for the new; yet the very same hunger also keeps this imagination in line with our actual needs and the possibilities of our material reality. In Bloch's uncommon materialism, the new would never come to exist in history unless it first existed in our imagination and haunted us in our daydreams.

We have here a curious inversion of materialism into its apparent opposite, into what to many appears as idealism. Yet this inversion is characteristic of much of German thought. We remarked earlier that Hegel's idealism could be read as sociological theory rendering an account of how the symbols operative in the mind are translated into the concrete institutions of society and how dialectical reason, operative in the forward movement of society, expresses itself in the practical reactions of people to the alienating trends hidden, and eventually manifest, in the concrete condition of their lives. Ernst Bloch also provides a philosophy that shows how the subjective is translated into objectivity, how the dream is the parent of tomorrow's world, and how human hope is the source of history that man creates – all conjoined to a material logic from below. This trend of thought is not startling to the readers of this book. For the sociologists we have studied recognized that symbols are both the reflection of society in the human mind and the guiding patterns of consciousness in the creation of social world. The symbols of the future have power in the production of society.

Bloch's anthropology of hunger ties his philosophy into the Marxian theory, which assigns a special historical role to the poor and dispossessed and the ensuing class struggle against oppression. Yet while the direction of history is determined by the quest for fulfillment of human hunger, Bloch stresses the indetermination within this general direction. For the emergence of the new in history depends on the dreams of people and the power of their hope, rooted in the latency of their material conditions. History then remains open and free. Bloch's intoxicating hope, in the face of the gigantic obstacles to humankind's pacification, was founded, curiously and unconvincingly, on the dynamics of matter revealed in human hunger. Bloch was a passionate atheist; he repudiated any divine lord ruling the world from above or any supreme spiritual principle directing the world from within. Bloch opposed the divine as a dangerous factor alienating people from their material foundation. What people have to learn, he argued, is to trust their material principles and create the world out of their hunger. Yet the theological reader finds in Bloch's writings a seductive religious quality: they witness an extraordinary faith in the inexhaustible fecundity of the matrix of human life; they betray the paradoxical conviction that in their vigorous actions people are simultaneously being carried forward, and they reveal an imagination haunted by the irrepressible daydream of a future realm in which people shall live in justice and peace. I honour Bloch's atheism; yet I am tempted to see in Bloch's vehement denial simply the radical refusal to pronounce the Holy Name.

Bloch's anthropology of hunger offers an interesting critique of the Freudian theory that attributes to sex a centrality in human life. The sexual drive is primary only among the well-fed classes – the poor and exploited are first of all hungry. According to Bloch, it is out of this primary, material self-symbolization of the poor that the whole of humankind's history must be understood. To illustrate the Blochian perspective, I wish to recount a dramatic incident that took place at a theological conference held in the United States in the 1960s. A well-known imaginative, psychotherapeutically oriented theologian wanted to discuss with his audience the methods used in theology. To do this well he tried to initiate the participants into the telling of their own private story. Only as we become familiar with our own story, beginning with childhood and the early relationship to mother and father, do we discover the bent of our mind and the orientation of reason that alone will be fruitful for us. Unless we recover our own emotional past, we might adopt a method of rational reflection that actually goes counter to our basic intuitions and strengthens our defences against conflicts repressed in early childhood. The lecturer then asked the participants of the conference to form groups of two; handing out large sheets of drawing paper and felt-tip markers, he then asked each pair to draw the plan of the house or apartment where they were born and lived as children, to indicate where mother and father slept, where their own bed was situated, etc. The pairs were asked to tell their childhood story to one another and, if possible, to verbalize the feelings that emerge as they tell their story. The source of people's creativity, the lecturer presupposed, lies in their infancy dreams and wishes, and only as they are able to overcome the defences that keep these desires hidden are they able to discover the bent and power of their thinking. The few African and Mexican Americans present vehemently objected to this procedure. "White, middle-class nonsense!" they shouted. Yet they were unable to analyze the reasons for their strong reaction. One young Mexican American priest stomped out of the hall. A fellow participant followed him and joined the angry priest on a walk around the building. After a little, when the priest's anger had subsided, he turned to his companion and said, "Now I'll tell you my story. When my people were annexed to the U.S. in 1848...." His companion was amazed. If you belong to the middle class, your story begins with the infancy relations to mother and father – the Freudian perspective – but if you belong to an oppressed people, the conditions of this oppression overshadow the childhood conflicts with mother and father and mark the structure of daily existence so strongly that even the personal story begins with the people's fall into servitude. Here human beings appear defined by their hunger – the Blochian perspective. Here, self-understanding is available only through the freedom history of one's own people or class. Women can use the Blochian analysis to refute the dependent image that Freud, so devastatingly, has painted for them. At the same time, there is no reason why Bloch's concept of hunger could not include eros and the sexual transcendence of self-love. For the kind of hunger that Bloch describes in his writings does not lead to a concentration on one's own egotistic desires, but, on the contrary, to the identification with the brother and sister in fellowship and common life, and hence to a self-transcendent conversion to the other.

So far, Bloch's utopia still remains too undefined. Not every dream of future happiness is utopian. In modern, capitalistic society we are constantly exposed to images of an ideal future based on an ever higher standard of living and the continuing quest for the egotistic fulfillment of pleasure and comfort. This, according to Ernst Bloch, is no utopian dream. For we can speak of utopia only if the imagination introduces a qualitatively new element in the form of human life. The utopian daydream does not prolong the present into the future, but it elevates and recreates the present in keeping with our unfulfilled potentialities. With this demand for the qualitatively new, Bloch distinguished utopian from other future dreams, just as Mannheim did after him, with the contrast between ideology and utopia.

Bloch distinguished between various kinds of hunger and their extensions into human longing. There are yearnings for objects that already exist in the world, and there are yearnings for objects that do not yet exist. The first yearning produces inauthentic feelings such as envy, greed and veneration. Envy and greed do not unfold but disguise the as yet unfulfilled powers of human life. But even the veneration of people who possess what one desires relates one inauthentically to the object of desire: for veneration leads to passivity and a person's ready submission to inequality. The yearning for objects that do not yet exist – that is, the strong feelings of expectancy in regard to the future – include anxiety, fear, hope and faith. Of these only hope is authentically human.[215] For anxiety and fear are born of alienation, and even faith makes people dependent on another, fosters inaction and eventually results in alienation. In hope alone do people authentically relate their yearning to the future. Only if the daydream is accompanied by hope does it release the potentialities of matter, guide active engagement and enable people to create the new. These critical reflections greatly limit the daydreams that may rightly be called utopian. Excluded are the narcissistic dreams that often possess us; excluded are dreams of revenge and the fantasies of resentment; excluded are the longings for self-aggrandizement and the contemplation of future victory over others. The philosopher of the daydream here develops a strict asceticism of the imagination. He excludes even religious faith, since it relies on promises made by another. The only authentically human daydream of the impossible is one that is rooted in the possibilities of our material nature.

Bloch moves one step further in distinguishing utopia from other imaginations of the future. He contrasts "concrete" with "abstract" utopias.[216] Concrete utopias are imaginations of future fulfillment that are sufficiently close to the possibilities of the present that they give rise to practical ideas of what to do and summon forth some form of action. Abstract utopias, on the other hand, present the imagination of the new future in such a remote way, wholly unrealizable in terms of present possibilities, that it paralyzes the practical intelligence, leads to inaction and makes people into empty dreamers. In the language of Mannheim, abstract utopias are really ideological. The ordinary use of the word "utopian" has come to refer precisely to the unrealizable dream of the perfect life, which makes no contribution to changing the world. What is regrettable in this common usage, however, is that it denigrates all utopias, even concrete utopias, and when the utopias die, as Mannheim told us, society will be caught in an inflexible cage. Concrete utopias alone, according to Bloch, can generate hope and become our entry into a new future.

* * *

Let us return to theology. Making use of the preceding analysis of future images, we suggest that the Church's teaching on eternal life can exercise a utopian function. The message of the kingdom, partially present among us and still approaching in all its power, proposes a vision of the future in which people live in justice and peace, conjoined in friendship and the common worship of the divine mystery. The eschatological reign of God, situated at the horizon of history, need not be envisaged as an imposition from above by a higher authority, but rather as the fulfillment of a liberation already begun, as the visible manifestation of divine grace now operative in people's efforts to create a fraternal (sisterly) society. The glory of the future is the unfolding of present grace.

This message of God's coming is utopian (not ideological) because it reveals the structure of sin in the present world. The promised realm of justice and peace is the measure by which Christians evaluate and judge present society. "Thy will be done on earth as it is in heaven." The heavenly city expresses a mandate for life in present society. The Christian message of eternal life, then, makes people critical of present institutions and elicits in them a longing for a more just and more equal social order. Indeed, the Christian message of eternal life exercises its utopian function, despite the setbacks and cruel disappointments people have suffered – and are at this time suffering – in history. The crucifixion of Jesus was not God's last word, nor is the shadow cast by the crucifixion on human history the end of the divine story. The Christian message of the Resurrection summons forth hope in the newness of life even on this earth. The eschatological message gives birth to self-actualizing hope, since the God in whom Christians believe is enabler and vivifier in history and empowers men and women to act on their own behalf. Faith in the divine promises does not make people inactive; it empowers them to act.

At the same time, the divine promises transcend the purely earthly possibilities, yet they do so without relativizing the importance of history. The message of eternal life is not an emergency door that allows us to escape from humankind's collective responsibility for life on this earth. The eschatological message is proclaimed in terms that overcome the harmful dichotomies between heaven and earth, soul and body, person and society. The divine promises recorded in the Scriptures do not sort out the order of their fulfillment. What will be fulfilled in history and what beyond history? The answer to this question depends on human freedom, a freedom that is the fruit of God's present grace. The message of God's final victory over evil announces the resurrection of all gracious life in a realm of justice and peace, in which every tear shall be wiped away.

The Christian message of God's coming reign produces a view of history at odds with many views currently held in culture and society. Christians disagree with all views that regard history as determined. According to certain thinkers, history has a built-in logic that moves it forward towards progress. Auguste Comte thought that the movement towards progress was assured by science and technology; Karl Marx's dialectical materialism supposed that the class conflict carried history from the realm of necessity to the realm of freedom; and thinkers like Herbert Spencer trusted that the principle of biological evolution would lead humanity towards ever higher levels. Christians are ill at ease with the language of determinism. The only determinism is that of hope. They gladly speak of God as the forward movement in history, as the ground, vector and horizon of all human life, but they insist at the same time that history remains open to the unexpected and hence is undetermined, and that it continues to depend on human freedom and the gracious moments of God's self-communication.

Christians also have little sympathy for the despairing views of history that see human society inevitably moving towards decline. We find these views among the social scientists, such as Pitirim Sorokin, who accept the cyclical model of civilization's rise and fall; among cultural pessimists, such as Max Weber, who regard today's rational society as the beginning of the iron cage; and among contemporary natural scientists who predict the end of human history on this globe or propose a strategic lifeboat theory of survival. None of these theories can be proved. For the demonstrations offered always presuppose that history is determined, which is precisely the issue in question. The last-named theorists of gloom,[217] who tell us that we have almost exhausted the earth's resources, tend to presuppose that the social and economic institutions will remain constant, and hence they prefer to speak of future doom rather than advocate radical political change with accompanying changes in people's lifestyles. These scientists try to measure the carrying capacity of the earth, but they do not reflect on its unrealized sharing capacity yet to be achieved.

The Christian symbols of the future demand that we speak of history in a paradoxical way. History is destined for redemption, yet undetermined; it is alive by a divine drift towards humanization, yet remains the locus of catastrophic sins; history is constantly renewed by God's saving grace, yet remains forever wounded by human malice. If people ask whether God's final victory will arrive as the crowning of human reconciliation in history or as a new creation after a total catastrophe, we are unable to give them an answer. The Bible does not tell us. What we do know is that God's redemptive presence summons and strengthens us to assume responsibility for the world and become reconcilers of people in conditions of justice and peace.

This paradoxical discourse is not sufficiently respected in Pierre Teilhard de Chardin's cosmic vision of the future. One has the feeling that the great thinker knows too much. He easily passes from the realm of hope to the realm of science and regards the revealed images of God's reign as information about the future, rather than symbols that through faith enter into the redemption of history.

The promised kingdom of God is a utopian message, but it is not "a concrete utopia" in the sense that Ernst Bloch gave to this term. A concrete utopia is an image of an alternative society that is close enough to the as yet unrealized possibilities of the present to become the guide for a realistic political project. A concrete utopia must be invented in a particular historical situation, taking account of ultimate values as well as the unexplored potential of the existing situation. This point was made by Gustavo Gutierrez[218] and accepted in Latin American liberation theology. It would be foolish to think that God's kingdom can ever be fully realized in history. God's kingdom is a utopian symbol that summons forth the new in any historical situation, yet it does not provide a model of society that guides people's political engagement. In Latin America of the 1960s, vast numbers of people thought that a radical social revolution towards greater justice and equality had become a historical possibility. The concrete utopia that guided the people, including the liberation theologians, was an original Latin American socialism, different from communism and different from the consumer society of the North, where the production of goods aimed at feeding the people, provided work for the great majority, employed the local natural resources, and used a simple technology adapted to the skills of the largely rural population. The realization of this concrete utopia would have incarnated many Gospel values, but after the revolution God's promised kingdom would still have stood as a utopian symbol over the new society.

Does the deprivatization of Christian teaching on sin, conversion, salvation and eschatology lead to a loss of interior life, a neglect of personal prayer and an indifference to religious experience? A Christian community that loses its rootedness in the saving acts of God, in its liturgical celebration and in the personal spirituality of its members will gradually lose access to the Spirit that keeps it alive and sends it on its earthly mission. The loss of inwardness will, in the long run, undermine the solidarity with others and weaken the Church's impact on society. The Christian community that tries to understand its mission in terms of solidarity and liberation must engage in contemplation of the mystery of God as matrix, vector and horizon of human history.

Social engagement is not deprived of the mystical dimension that is part of the Christian life. According to the ancient teaching, especially of St. Augustine, the good we do is God's free gift to us. In this Christian perspective, action equals passion. While we see, we are being enlightened; while we act, we are being carried forward; while we love, we are being saved from selfishness; and while we embrace all people in solidarity, we are being freed inwardly to cross one boundary after another. Every step

towards greater humanization is due to the expansion of new and gracious life in us. We are alive by a power that transcends us. Because of
the wide-spread suffering in today's world, we find it difficult to worship
God as lord of history. We then remember that God is not only the life of
our life but also the abiding pain we experience in the face of a suffering,
oppressed and hungry humanity.

11

After Thirty Years

S tudying sociology at the New School for Social Research over 30 years ago, I became convinced that dialogue with sociology was of great importance in the exercise of theology. I wrote *Religion and Alienation* to introduce students of theology to the sociological tradition. In rereading the preceding chapters, I discover in them five reasons why theologians should engage in dialogue with sociological thinkers.

Dialogue with Sociology

The social thinkers studied in this book offer critiques of religion that deserve to be taken seriously. The young Hegel had the sociological intuition that doctrine or the conceptual formulation of religion has an impact on culture and society. He argued that traditional theism – God ruling the world from above – has generated a hierarchical society of unfree people, each depending on decisions made by their superiors. Hegel proposed the idea that proclaiming the transcendent God as immanent in human history would rescue people from their dependency and release their personal creativity. Hegel may have exaggerated the power of religion to influence culture and society, yet his proposal anticipated a theological movement in the 20th century often called panentheism.[219]

Marx used the term "ideology" to designate a set of ideas or symbols that disguises the oppressive features of society and legitimates the existing power structure. According to Marx, religion was the most effective ideology because it invoked the sacred to bless the secular authorities, demand that people obey them, and console the oppressed and exploited with promises of heaven. Subsequent sociologists – we mentioned Karl Mannheim – recognized that religion was a much more complex phenomenon. They did not deny that in many situations religion has exercised an ideological function, yet they also acknowledged that religion has at times exercised a utopian function, making people impatient with the unjust conditions, delegitimating the existing powers, and creating a yearning for an alternative society.

According to Freud's radical critique, religion is a pathological phenomenon that prevents people from becoming independent and produces debilitating guilt feelings. We saw that subsequent psychologists – we mentioned Erich Fromm – admitted that religion may exercise a pathogenic function, but they also recognized that the same religion may have a therapeutic impact.

Theologians, I argue in this book, want to take the critiques of religion seriously. They want to detect the ideological and pathogenic trends in their own religious tradition and then, rereading the Scriptures and rethinking the divine promises, interpret the Gospel as a message of liberation, freeing people from all the enemies of life. In Chapter 9 of this book, I defined "critical theology" as the ongoing dialogue of theology with the critical thought of the Late Enlightenment. Critical theology, I argued, questions the Christian tradition in the light of the suspicions raised by the theories of alienation and then discerns in the Christian Gospel the gift of grace that rescues people from alienation. In subsequent writings, I have defined critical theology more briefly as the exploration of the emancipatory power of the Gospel.[220] This is, in fact, what I did in Chapter 9 of this book, where I interpret the notions of sin, conversion and new life as a theology of human liberation.

A second reason why theologians should engage in dialogue with sociologists is that they tend to offer a profound critique of modern society that is at odds with the dominant political ideology. Modern society was created by two protest movements against the feudal-aristocratic order: the democratic revolution, symbolized by the French Revolution, and the industrial revolution, based on steam power and driven by capitalism. Both revolutions demanded freedom: democracy brought freedom from arbitrary royal power, and industrial capitalism brought freedom from the royal control of the economy. The philosophy behind these revolutions was the eighteenth century Enlightenment thought of England and France that looked upon reason as the organ of human liberation and rejected as irrational the cultural and political traditions of the past. Political thinkers in solidarity with the new ruling class – the bourgeoisie – welcomed the creation of modern liberal society and thought that human reason would continue to guide this society in the direction of greater progress. This liberal philosophy, supported by scientific discoveries and technological innovations, produced an optimistic cultural climate in Europe and the United States. Many people came to believe in inevitable progress.

The sociologists looked upon modernity in a radically different light. We studied two major critiques of modern society, both of them with ethical implications and hence demanding the attention of theologians. The first critique, offered by Marx, focused on the oppression and exploitation of the labouring class in capitalist society. The accumulation of capital by the owning classes not only deprived the workers of the full fruit of their labour, it also produced conditions of labour that damaged the humanity of the workers. While regarding itself as rational, liberal society was in fact riddled with contradictions. Though progressive political parties and the power of organized labour eventually improved the conditions of workers in capitalist societies, the exploitative mechanism continued to operate, this time defining the unequal relation of the industrial North to the poor countries of the South. While Marxist theory revealed the oppressive character of modern society, it still clung to the Enlightenment idea that reason was moving history forward to a realm of freedom. Reason, Marxists believed, dwelled in the working class; reason would guide its struggle against the ruling class, lead to a revolution and create a classless society.

The other critique of modern society was formulated by Toennies in his famous theory of Gesellschaft.[221] The rationality implicit in modern institutions, Toennies argued, undermined the traditions based on solidarity and produced a culture marked by individualism, utilitarianism and secularism. The ethical values inherited from Gemeinschaft-type societies evaporated in modernity so that modern society was no longer able to define a common good. People were now alone, conscious of their independence and self-responsibility, each promoting his or her own advantage, and related to one another and to society as a whole only in a contractual manner. Toennies still thought that the remnants of Gemeinschaft values would be the starting point for the creation of a new solidarity, yet Max Weber, writing a generation later, no longer shared this hope. He thought that the domination of formal reason – also named instrumental or techoscientific reason – was irreversible, leading to the waning of religion, the decline of culture, the loss of values, and the integration of people into a fully bureaucratized society.

Theologians may not agree with these two judgments on modern society, yet they want to wrestle with them. They wish to confront the sinister side of contemporary society so that they can proclaim the Christian Gospel as God's gracious rescue from the sinful forces that destroy human beings. Further on, we shall have more to say about the Marxian and Weberian critique of modernity.

Learning from sociological studies is important for theologians because the Christian faith is incarnate in historical churches – that is in social institutions subject to change and development. For pastoral reasons, these must be studied scientifically. An ecclesiology that does not take sociology into account will be abstract and lack credibility; ecclesiastical policy making without the help of sociological research will be ineffective. This aspect has not been explored in the preceding chapters. Yet it seemed important to me to insist in Chapter 7 that the famous theory of secularization has never been empirically demonstrated; in other words, that there is no fixed law relating modernity to religion.

Christian ethicists also want to be in dialogue with sociology since human behaviour is a composite of personal freedom and social determination. We have shown in Chapter 9 that the moral evaluation of personal behaviour demands a twofold inquiry, analyzing personal choice as well as social conditions. The traditional separation of personal and social ethics is quite inadequate. We cannot gain an understanding of personal actions unless we also study the historical context in which they occur. Émile Durkheim even demonstrated that while suicide was a free and arbitrary choice, the suicide rate in a given society was determined by social conditions.

There is a final reason why the dialogue with sociology is of great importance for theologians. We have seen that sociological thinkers recognize an inevitable interrelation between culture and consciousness on the one hand and the material institutions of people's lives on the other. Marx referred to these two realties as "superstructure" and "infrastructure." Yet we have seen that sociologists are not in agreement on the manner of interaction between ideas and their material base. In scientific Marxism, culture and consciousness are simply projections of the material infrastructure, yet this materialistic theory is not persuasive. Even Marxist philosophers do not accept this extreme position. The opposite extreme is the idea that culture and consciousness are produced and developed quite independently from their historical location. An idealism of this sort is the implicit assumption of most philosophers and theologians: they assume that ideas float above history, develop according to a logic intrinsic to them, and hence are independent of the social context of their authors.

This kind of idealism is implicit, for instance, in theories offered by theologians to account for the development of doctrine. They usually assume that an extended reflection on doctrines either made explicit what was implicitly contained in them or discovered rational consequences that were previously not recognized. These theories pay no attention to the changing political, economic and social conditions under which the doctrinal development has taken place.

The great majority of sociologists are neither materialists not idealists: they acknowledge an ongoing interaction between ideas and their social base. While they hold different theories about this interacting process, assigning more or less independence to one of the two factors, they all agree that an idea cannot be fully understood unless the relationship to its social base has been clarified. We mentioned in particular Karl Mannheim's sociology of knowledge and his insistence that all knowledge is *seinsgebunden*, grounded in concrete historical circumstances. This idea has been part of biblical studies since the end of the nineteenth century, when it was taken for granted that the meaning of a biblical text could not be understood without taking into account its *Sitz im Leben*, its historical context. Yet theologians have shied away from this principle when exploring the meaning and development of doctrine. The principle that our location in history affects our reading of reality has far-reaching consequences for the practice of theology.

Religion and Alienation

Reading my book 30 years later, I am keenly aware that it was written in an historical context different from the present one. My theological reading of the sociologists was seinsgebunden, related to the hopeful mood that pervaded the culture of the 1960s and '70s, especially in the Catholic Church. I shall analyze this cultural mood further on and compare it with today's gloomy outlook produced by changes in the economic and political order. But first let me show that my reading of the sociologists was influenced by the hope that we were on the way towards a more just society.

In Chapter 9, I admired Richard Niebuhr's prediction that after World War II the Christian churches would come to acknowledge Jesus Christ as the transformer of culture. Niebuhr believed in the 1950s that the churches were about to recognize the emancipatory power of the Gospel. Looking at the churches in the 1970s, I realized that the predicted evolution had taken place both among the members of the World Council of Churches

and in the Catholic Church at Vatican Council II (1962–1965.) Following the Niebuhrian terminology,[222] we can say that Protestants moved
forward from type 4, Christ and Culture in Paradox, and Catholics from
type 3, Christ above Culture, to embrace type 5, Christ, Transformer of
Culture. I rejoiced in this development, marvelled at the documents of
the Vatican Council, especially *Gaudium et spes*,[223] and expected that the
emancipatory and socially involved understanding of the Gospel would
continue to spread in the Christian churches. In the 1970s and early
'80s, the Canadian Catholic bishops published a series of pastoral letters,
influenced by Latin American liberation theology, that applied the emancipatory meaning of the Gospel to the Canadian situation.[224] What I did
not foresee was that, despite their progressive policy statements, many
churches, including the Catholic Church, would – from the mid-1980s
on – become increasing silent on issues of social justice. Nor did I foresee
the spread of a conservative piety in the churches that would detach faith
from commitment to justice and focus on personal fulfillment or personal
sanctity. Nor did I anticipate the emergence of fundamentalist trends in
the Christian churches.

Most of the social thinkers studied in this book belong to what has
been called the Late Enlightenment. I was impressed by cultural historians,
such as H. Stewart Hughes,[225] who thought that these social thinkers had
corrected the excessive rationalism of the eighteenth century Enlightenment, which trusted in the power of reason to advance the emancipation of
humanity. The sociologists I studied must have smiled at René Descartes's
famous *cogito ergo sum* argument, the idea that humans were isolated
agents, wrestling to find the truth, doubting the inherited wisdom, and
certain of their own existence only because they were thinking. According
to the sociologists, there are no isolated humans: human beings are born
into a community and come to be by participation in the language, the
symbols and the institutions of that community. They may start to doubt
and use their reason to question the received wisdom, but they do this
with presuppositions inherited from their cultural history. Humans are
never isolated thinkers: they are inevitably interdependent beings. Even
individualism and alienation are culturally mediated.

According to the Early Enlightenment, human reason was to bring
liberation to the human family. Reason would rescue people from the
ideas of the past that had blinded them, open their eyes to reality and
allow them to discover universal truths. Leaving their history behind,
people from all parts of the world would arrive at the same rational con-

clusions, the same clear and distinct ideas. But the social thinkers of the Late Enlightenment saw the world quite differently. They entertained a pluralistic idea of humanity: people were shaped by different languages, customs and cultures; and reason itself played different roles in different cultural contexts. The sociologists moved beyond the individualism and universalism of the Early Enlightenment. Recognizing the importance of symbols in the self-constitution of cultures and peoples, these social thinkers corrected the rationalism of the Early Enlightenment. We have documented this in the preceding chapters. Nor did the sociologist neglect the role of the emotions in the construction of society. While the Early Enlightenment was often hostile to religion, the Late Enlightenment thinkers, while not religious themselves, opened the door to an appreciation of religion. I became persuaded that dialogue with the sociologists would arrive at insights helpful for the renewal of the Christian faith and useful for the social struggle for a more just society.

At the end of chapters 3 and 9, I refused to accept the radical Weberian critique that modern society or Gesellschaft was about to be totally dominated by instrumental reason, tightly controlled by bureaucratic administration, caught in "an iron cage," and forever closed to the emergence of a new utopia. I argued that the cultural pessimism of German social thinkers was related to the cultural change produced by the late arrival of industrialization in Germany, which created malaise among the intellectuals. More substantially, I argued against Toennies and Weber that modernity also had a positive cultural effect, beyond the individualism and utilitarianism denounced by them. Tocqueville and Durkheim, the French social thinkers, clearly recognized that the institution of democracy produced a culture that fostered social responsibility. Citizenship presupposes an ethical understanding of the human person. Democratic institutions summon people to move beyond their personal interests, care for the common good, and think in political terms about the future of their society. I have called "historical consciousness" the discovery that we are co-responsible for our collective existence. Built into this consciousness is the desire to participate in the decisions that affect our lives. I therefore refused to believe, following Toennies and Weber, that democratic institutions had become totally controlled by bureaucracies that made decisions based on technocratic reason alone. The experience of the 1960s persuaded me that democracy was based on an ethical ideal, generated the desire to be co-responsible, and created a restless anticipation of a more just society, open to greater participation. Democracy produced a critique of communism, pointing to its hierarchical structure and the absence of popular participation. Democracy also produced a critique of capitalism, pointing to the hierarchical structure and the exclusion of labourers and employees from participating in the decisions that affect their work. I might add that Catholics living in democratic societies are often torn apart by the culturally induced desire to be responsible participants and their condemnation to silence by the ecclesiastical hierarchy.

These are three lines of thought that reveal the hopeful cultural mood in which I wrote *Religion and Alienation*. In the subsequent sections, I wish to compare the historical situation of the 1970s, when I wrote the first edition of this book, with the historical situation of the present.

Welfare Capitalism

After World War II, the societies of the West adopted some form or other of welfare capitalism. This development had several causes. Both labour unions and progressive political parties demanded that the government involve itself in the promotion of the economy. The shortcoming of the unregulated market system had been revealed in the Great Depression, and the unemployment it produced had lasted until the beginning of the war. The British economist John Maynard Keynes had recommended government intervention in the national economy, a principle already applied in President Roosevelt's New Deal in the '30s that a decade later, after the war, would receive universal support in the West. The British government argued that it would be a scandal to have the soldiers return from the war to conditions of unemployment. The capitalist class, persuaded by political pressures and the fear of another depression, was willing to enter into an unwritten contact with the government in support of full employment, respect for labour unions and welfare payments for people in need. In return the government would create advantageous conditions for the development of privately owned industries.

Government-guided capitalism – or Keynesian capitalism, as it is called – was enormously successful from the end of the war up until the 1970s: it produced great wealth in Western societies and raised the standard of living even for worker and employees. That a good deal of the wealth was derived from exploiting the developing world was not noticed at the time. The extraordinary economic success of the industrialized West produced an optimistic culture: people came to believe that built into history was an orientation towards progress. In Western societies this spirit led to the creation of reform movements of various kinds, supporting social democracy, reducing economic inequality, defending the human rights for the disenfranchised, overcoming racist discrimination, and demanding the extension of social services.

It was in this culture of hopefulness that Vatican Council II took place. Urged by the bishops of the successful industrialized countries of northwestern Europe, the Church willingly engaged in open dialogue with the modern world. The Council proclaimed religious liberty, supported human rights, recommended democracy, condemned all forms of prejudice and discrimination, blessed the ecumenical movement, encouraged inter-religious dialogue, supported the peace movement, and expressed the hope that the reform capitalism that had created the successful welfare society in the North could be extended to the poor countries of the South.

The section on socio-economic life in *Gaudium et spes* characterises the present situation in these words: "We are at a moment in history when the development of economic life could diminish social inequalities if the development were guided and co-ordinated in a reasonable and human way." (# 63) The chapter then shows at length the dehumanizing poverty existing in many parts of the world and the exclusion of people from the necessities of life and their right to act on their own behalf. What is demanded, therefore, are "numerous reforms at the socio-economic level, along with universal changes in ideas and attitudes." (# 63) This sounds quite modest. The chapter then proposes policies and ideas for the management of the economy and the redistribution of wealth that are in line with the ideals of social democracy.

The section on culture in *Gaudium et spes* contains a paragraph that expresses the hopeful mood of the 1960s (# 55).

> From day to day, in every group or nation, there is an increase in the number of men and women who are conscious that they themselves are the authors and the artisans of the culture of their community. Throughout the whole world there is a mounting increase in the sense of autonomy as well as of responsibility. This is of paramount importance for the spiritual and moral maturity of the human race. This becomes more clear if we consider the unification of the world and the duty which is imposed upon us, that we build a better world based upon truth and justice. Thus we are witnesses of the birth of a new humanism, one in which man is defined first of all by this responsibility to his brothers and to history.

The View from the South

The Latin American bishops, meeting three years after the Council in Medellín, Colombia, did not share the idea that a mounting increase in the sense of autonomy and responsibility was taking place around the world. They saw the world from a different perspective.

That the successful welfare capitalism of the North should be exported to the poor countries of the South was an opinion shared by many people. They believed that this economy would help these countries to overcome their poverty. In the 1960s, promoting economic development in Latin America became a policy of the U.S. government, in view of countering the growing influence of socialist ideas. The United States promoted capital investment and northern-style industrialization on the southern continent, uncontrolled by local governments. Yet since unregulated capitalism is an economic system that enriches the centre at the expense of the periphery, the export of capitalist development to Latin America was counterproductive: it created a new kind of poverty. The capitalist development steered from the North expelled local populations from the land, undermined their subsistence economy, chased them into poverty-stricken shantytowns, produced exploitative working conditions, and enriched a small technically trained local elite loyal to the new masters.

These were the conditions that generated radical movements in Latin America seeking to replace the capitalist economy by a socialist economy. In the 1960s and '70s, many Latin Americans on all levels of society believed that a historical moment had arrived, making a socialist revolution a realistic possibility. Their conviction was shared by many Catholics whose social engagement was inspired by their faith. In this context, liberation theology was born.[226] Even the Latin American Bishops Conference meeting at Medellín in 1968 rejected the capitalist colonialism imposed on their continent and encouraged a revolutionary hope for a more just and more humane society.[227] Looking at the world not from the centre, as the Vatican Council had done, but from the periphery, the Latin American bishops recognized an ever-extending system of wealth creation that threatened to enslave the population on the southern continents. Their perspective was adopted by the World Synod of Bishops meeting in Rome in 1971:

> Looking at the situation of the world, we have perceived the serious injustices that are building around the world of men a network of domination, oppression and abuses, which stifle freedom and keep the

greater part of humanity from sharing in the building up of a more just and more fraternal world.[228]

It is worth mentioning that the socialist economy envisaged by Latin Americans was not an imitation of Soviet-style communism – that is, the introduction of state-owned and state-controlled industrial development. What they hoped for was an economy that relied on local resources, involved the local people in production, used a simple technology adjusted to their skills, and produced the goods and services needed by the population. What they envisaged was a distinctive civilization, different from the industrial capitalism or communism of the North.

Latin American liberation theology and the messages of the Latin American Bishops Conference exerted a strong influence on the entire Catholic Church. "The preferential option for the poor"[229] became a principle adopted by socially engaged Catholics in many parts of the world, including Canada and the US. This option called for a double commitment: to look at society from the perspective of its victims, and to offer public support of their struggle for greater justice. This option was practised by groups of Catholics in many parts of the world, often referred to as the Catholic Left. What is truly remarkable is that it was even endorsed by papal documents and pastoral letters of national bishops conferences, outstanding among them the Canadian bishops' conference. Over the years I have analyzed this development in several publications.[230]

When I wrote *Religion and Alienation* in the early '70s, I recognized two distinct orientations among socially engaged Christians in the North: a reformist one, supporting social democracy in continuity with the inherited institutions, and a radical one, hoping for the collapse of the present order and the construction of a new, more just and more participatory society. I then argued that, contrary to the custom of the secular Left, reformist and radical Christians should remain friends, committed as they were to the same Gospel.

Neo-liberal Globalization

In the early eighties the world began to change. I remember that looking at the world situation in 1991, right after the first Gulf War, I was greatly discouraged. I thought a major transformation had taken place. I wish to republish here the major part of an article I wrote at that time for *The Ecumenist*.

The '60s and '70s were a time of cultural optimism. For Christians, this was the time of Vatican Council II and the subsequent ecumenical rapprochement between the Catholic and the Protestant churches in North America. This religious excitement happened against a background of historical struggles that promised to make the world a more just and peaceful place. Those were the days of the anti-colonial struggles in what we then began to call the Third World and the movements of Latin Americans to liberate themselves from economic dependency on the system that exploited them. Those were the days of the civil rights movement in the United States. Seeing that it was possible to change society if people gather in solidarity and strength, other groups, including women, began to organize, and march, and demand justice for themselves. The Church heard in these movements the voice of biblical prophecy. Catholics discovered as they had not done before in quite the same way that faith and justice were interconnected. Discipleship demanded what in Catholic ecclesiastical documents was called "the preferential option for the poor." Christian *agape* increasingly unfolded itself as social solidarity extended to the victims of society. Over a period of about 25 or 30 years we lived, prayed and struggled as if the conversion of society to greater justice was a historical possibility in our own generation.

This period, I believe, is over. The Gulf War was for me the publicly approved massacre that sealed in blood the new politico-economic orientation, begun over a decade ago, that sought to enhance the material well-being of a privileged minority and assign to the margin the rest of the globe's population. At present, it seems to many analysts, there exists no real hope that society will change for the better: not in North America (the United States and Canada), not in the developing world, and not on the international level.

The United States and Canada have turned their back on Keynesian-inspired welfare capitalism and foster instead neo-conservative or, better, neo-liberal monetarist policies that promote the economy by relying exclusively on the mechanism of the free market. This social project calls for privatization, deregulation, cutting welfare programs, increasing the price of public services, lowering the wages of public employees, fighting the unions, creating conditions such as tax breaks that are favourable for domestic and foreign investment, etc. Even socialist or social democratic governments ... are found to follow the neo-liberal trend. The new adjustment policies have had devastating effects on the majority of the people. For growing crowds, unemployment has become a chronic condition; the jobs available are temporary or part-time; welfare support decreases. Working people live in constant fear. Young people have little hope. Even middle-class people live in fear that the forces of marginalization will also engulf them. Under such pressures, society tends to become angry and less tolerant, with harmful consequences for the visible minorities.

The Third World countries, burdened by their debt, have been largely deserted by the rich nations of the North. The international monetary organizations impose "structural adjustment policies" on the poor countries which demand that they cut their programs of social support and create conditions favourable for foreign investment, even if this should mean tax exemption, forbidding labour unions, or creating "free zones" where companies are dispensed from ecological and labour regulations. In most countries of the developing world, strong-arm governments prevent the organization of popular-based opposition movements. Nicaragua's attempt to create an alternative society has been successfully undermined. The popular liberation movements, which in the churches generated liberation theology, are largely dead.

On the international level, the collapse of the eastern European communist regimes and the arrival of democratic freedoms – a source of great joy – ended the Cold War and created an opportunity for a new global solidarity. But this is not what happened. Capitalist empire, no longer checked by a balance of power, decided to create conditions that would guarantee its rule over the world. The new regime protects the interests of the developed nations, regulates the flow of money all over the world, controls oil and other natural resources, and pacifies the unruly by military force.

The new order, mighty at this time, is unsuccessfully challenged by the chaos created among the peoples that have been pushed to the margin. A microcosm of the new international order is the American city with its slums of the poor and despised, wounded by crime and drugs and supervised by police power. But there is one challenge that cannot be controlled for long: encroaching ecological disaster.

In my judgment, the present is a time of mourning.

The period beginning with the 1960s was experienced by the Church as a "kairos," a special time when major social change towards greater justice was a historical possibility. At that time, Christian faith and love generated the impulse to social solidarity with the poor and the powerless. Christians entered upon a new spirituality. They experienced God as the Light that made people discover the nature of their bondage and the Life that enabled them to assume responsibility for their social existence. Faith, love and justice here became closely intertwined. The surrender to God acquired political meaning. The preferential option for the poor became the contemporary form of discipleship.

In my judgment, this "kairos" is over. We now live in "the wilderness." The new politico-economic situation and the corresponding cultural trends have, moreover, affected the life and the policies of the Christian churches. Retrenchment is the order of the day. Will the World Council of Churches survive the present trend where each church concentrates on its own confessional identity? In the Catholic Church, the new emphasis on identity is making the hierarchy more self-involved, putting the brakes on its involvement with other churches, its association with other religions, and its co-operation with social movements. Fear is becoming the Church's counsellor.

Living in the desert, mourning and lamentation have their place – so the Scriptures tell us. Still, Christians are summoned to hope, even as they sojourn in the wilderness.... Christians for whom faith and justice have become intertwined will want to keep their networks, centres and institutions alive. They will continue to search for opportunities to involve themselves in action. Catholics will use the radical critiques of liberal capitalism offered in John Paul II's social encyclicals as the starting point for the social analysis of the present situation. And they will be ready, if they hear the call, to enter upon a new spirituality, a new, possibly painful experience of God, where the peace that passes all understanding becomes a blessed restlessness.[231]

This brief analysis of the new era is still valid. Since 1991, the situation has become worse – both through the military extension of American empire and the spreading globalization of the unregulated market system. I have written about these developments in other publications.[232] Let me mention in this connection that Pope John Paul II opposed the first Gulf War, criticized the bombing of Afghanistan and argued against the pre-emptive American strike against Iraq. In his book *Memory and Identity*, he identifies as a source of evil not only fascist and communist totalitarianism, but also recognizes the evil potential of Western democratic empire, with its attendant disparities of global political and economic power. The imperial power that imposes economic conditions on the poor countries of the South may become "another form of totalitarianism, subtly concealed under the appearances of democracy."[233]

The Dialectic of Modernity

Today, modernity has revealed its sinister side, which I did not recognize when I wrote this book 30 years ago. As a theologian, I am now in dialogue with social thinkers who shed light on the present condition and offer proposals for reconstruction. I shall first discuss my theological conversation with the Frankfurt School of social research and then, in a later section, turn to the critical thought and practical proposals of Karl Polanyi.

The sinister side of modernity has been explored by a group of social philosophers, known as the Frankfurt School, with whom I was not acquainted 30 years ago. In the early 1920s, Max Horkheimer and Theodor Adorno, joined by a number of colleagues, created an institute of social research in Frankfurt, Germany, usually referred to as the Frankfurt School, which became well known for its cultural pessimism.[234] After 1933, the beginning of the Nazi regime, this pessimism was recognized as prophetic.

The Frankfurt philosophers took with utmost seriousness and sought to combine the two critiques of modernity that we have studied in this volume: the Marxian critique of class oppression and the Weberian critique of the domination of instrumental reason. The Frankfurt thinkers were Marxists deeply disappointed by Marxism. Before 1914, the socialist parties of Europe represented in the parliaments of their country had bragged that they would oppose the imperialistic war threatening to tear Europe apart; yet when the time came, in 1914, the socialist parties, each in its own country, voted in favour of the war. The second great disappointment was the turn of the Russian revolution into a dictatorship. The Frankfurt philosophers concluded that the analysis of the economic infrastructure, on which Marxist theory relied, was unable by itself to explain what was happening in the world. What was needed as well, they argued, was a cultural analysis. People are not only prisoners of economic powers; they are also locked into cultural presuppositions from which they are unable to escape. These cultural presuppositions, they argued, include the understanding of reason itself. Following Max Weber, they denounced the cultural domination of instrumental reason. According to the famous theory of the Frankfurt School, called "the dialectic of the Enlightenment,"[235] the humanistic project of the Early Enlightenment, intended to liberate humans by the power of reason, has been turned into its very opposite and become the great obstacle to human liberation.

Enlightenment reason, according to the Frankfurt School, had been a creative human faculty that included "substantive reason" dealing with ends and "instrumental reason" dealing with means. Substantive reason reflected on the human vocation and the nature of the good, while instrumental reason produced the sciences and guided technological development. According to the Frankfurt School, the internal logic of capitalism and the cultural impact of positivism have led to the collapse of Enlightenment reason and reduced it simply to instrumental reason. What disappeared was rational reflection on the end and purpose of human striving. Reliance on instrumental reasons alone, they argued, was the prison of modernity. Since techno-scientific reason was unable to define human values, modern society was drifting into a vulgar utilitarianism. Overwhelmed by bureaucratic administration, democracy had lost its creative ethical function. The world now became increasingly a set of objects to be scientifically controlled for the chosen purposes of the powerful. Even human beings, according to this analysis, became increasingly objects to be manipulated or even discarded according to the wishes of men exercising authority.

After World War II, Horkheimer and Adorno argued that the Holocaust should not be understood as a regression of a civilized nation into barbarism, but rather as the revelation of the sinister side of modernity, the willingness to use technocratic reason to control and, if need be, eliminate human beings to fulfill the arbitrary wishes of the powerful. We may well admit that in our day, governments, following technocratic reasoning, have made administrative decisions that inflict death upon masses of innocent people by bombings or starvation.

Still, the Frankfurt philosophers objected to the complete rejection of the Enlightenment as it was done by conservatives, existentialists and fascists in the 1920s and '30s. Further on I shall extend their objection to today's postmodern protest against the Enlightenment. The Frankfurt School offered a passionate defence of the Enlightenment's ethical achievements – democratic co-responsibility and human rights – and dreaded what would happen to people if their human rights were no longer respected. Nor was the Frankfurt School opposed to instrumental reason: it simply advocated the de-centering of techno-scientific reason to make room for the retrieval of substantive rationality.

Using a Hegelian vocabulary, the Frankfurt philosophers called their position "a dialectical negation" of the Enlightenment. They called it dialectical because they tried to retrieve the original Enlightenment's ethical vision. At the same time, they denounced as irresponsible a "non-dialectical negation" that would repudiate the Enlightenment altogether. The urgent task of society, they argued, was the recovery of the emancipatory values of the original Enlightenment and the promotion of a new ethical culture. What they had in mind was probably the reappropriation of the Kantian ethic: the categorical imperative, the commitment never to treat human beings simply as means, and the axiom that an action is ethical if the tenet that guides it can be applied universally.

Theirs was a dark analysis of contemporary society. What, we may ask, are the cultural resources for the moral conversion necessary to save our civilization? One does not see how a purely philosophical ethic can obtain cultural power. Are there new social movements that promote an ethic of solidarity? We shall return to this topic further on. Then I shall also mention that, according to Hans Küng, a new paradigm is emerging in the world religions, making them redefine their mission in humanistic terms – promoting human rights, protecting the earth and reconciling the divided human family.

The Frankfurt School developed an intellectual approach called "critical theory," which has important implication for theology. "Classical theory," the Frankfurt philosophers argued, is a set of ideas that seeks to define a universal condition, which can then be applied to individual cases. The natural sciences produce classical theories, providing universally valid information regarding what is happening in particular cases. Weber's sociological theory, that religion is the product of the charismatic gifts of a founding personality, and Durkheim's sociological theory, that religion is the product of society's effort to realize its potential, are both classical theories: their authors believe they have been empirically demonstrated and thus can be applied to any particular religion.

"Critical theory" is something quite different. It refers to the method of reasoning used in pursuit of truth. At the beginning of any inquiry, critical theory demands that one analyze the present historical situation, detect the structures of oppression and exclusion that damage human life, and recognize the cultural symbols and intellectual traditions that disguise these scandals and reconcile educated people with the existing society. Such disguise may well be spread by our schools and universities. Critical theory demands that the rational inquiry into a particular issue not re-enforce the dominant symbols of disguise, but instead raise the awareness of the ongoing dehumanizing drama. The search for truth therefore begins with negation. According to critical theory, truth is not available to inquirers who rely simply on their intelligence; required also is an emancipatory commitment on their part. Knowledge acquired without the commitment to human liberation inevitably re-enforces the existing historical conditions, including their destructive impact.

The Frankfurt School presented its critical theory to social scientists and philosophers, yet it also applies to the exercise of theology. In fact, theologians recognize in critical theory's emancipatory commitment an echo of biblical prophecy denouncing unjust conditions as well as an echo of the patristic teaching that truth is not available without love, that truth and love are interrelated and dependent on one another. According to St. Augustine, reason can be trusted only when it is grounded upon love. The separation of love and knowledge entered into theology through a narrow understanding of scholasticism.

In the preceding chapters I have applied critical theory, even though I was not as yet acquainted with the Frankfurt School. My theological method involved negation and retrieval: I negated the ideological distortions of the Christian tradition; then, rereading the Scriptures, I tried to retrieve the original salvific meaning of revelation. Thus I explored the anti-Jewish rhetoric present in Christian preaching and acknowledged its devastating historical consequences, and then explained how, after the Holocaust, the Church redefined its relationship to the Synagogue in a manner that fosters respect and co-operation. Thus I negated the individualistic interpretation of the Gospel, presenting it simply as a message of personal salvation and then, rereading the Scriptures, tried to retrieve the social dimension of the Gospel and its promise of human liberation. Critical theology also negates the patriarchal inheritance of the Christian tradition and, rereading the Scriptures in the light of new religious experiences, tries to retrieve the prophetic promise of gender equality. While at this time critical theory attracts little attention at university departments of philosophy and social science, it is commonly applied by theologians who search for the meaning of the Gospel in today's society. In response to the ecological crisis, to give another example, theologians have examined to what extent Christian teaching has presented nature simply as an object for human use and thus facilitated the industrial exploitation of the earth, and then, as a second step, have retrieved the biblical awe and admiration before nature as an image of divine wisdom and beauty. "The emancipatory commitment" of secular critical theory is replaced in critical theology by faith in the divine promises and the emancipatory message of the Gospel.

Let me mention another principle that is part of Frankfurt School critical theory: "the end of innocent critique."[236] A critique is deemed innocent, or naively unaware of its consequences, if i) it rejects a system or institution non-dialectically, i.e. without retrieving the true insights achieved by it, and if ii) it does not examine the social impact of the critique if it should achieve cultural dominance. The Frankfurt School's critique of the Enlightenment was not innocent. We saw that it was "a dialectical negation." It advocated the retrieval of ethical reason and universal solidarity, and instead of repudiating science and technology altogether, it simply wanted to reduce their cultural power. Yet the Frankfurt School accused Marxism of offering an innocent critique of liberalism. Why? Because Marxists did not retrieve from liberalism its great achievements, the civil liberties, and, second, because Marxists did not ask themselves what would be the social consequences of their critique if it became the dominant opinion. Marxists remained unaware that their principles, if uncorrected, would produce pre-liberal tyrannical governments. Conversely, the Frankfurt School objected to the innocent critique of Marxism offered by the great defenders of capitalism. In my study of two encyclicals, *Laborem exercens* (1881) and *Sollicitudo rei socialis* (1987),[237] I have been amazed by the ability of Pope John Paul II to offer dialectical negations of both communism and capitalism, denouncing their dehumanizing impact as well as honouring the positive contribution they have made to the vision of a more just and more humane society.

The Postmodern Proposal

An important cultural transformation has taken place since the '60s and '70s that many social scientists and political thinkers have interpreted as the passage from welfare capitalism to neo-liberal globalization. We have followed their interpretation. Yet there exists another interpretation of this cultural change, defended by philosophical thinkers and widely accepted by intellectuals and artists. They claim that we have left modernity behind and now live in a postmodern age.

What is meant by postmodern is not quite clear. The term was introduced in Jean-François Lyotard's 1979 book, *La condition postmoderne*.[238] Like many French philosophers, Lyotard had been a communist who, after the revelation of Stalin's massive crimes against humanity, suffered from guilt feelings, abandoned his Marxism, and sought a new approach for understanding society. He argued that the totalitarianism and the clashing of empires that have characterized modernity were the result of

Enlightenment thought, which introduced two dangerous innovations: i) the belief that reason guides history in the direction of progress and human liberation and ii) the belief that reason allows us to arrive at universal truths and values. These two beliefs, Lyotard argued, allow intellectuals to impose their vision of progress on society and claim universal validity for their ideas, thus legitimating political dictatorship. Modernity has created totalitarianism.

Today, Lyotard continues, we live in a postmodern age. People repudiate totalitarianism; they are sick of emancipatory ideas and movements, socialist or liberal; they mistrust all great narratives – les grands récits – promising liberation or redemption. In the postmodern age, people no longer believe in universal truths and values; they accept radical pluralism, acknowledge otherness, and want to be left alone to define their identity as they wish. Let many flowers bloom.

Lyotard's characterization of modernity is puzzling, especially for readers of this book. Was the young Hegel, who rejected reliance on reason, already postmodern? Tocqueville, we recall, did not believe in inevitable progress: he warned that liberal democracy may turn into tyrannical rule. Toennies and Weber, as we have seen, were keenly aware of the dark side of modernity, and even Durkheim, while trusting in reason, was greatly troubled by the spread of anomie produced by modernity. We saw, moreover, that Durkheim and Freud represented an intellectual current that moved beyond the exclusive trust in reason of the Enlightenment to the recognition that symbols and the imagination play an indispensable role in the self-constitution of society. Were these social thinkers postmodern before their time? Was Kierkegaard postmodern when he repudiated universal reason? In a previous chapter, we saw that Weber and Durkheim recognized that ideas and values were culturally produced and hence differed from one civilization to another: in other words, they recognized pluralism. According to the interpretation I have followed in this book, the sociologists were representatives of the Late Enlightenment, which corrected the excessive rationalism of the Early Enlightenment. By disregarding this long list of thinkers, Lyotard's characterization of modernity lacks credibility.

Let me add that ethical pluralism is not a new idea. In fact, the belief in ethical pluralism produced by social scientific studies at the beginning of the 20th century raised dangerous political questions that are still with us today. If values are simply the product of a particular culture, different from one to the other, then there is no reason to believe that order in the world can be grounded upon a common agreement or shared reasoning. In that case – some German philosophers argued – order in the world must be imposed by a powerful nation whose history has prepared it for this mission. Can you guess which nation these philosophers had in mind? Today it is Samuel Huntington and friends who insist on otherness and ethical pluralism and believe that world order must be imposed by a superpower exercising a universal mission.[239]

If Lyotard and other postmodern philosophers denounce the messianic dimension present in Marxism, liberalism and other evolutionary theories, they have our support. But they go much further. Lyotard argues that even the Frankfurt School, despite its devastating analysis of modernity's sinister side, was still caught in the modern illusion.[240] Why? Because its followers yearned for human emancipation and hoped beyond hope for the retrieval of universal solidarity, rescuing the victims of society. Postmodern thought tries to remain indifferent to the poor and oppressed because the idea that they can be liberated is a dangerous illusion.

Postmodern thought rejoices in the pluralism of truth. The various circles or networks to which people belong define reality in different ways, each according to a creativity of its own. Postmodern thought honours the freedom of artists to break inherited standards and follow their own inspiration. The postmodern attitude delivers us from rationalist illusions, from linear thinking and logical consistency, and allows us to acknowledge the total otherness of others. According to Lyotard, cross-cultural dialogue is a modern illusion. Why? Because dialogue assumes that the partners share a common reason – the modern illusion – making communication possible. Lyotard tells us that human life is a game that people define as they wish. Their discourse defines reality for them. The words we use do not refer to an existing reality beyond them: they are simply self-referential; they constitute their own universe; they cannot be tested by relating them to an objective situation. Reality is here principally linguistic.

Since Lyotard is an honest philosopher, he is ready to tell us how he sees present-day society, even if he is unable to convince his readers. Lyotard argues that contemporary capitalism is no longer committed to the accumulation of capital and no longer generates class conflict. Capitalism has transcended its historicity: it has achieved a self-perpetuating stability. Organized in giant transnational corporations, the world economy is guided by management teams that operate on purely technical, value-free, scientific grounds. Lyotard argues that the world economic system, geared to maintaining and improving its performance, no longer has a historical subject, which means that no one, no group of persons, no government is able to assume responsibility for its operation. The economic activities that sustain human life constitute a mobile but stable roof over our heads, allowing us to concentrate our minds on issues that appeal to us.

If this analysis were a brilliant caricature, it would be worthwhile to explore its meaning, but as a serious proposal the analysis is outrageous. The victims of neo-liberal capitalism disappear here completely. The idea that we live in a postmodern age gives permission to philosophers to think seriously and creatively – without attention to the poor and oppressed. Yet it would be wrong to think that Lyotard had sympathy for right-wing political movements. When interviewed, he declared that he opposed the French war in Algeria and the US war in Vietnam, but when asked on what grounds he did so, he did not reply. Posing questions that demand a purely rational reply, he felt, was an exercise of violence.[241]

The French postmodern thinkers were greatly embarrassed by Jean-Marie Le Pen's political movement, *le Front National*, which foments hostility to immigrants because of their cultural difference and the impossibility to integrate them into French society. Le Pen uses the postmodern emphasis on difference and the absence of cross-cultural values to promote his right-wing political cause. In their hearts, the postmodern thinkers wanted differences to be respected, but they were unable to say so, for then "respect for otherness" would be a universal value that they had so dramatically ruled out. To counter Le Pen, the French thinkers now advocated the idea of hospitality.

Using the vocabulary of the Frankfurt School, we can say that overcoming the oppressive implications of universal values by putting exclusive emphasis on difference is "an innocent critique" since i) it does not try to save the valid insight of the rejected theory nor ii) examine the social impact of its critique if it acquired cultural power. Against the postmodern emphasis on otherness, I propose that, in the face of the contemporary ideologies of exclusion, every sentence acknowledging the difference between people must be followed by a sentence that recognizes the similarity between them. The emphasis on otherness evokes an unintended fascist memory, unless it is immediately supplemented by an equal emphasis on likeness. Despite our differences, we must celebrate our common humanity. Can we be sure that all humans have much in common? Yes, for all of them suffer when they are despised and excluded.

The postmodern emphasis on difference raises critical political issues. According to the theory of "the clash of civilizations," proposed by

Samuel Huntington and welcomed by circles close to the White House, the civilizations of the world are different and at odds with one another.[242] They are all based on religious traditions that mediate incompatible values and thus produce tensions and lead to war. A special threat, according to Huntington, is the clash between the West and the Muslim world. But that the world religions foster incompatible values is empirically disproved by the many inter-religious networks – for instance, the World Conference of Religions for Peace[243] – dedicated to mutual respect, economic justice and peaceful co-operation. Present tensions between civilizations are created by the political, economic and cultural policies of powerful governments that use religion to legitimate their actions. Against Huntington's clash of civilizations, the United Nations and Pope John Paul II have advocated "the dialogue of civilizations" promoting mutual understanding, respect for difference, and the discovery of common values.

Postmodern thought, invented in France, has spread rapidly in the academies of the United States. It has allowed intellectuals to think deeply without attending to the harmful impact of neo-liberal globalization and American political and military policies. I am not suggesting that intellectuals who regard themselves as postmodern are supporters of neo-liberal ideas and policies. In private conversation, they are likely to criticize the political and military policies of their country and think of themselves as left-wing liberals. Yet the postmodern option allows them to engage in intellectual inquiry and do important scholarly work without taking the victims of society into account. They therefore join, willy-nilly, the vast intellectual and cultural project that tries to reconcile people to the scandalous disorder that is today's global society.

Theology should not wish to join this game. The crucifixion of Jesus by empire and the religious and secular elites supporting it – the *memoria passionis Christi*[244] – should prevent Christian theologians from using their intelligence to overlook the suffering inflicted on people by powerful economic, political and military institutions. From dialogue with sociology, theologians learn to take into consideration the social implications of their own discourse. Does it raise critical questions regarding the existing order, they ask themselves, or does it make its victims invisible?

The postmodern thinkers are correct when they claim that after the '60s and '70s, we moved into a new cultural age. But this age is still part of modernity; it is created by the invention of new technologies, the unregulated market system, the bureaucratization of democracy, the militarization of the globe, the obscene gap between rich and poor, the obsession with status and consumption, the spread of chronic unemployment, and the loss of humanistic values. The individualism and utilitarianism generated by liberal capitalism are penetrating all spheres of life and undermine the inherited institutions that foster human solidarity. It is my impression that since anticipating reform or reconstruction seems increasingly unrealistic, intellectuals turn to issues that do not raise social questions and call themselves postmodern.

The Church's teaching has always interpreted the grave economic and political problems of society as moral crises, as historical events revealing the love of wealth and power and the indifference to justice and human solidarity. In the past, we often added that this absence of ethical commitment was related to the secularization of society. Because people no longer believed in God, they became indifferent to the common good, promoted their own interests and made their society increasingly unjust. Today we can no longer say this. For in many parts of the world, intensely religious people support political or military policies – in the name of God – that produce violence and oppression. The fundamentalist currents in the world religions make it difficult for religious people dedicated to peace and justice to have their voices heard. Still, lively movements in the world religions promote universal solidarity.

Let me return to the dialectical negation of the Enlightenment – proposed by the Frankfurt School – demanding that society retrieve emancipatory reason and universal solidarity. Yet what are the moral resources for an ethical conversion of this kind? At one time, the institution of citizenship generated an ethical summons to social co-responsibility. At the present, people see themselves increasingly as customers who want to be served well for their money, and even governments increasingly look upon them as clients, not as citizens. There are – thank God – still many social movements, inspired by social solidarity and respect for nature, that promote an alternative vision of society, movements that are today also supported by many people of faith.

Countervailing Movements

Despite the Frankfurt School's persuasive analysis of the sinister side of modernity, we will not overlook Max Weber's theory of social change examined Chapter 8.[245] He argues that the alienation produced by the dominant system is likely to generate countervailing movements guided by an imagination that promises rescue. His theory is verified by contemporary developments. We are in fact witnessing a multiplication of countervailing movements, often organized internationally, that defend human rights, demand social justice, oppose violence and war, foster the emancipation of women and protect the natural environment. These movements agree that the present system, defined by neo-liberal globalization and American empire, is leading the human family into a humanitarian and ecological catastrophe, even if they disagree about many issues of public policy. These movements promote an alternative form of globalization, a globalization-from-below, that enables a multitude of actors, making use of the new technology (e-mail, the Internet and jet transport), to create worldwide co-operation in the pursuit of an alternative society. The concrete symbol of this co-operative effort is the World Social Forum, which has held yearly meetings at Porte Allegre in Brazil, attracting each time tens of thousands of participants. The political scientist Richard Falk has argued that the utopian imagination that inspires these diverse actors has a certain religious quality. His book *Religion and Humane Global Governance*[246] contains a chapter on the spirituality that animates the secular activists, the majority, and a chapter on the part played by activists identified with a religious tradition.

Since these countervailing movement are organized according to principles at odds with the dominant system, they create a new consciousness among the people engaged in them. These movements are democratic and egalitarian, allowing everyone to speak; they uphold the equality of men and women, contesting the patriarchal inheritance of society; they practice co-operation across boundaries, a spirit at odds with the obsessive competitiveness that drives contemporary society; they make the participants conscious of their power to act as social agents, against the effort of capitalism to define people as customers and clients; and they generate solidarity across national boundaries and facilitate transversal activities, involving people internationally. These alternative movements may well be the training ground for the creation of an alternative global society – not immediately, but after the shock waves created by environmental disasters or the revolts of the excluded masses awaken the sleeping middle classes.

The energy that drives these international movements is, to a large extent, generated by people's involvement locally – in their neighbourhood, their city or their region. This involvement is often referred to as community development. Thanks to the neo-liberal globalization described in a previous section, Western capitalist societies are increasingly divided into three sectors: i) the economic and political elites and their families, ii) people with a good income – merchants, professionals, technicians and organized workers, and iii) the "third sector" made up of minimum-wage workers, part-time workers, occasional workers, the unemployed and the unemployable. In all capitalist societies, the third sector is growing. It is in this sector that the new growth of community development is taking place.

The social theory of political economist Karl Polanyi (1886–1964) has provided a theoretical basis for understanding the broad significance of community development, including especially the social economy or, as it is sometimes called, community economic development. His major study, *The Great Transformation*,[247] offers a critique of liberal capitalism that has a certain similarity with Marxism, yet it reveals an attention to culture and human values that is absent from Marxism and it produces recommendations for what should be done that also differs from Marxist political theory.[248] Since I dealt with the Marxist theory of alienation in Chapter 2, I wish to introduce the similar, yet significantly different, proposal of Karl Polanyi.

In his critical analysis of liberal capitalism, Polanyi does not restrict his attention to the exploitation of workers in the factory system, but attends more especially to the harmful effects that capitalist industrialization has on traditional societies. While his historical analysis focused on the impact of the Industrial Revolution on Great Britain beginning in the late eighteenth century, his theory sheds light on the dramatic changes produced in our own day by industrialization in the societies of the South. The workers are mainly rural people lifted out of their villages and employed in industries removed from their communities. Because of his attention to culture, Polanyi recognizes that in traditional societies, people's daily labour rendered a service to the community, strengthened its social cohesion and gained them public respect. Here people worked to assure their honoured place in the community. Polanyi disagrees with social thinkers who believe that the profit motive is a universal human inclination. It is only when people become wage labourers in capitalist industries, when their daily labour is "disembedded" from their social matrix and they lose their inherited values and cultural identity, that they labour to make the money needed for their survival. It is the economic system that makes people hunt after money: the poor for the sake of survival, and the rich to increase their profit.

The spread of the unregulated market system in traditional societies produces cultural disintegration and weakens social solidarity. This damage has devastating consequences in parts of the world where the majority of people rely on a subsistence economy for their survival. Material poverty, Polanyi argues, is not a tragic human condition if people belong to communities that have survival skills and a strong sense of solidarity – this is how humanity has survived for thousands of years. Yet material poverty is body-and-soul destroying if people are isolated and have no community support. Capitalist industrialization produces the second kind of poverty in the countries of the South and, thanks to today's neo-liberal policies, this poverty is again spreading in the wealthy countries of the North.

What, in this situation, is to be done? According to Polanyi, the remedy for impoverishment-cum-cultural-disintegration is not the collective ownership of the means of production nor, primarily, the social democratic transformation of capitalism. For him, the present condition is primarily a social problem, not a political one. People spend most of their energy in their daily work, yet if this work simply serves the market and does not benefit the community, then the expended energy will not generate solidarity or create a culture of co-operation. Society can be transformed only by forces at the community level. What has to take place, according to Polanyi, is the re-embedding of economic activity in people's social relationships. Co-operative daily labour organized democratically, he argued, would create trust and solidarity and foster the spirit of community. Here the motivation for people's work would not be to increase their personal profit, but rather to contribute to the progress of their community and assure their own well-being within it. Engagement in the social economy, Polanyi argued, would transform people's consciousness and lay the cultural foundation for a political movement to change the dominant structures of society. According to Polanyi, the struggle for a more just and humane society is first of all a social movement, reorganizing people's daily labour, before it can become a political movement for the reconstruction of society.

Karl Polanyi's work offers a social theory that supports community-based models of economic development. The social economy is a countervailing movement in Max Weber's sense, provoked by the alienation created by unregulated capitalism and guided by a set of principles at odds with the dominant culture. In this and similar movements, people feel that they are not paralyzed by neo-liberal globalization, for in their daily activities they operate according to a set of alternative values. Community development, carried on in this spirit, is not a liberal reform movement; it is rather, using the lingo of political scientists, a non-reformist reform movement – non-reformist because it is guided by principles at odds with the dominant system.[249]

Universal Solidarity

For the Frankfurt School, we recall, the only possibility of avoiding the dehumanization of our civilization was the retrieval of emancipatory values and the conversion to universal solidarity. Will this transformation occur? One resource for a new ethical culture may be the social movements briefly discussed in the previous section. Another source may well be the theological evolution taking place in the world religions.

Studying the changed attitudes in the world religions and participating in several inter-religious organizations, Hans Küng has concluded that a new paradigm is emerging in these religions.[250] Responding to the injustices, the conflicts and the misery that characterize today's world, significant circles in the world religions are interpreting their sacred mission as a commitment to promote universal solidarity and respect the natural environment. Fidelity to the Absolute as they see it makes believers yearn for an alternative society of mutual respect and the sharing of resources. In Christianity, these circles have begun to influence even the leaders of the churches, Protestant and Catholic. In a recent book, *Amazing Church*, I documented the emergence of the new paradigm in the Catholic Church, supported by Vatican Council II and Pope John Paul II's passionate support for human rights, economic justice, solidarity with the poor, environmental care and inter-religious co-operation in the service of humanity.[251] Some critics claim that the bold policies advocated in the papal encyclicals function as public relations discourse and do not correspond to the Pope's actions and pastoral policies. Still, for Christian believers, the yearning for universal solidarity and the social engagement to stem the tide of oppression and exclusion is religiously meaningful, even if the social movement they support should eventually fail. For in their pain, their longing and their hope, God dwells.

Notes

Chapter 1

[1]   *Early Theological Writings*, trans. T. M. Knox and R. Kroner, Harper & Row, New York, 1948. Cf. *Hegels Theologische Jugendschriften*, edit. Hermann Nohl, J. C. B. Mohr, Tülbingen, 1907.

[2]   The interpretation of Hegel's early essay presented in this chapter has been derived in reliance on P. Asveld, *La pensée religieuse du jeune Hegel: liberté et aliénation*, Publication universitaire de Louvain, Louvain, 1953, and B. Bourgeois, *Hegel à Francfort*, J. Vris, Paris, 1970.

[3]   On extrinsicism, see G. Baum, *Man Becoming*, Seabury Press, New York, 1979, pp. 3-13.

[4]   Ludwig Feuerbach, *The Essence of Christianity* (1841), Harper & Row, New York, 1957.

[5]   Richard Schacht, *Alienation*, Doubleday, New York, 1971, analyzes the concept of alienation in the philosophical writings of the mature Hegel, especially in his *Phenomenology of the Spirit*. The author is curiously insensitive to Hegel's early theological writings.

Chapter 2

[6]   Karl Marx and Friedrich Engels, *The German Ideology*, International Publishers, New York, 1947, pp. 14, 15, 19.

[7]   The first section of *The German Ideology*, op. cit., pp. 3-79, deals with Marx and Engel's response to Feuerbach. More especially, confer Marx's famous "Theses on Feuerbach," op. cit., pp. 197-199. The Theses are also found in *Karl Marx: Selected Writings in Sociology and Social Philosophy*, trans. and ed. T. B. Bottomore, McGraw-Hill, New York, 1964, pp. 67-69.

[8]   From the 3rd thesis on Feuerbach. Cf. preceding note.

[9]   "Contribution to the Critique of Hegel's Philosophy of Right, Introduction," *Karl Marx: Early Writings*, trans. T. B. Bottomore, McGraw-Hill, New York, 1964, p. 43.

[10]   These manuscripts are published in *Karl Marx: Early Writings*, op. cit., pp. 61-221.

[11]   Ibid., pp. 75, 85.

[12]   Ibid., p. 192.

[13]   Ibid., p. 124.

[14]   Ibid., p. 125.

[15]   Ibid., pp. 189-190.

[16]   Ibid., p. 193.

[17]   Cf. Max Weber's remarks on marginal intellectuals, *The Sociology of Religion*, trans. E. Fischoff, Beacon Press, Boston, 1968, pp. 124-126.

[18]   Paul Tillich, *Die sozialistische Entscheidung*, in *Gesammelte Werke*, vol. 2, Evangelisches Verlagswerk, Stuttgart, 1962.

[19]   *Karl Marx: Early Writings*, p. 43.

[20]   See pp. 77-81.

[21]   *Karl Marx: Early Writings*, pp. 3-33.

[22]   For a discussion of Marx's "On the Jewish Question," see Emil Fackenheim, *Encounters Between Judaism and Modern Philosophy*, Basic Books, New York, 1973, pp. 145-148. Also confer Edmund Silberer, "Was Marx an Antisemite'?" *Historia Judaica*, Vol. XI, 1949, pp. 3-52, and Shlomo Avineri, "Marx and Jewish Emancipation," *Journal of the History of Ideas*, 1964, pp. 445-450.

[23]   Max Weber, *The Sociology of Religion*, pp. 80-137.

[24]   "Contribution to the Critique of Hegel's Philosophy of Right, Introduction," *Karl Marx: Early Writings*, pp. 43-44.

[25]   See below pp. 94 and 109.

Chapter 3

[26]   Robert Nisbet, *The Sociological Tradition*, Basic Books, New York, 1966.

[27]   Auguste Comte, *Cours de philosophie positive*, vol. I, La Société positiviste, Paris, 1893, p. 243.

[28]   Alexis de Tocqueville, *Democracy in America*, Vintage Books, New York, 1945, vol. 2, pp. 104-106.

[29]   Karl Marx, *The Communist Manifesto*, Appleton-Century-Crofts, New York, 1955, p. 12.

[30]   Ferdinand Toennies, *Community and Society* (1887), trans. C. P. Loomis, Harper & Row, New York, 1963.

[31]   Alexis de Tocqueville, *Democracy in America* , vol. 1, p. 15.

[32]   Max Weber, *Basic Concepts in Sociology*, The Citadel Press, New York, 1969, pp. 51-55. Cf. also Talcott Parsons, *The Structure of Social Action*, Vol. 11, Free Press, New York, 1968, pp. 601-610, and Julien Freund, *The Sociology of Max Weber*, Vintage Books, New York, 1969, pp. 59-70.

[33]   F. Toennies, *Community and Society*, p. 65.

[34]   Ibid., p. 76.

[35]   Ibid., p. 77.

[36]   Ibid., p. 83.

[37]   Ibid., p. 219.

[38]   Ibid.

[39]   Ibid., p. 222.

[40]   "Contracts of any type could not be sustained for a moment, Durkheim argues (in his *The Division of Labor*), unless it was based on conventions, traditions, codes in which the idea of an authority higher than contract was clearly resident": quoted in R. Nisbet, *The Sociological Tradition,* Basic Books, New York, 1966, p. 91.

[41]   F. Toennies, *Community and Society*, p. 231.

[42]   Ibid., p. 159.

[43]   Ibid., p. 125.

[44]   Cf "Science as a Vocation," *From Max Weber*, edit. Gerth and Mills, Oxford University Press, New York, 1958, p. 155.

[45]   For Max Weber on bureaucracy see especially *From Max Weber*, pp. 196-244.

[46]   The term "iron cage" is from M. Weber's *The Protestant Ethic and the Spirit of Capitalism*, Charles Scribner's Sons, New York, 1958, p. 181.

[47]   Herbert Marcuse, *One-Dimensional Man*, Beacon Press, Boston, 1964.

[48]   Karl Mannheim, "Conservative Thought," *Essays on Sociology and Social Psychology*, Routledge & Kegan Paul, London, 1953, pp. 74-164.

[49]   Stewart Hughes, *Consciousness and Society: The Reorientation of European Social Thought, 1890–1930*, Vintage Books, New York, 1961.

[50]   Fritz Ringer, *The Decline of the German Mandarins: The German Academic Community, 1890–1933*, Harvard University Press, Cambridge, MA, 1969.

[51]   Max Scheler, *Ressentiment*, Free Press, New York, 1961.

Chapter 4

[52]   The presentation of biblical themes in this chapter relies heavily on Xavier Léon-Dufour's *Vocabulaire biblique*, Jean-Jacques von Allmen's *Vocabulaire biblique*, and the notes and comments of *La Bible de Jérusalem*.

[53]   Rosemary Ruether, "The Pharisees in First Century Judaims," *The Ecumenist,* 11, Nov.-Dec. 1972, pp. 1-7; Jacob Neusner, *From Politics to Piety: The Emergence of Pharisaic Judaism*, Prentice-Hall, Englewood,NJ, 1973.

[54]   Rosemary Ruether, *Faith and Fratricide*, Seabury Press, New York, 1974.

[55]   Cf. Gregory Baum, "Theology After Auschwitz: A Conference Report," *The Ecumenist*, 12, July-August 1974, pp. 65-80.

Chapter 5

[56]   Émile Durkheim, *The Elementary Forms of Religious Life*, trans. J. W. Swain, Free Press, New York, 1965.

[57]   Ibid., p. 470.

[58]   Ibid., p. 474.

[59]   James Frazer, author of the 2-volume work *The Golden Bough*, published in 1890.

[60]   *The Elementary Forms of Religious Life*, pp 57-62.

[61]   Ibid., p. 63.

[62]   Max Weber, *The Sociology of Religion*, trans. E. Fischoff, Beacon Press, Boston, 1964, pp. 20-31.

[63]   Ibid., Introduction, p. xxx.

[64]   See Ibid., Introduction, pp. xxxii-xxxiii, and Index, under "rationalization," p. 300. For Weber on rationalization, see also *From Max Weber*, eds. Gerth and Mills, Oxford University Press, New York, 1958, Index, under "rationalization," p. 484; Julien Freund, *The Sociology of Max Weber*, Vintage Books, New York, 1969, pp. 17-24; and Robert Nisbet, *The Sociological Tradition*, Basic Books, New York, 1966, pp. 141-150.

[65]   *The Sociology of Religion*, pp. 32-45.

[66]   Ibid., pp. 46-59.

[67]   See below, p. 122.

[68]   On functionalism, see Irving Zeitlin, *Rethinking Sociology*, Prentice-Hall, Englewood Cliffs, NJ, 1973, pp. 3-62, and Thomas O'Dea, *The Sociology of Religion*, Prentice-Hall, Englewood Cliffs, NJ, 1966, pp. 1-19.

[69]   See Milton Yinger, *The Scientific Study of Religion*, Macmillan, London, 1970, pp. 69-71, 74-77, where the author documents the trend in much of contemporary social anthropology to regard religion and magic as functional equivalents.

[70]   See Albert Pierce, "Durkheim and Functionalism," in Émile Durkheim et al., *Essays on Sociology and Philosophy*, ed. Kurt Wolff, Harper & Row, New York, 1960, pp. 154-169, and Robert Bellah's "Durkheim and History," in Robert Nisbet's *Emile Durkheim*, Prentice-Hall, Englewood Cliffs, NJ, 1965, pp. 153-176.

[71]   Erich Fromm, *Psychoanalysis and Religion*, Bantam Books, New York, 1967.

[72]   Ibid., p. 18.

[73]   Ibid., p. 19.

[74]   Ibid., p. 22.

[75]   Ibid., p. 37.

[76]   Ibid., p. 48.

[77]   See Edgar Bruns, *The Art and Thought of John*, Herder & Herder, New York, 1969, pp. 78-86.

[78]   Max Weber, *The Sociology of Religion*, pp. 80-137.

[79]   Karl Mannheim, *Ideology and Utopia*, trans. L. Wirth and E. Shils, Harcourt, Brace & World, New York, no date, p. 78.

[80]   Ibid., pp. 192-196.

[81]   Ibid., pp. 262-263.

[82]   Ibid., pp. 43-47.

[83]   Ibid., pp. 47-48, 98-108. Also see Karl Mannheim, "On the Interpretation of Weltanschauung" and "Historicism," *Essays on the Sociology of Knowledge*, ed. Paul Kecskemeti, Routledge & Kegan Paul, London, 1952, pp. 33-133.

[84]   Charles Reich, *The Greening of America*, Random House, New York, 1970.

[85]   Karl Mannheim, *Ideology and Utopia*, pp. 211-218.

[86]   Rosemary Ruether, *The Radical Kingdom*, Harper & Row, New York, 1970. In the following section, I also rely on Rosemary Ruether's as yet unpublished manuscript, "Messiah of Israel and Cosmic Christ." Cf. also Harold H. Rowley, *The Relevance of the Apocalyptic*, Lutherworth, London, 1964 and David S. Russell, *The Method and Message of Jewish Apocalyptic*, SCM, London, 1964.

[87]   See above p. 87.

[88]   Peter Berger, *The Sacred Canopy*, Doubleday, New York, 1967, p. 100.

[89]   Peter Berger and Thomas Luckmann, *The Social Construction of Reality*, Doubleday, New York, 1967, pp. 95-97.

[90]   Peter Berger, *Invitation to Sociology*, Doubleday, New York, 1962, pp. 25-53.

[91]   Cf. Richard Schacht, *Alienation*, Doubleday, New York, 1971, pp. 45-62.

Chapter 6

[92]   Cf. Stewart Hughes, *Consciousness and Society: The Reorientation of European Social Thought*, 1890–1930, Vintage Books, New York, 1961.

[93]   Sigmund Freud, *The Interpretation of Dreams*, Avon Books, New York, 1965, especially pp. 155-167, 385-439. For dreams as symbols, also see the chapters "Symbolism in Dreams" and "Archaic and Infantile Features in Dreams" in Freud's *A General Introduction to Psychoanalysis*, Pocket Books, New York, 1953, pp. 156-177 and pp. 209-223.

[94]   For the primary processes and the archaic roots of the unconscious mind, see Sharon MacIsaac, *Freud and Original Sin*, Paulist Press, New York, 1974, pp. 26-28, 60-62.

[95]   "The era to which the dream-work takes us back is 'primitive' in a twofold sense: in the first place, it means the early days of the individual – his childhood – and, secondly, insofar as each individual repeats in some abbreviated fashion during childhood the whole course of the development of the human race, the reference is phylogenetic....

It seems to me that a symbolism, which the individual has not acquired by learning, may justly claim to be regarded as phylogenetic heritage." S. Freud, *A General Introduction to Psychoanalysis*, "Archaic and Infantile Features in Dreams" (translation adjusted), pp. 209-210. The phylogenetic unconscious is the underlying theme of Freud's study *Moses and Monotheism* (Vintage Books, New York, no date).

96   For Wilhelm Reich's early criticism of Freud, see Paul A. Robinson, *The Freudian Left: Wilhelm Reich, Geza Roheim, Herbert Marcuse*, Harper & Row, New York, pp. 19-52.

97   Emily Hewitt, "Anatomy and Ministry: Shall Women Be Priests?" *The Ecumenist*, vol. 11, July-Aug. 1973, pp. 70-75.

98   See Vatican Council II, especially the Declaration of the Church's Relationship to Non-Christian Religions (*Nostra aetate*) # 2: "The Catholic Church rejects nothing that is true and holy in the world religions... and respects their ways of conduct and of life... which often reflect a ray of that Truth which enlightens all humans."

99   *Nostra aetate*, # 4: "The Jews remain most dear to God because of the promises to their fathers, for God does not repent of the gifts He makes nor of the calls He issues (Rom 11:28-29)."

100   Émile Durkheim, *The Division of Labor in Society*, Free Press, New York, 1964, p. 172.

101   Émile Durkheim, *Suicide*, Free Press, New York, 1951, pp. 304, 305, 307, 309.

102   Ibid., pp. 312-320.

103   Ibid., p. 312.

104   Émile Durkheim, *The Elementary Forms of Religious Life*, Free Press, New York, 1965, p. 29. Cf. "The Dualism of Human Nature and Its Social Condition," in Émile Durkheim et al., *Essays on Sociology and Philosophy*, ed. Kurt Wolff, Harper & Row, New York, 1960, pp. 325-340.

105   Émile Durkheim, *Suicide*, p. 312.

106   Ibid.

107   Émile Durkheim, *The Elementary Forms of Religious Life*, pp. 474-475.

108   Ibid., p. 475.

109   Ibid, p. 470.

110   Émile Durkheim, "The Determination of Moral Facts," *Sociology and Philosophy*, Cohen & West, London, 1953, p. 38.

111   Ibid.

112   Robert Bellah, "Civil Religion in America," *Religion in America*, ed. W.G. McLoughlin, Beacon Press, Boston, 1966, pp. 3-23, reprinted with comments and a rejoiner in *The Religious Situation 1968*, edit. D. R. Cutler, Beacon Press, Boston, 1968, pp. 331-394; also available in Robert Bellah, *Beyond Belief*, Harper & Row, New York, 1974.

[113]   For a survey and analysis of the controversy and for evidence of its continued vitality, see *American Civil Religion*, eds. R. E. Richey and D. G. Jones, Harper & Row, New York, 1974.

[114]   Ibid., pp. 255-272.

[115]   Robert Bellah, *Beyond Belief*, p. 168.

[116]   Will Herberg, *Catholic, Protestant, Jew*, rev. ed., Doubleday, New York, 1955.

[117]   Ibid., p. 88.

[118]   Ibid.

[119]   Cf. the discussion of Civil Religion in Andrew Greeley's *The Denominational Society*, Scott, Foresman and Company, Glenview, IL, 1972, pp. 156-174.

[120]   Robert Bellah, "Coming Around to Socialism: Roots of the American Taboo," *The Nation*, vol. 219, Dec. 28, 1974, pp. 677-685.

[121]   M. Darrol Bryant, "Beyond Messianism: Toward a New 'American' Civil Religion," *The Ecumenist*, vol. 11, May-June 1973, pp. 45-51.

Chapter 7

[122]   Cf. Hermann Lübke, *Säkularisierung, Geschichte eines ideenpolitischen Begriffs*, Verlag Karl Albert, Freiburg, 1965.

[123]   Bryan Wilson, *Religion in Secular Society*, Pelican Books, London, 1969.

[124]   David Martin, *The Religious and the Secular*, Routledge & Kegan Paul, London, 1969.

[125]   Andrew Greeley, *Religion in the Year 2000*, Sheed & Ward, New York, 1969, and "The Present Condition of American Religion," and "The Secularization Myth," *The Denominational Society*, Scott, Foresman and Company, Glenview, IL, 1972, pp. 86-107, 127-155.

[126]   Bryan Wilson, op. cit., p. 112.

[127]   Ibid., p. 122.

[128]   Peter Berger, *The Sacred Canopy*, Doubleday, New York, 1967, p. 108.

[129]   Will Herberg, *Catholic, Protestant, Jew*, Doubleday, New York, 1955.

[130]   Alexis de Tocqueville, *Democracy in America*, ed. Phillips Bradley, Vintage Books, New York, no date, Vol. 2, pp. 21-33.

[131]   Ibid., pp. 30-31.

[132]   Ibid., pp. 32-33.

[133]   For Durkheim's description of these Gemeinschaft-type corporations, see his *Suicide*, Free Press, New York, 1968, pp. 378-384. For a summary of Durkheim's position, see Robert Nisbet, *The Sociological Tradition*, Basic Books, New York, 1966, pp. 155-158.

[134]   Cf. Andrew Greeley, *The Denominational Society*, p. 2: "In our model of American religion, we view the denomination as the point of intersection of meaning and belonging functions in a society where an urban, industrial order emerged in a society that had no established church."

[135]   Ibid, p. 2.

[136]   *Democracy in America*, vol. 2, p. 23.

[137]   Peter Berger, *The Sacred Canopy*, pp. 113–121.

[138]   Bryan Wilson, *Religion in Secular Society*, p. 42.

[139]   Richard Niebuhr, *The Social Sources of Denominationalism*, New York, H. Holt & Co., 1929.

[140]   S.D. Clark, *Church and Sect in Canada*, Toronto, University of Toronto Press, 1948.

[141]   *Religion in Secular Society*, pp. 43, 210-211, 219-220.

[142]   See Andrew Greeley, "The Protestant Ethic: Time for a Moratorium," *Sociological Analysis*, vol. 25 (Spring 1964).

[143]   *Religion in Secular Society*, p. 53.

[144]   Friedrich Gogarten, *Demythologising and History*, London, SCM Press, 1955.

[145]   Harvey Cox, *The Secular City*, New York, Mcmillan, 1965.

[146]   *The Sacred Canopy*, pp 113-121.

[147]   Talcott Parsons, "Christianity and Modern Industrial Society," *Religion, Culture and Society*, ed. Louis Schneider, John Wiley & Sons, New York, 1964, pp. 273-298.

[148]   David Martin, *The Religious and the Secular*, Routledge & Kegan Paul, London, 1969.

[149]   Oswald Spengler, *The Decline of the West*, Alfred A. Knopf, New York, 1939.

[150]   Pitirim Sorokin, *The Crisis of Our Age: the Social and Cultural Understanding*, Dutton, New York, 1941.

[151]   Robert Bellah, *Beyond Belief,* Harper & Row, New York, 1970.

[152]   Andrew Greeley, *Unsecular Man*, Schocken Books, New York, 1972.

[153]   Max Scheler, "Uber die positivistische Geschichtsphilosophie des Wissens," *Schriften zur Soziologie und Weltanschauungslehre*, 2nd ed., Franke Verlag, Bern, 1963, and *Ressentiment*, Free Press, New York, 1961.

Chapter 8

[154]   For a history of the controversy and the application of Weber's method to other cultures, see S. N. Eisenstadt, ed., *Protestant Ethic and Modernization*, Basic Books, New York, 1968.

[155]   See above pp. 54-55.

[156]   See above chapter 5, note 64.

[157]   See above pp. 60.

[158]   Max Weber, *The Sociology of Religion*, Introduction by Talcott Parsons, Beacon Press, Boston, 1964.

[159]   Ibid.

[160]   Ibid., Introduction, p. xxx.

[161]   *From Max Weber*, eds. H. H. Gerth and C. Wright Mills, Oxford University Press, New York, 1958, p. 152; cf. pp. 118-127.

[162]   Max Weber, *On Charisma and Institution Building*, ed. S. N. Eisenstadt, University of Chicago Press, Chicago, 1968; also *From Max Weber*, pp. 245-252.

[163]   Max Weber, *Theory of Social and Economic Organization*, Free Press, New York, 1968, pp. 329-340. Cf. Robert Nisbet, *The Sociological Tradition*, pp. 141-150.

[164]   See above p. 95.

[165]   See below p. 208.

[166]   Herbet Marcuse, *One-Dimensional Man*, Beacon Press, Boston, 1964.

[167]   Max Weber, "Science as a Vocation," in *From Max Weber*, 129-156, 155.

[168]   Max Weber, *The Protestant Ethic and the Spirit of Capitalism,* Charles Scribner's Sons, New York, 1958, p. 181.

[169]   Robert Merton, "Bureaucratic Structure and Personality," *Reader in Bureaucracy*, eds. R. Merton et al., Free Press, New York, 1952, pp. 361-371.

[170]   *From Max Weber*, pp. 151-152.

[171]   Gregory Baum, *Man Becoming*, Herder & Herder, New York, 1970, pp. 235-245.

[172]   Richard Niebuhr, *Christ and Culture*, Harper & Row, New York, 1951.

[173]   See above p. 100.

[174]   *Christ and Culture,* p. 218.

[175]   C. H. Hopkins, *The Rise of the Social Gospel in American Protestantism*, 1865–1915, Yale University Press, New Haven, 1940, p. 320.

[176]   Richard Allen, *The Social Passion: Religion and Social Reform in Canada, 1914–28*, University of Toronto Press, Toronto, 1973, pp. 7-8.

[177]   *The Church in the Modern World*, # 55, in Walter Abbot, ed., *The Documents of Vatican II*, Herder & Herder, New York, 1966, p. 200.

[178]   Ibid., pp, 213-214.

[179]   See the "Hartford Appeal for Theological Affirmation," *Worldview*, April 18, 1975, pp, 39-41, and the responses to the Appeal in *Worldview*, May 18, 1975, pp, 22-27, and June 18, 1975, pp, 45-47.

[180]   Max Weber, *The Sociology of Religion*, pp, 55-59.

[181]   Ibid.

[182]   *The Church in the Modern World, # 55*, in *The Documents of Vatican II*, pp, 260-261.

Chapter 9

[183]   The language of "privatizing" and "deprivatizing" the Gospel was introduced in Catholic theology by Johann Baptist Metz; see, for instance, "The Church's Social Function in the Light of a 'Political Theology,' " *Concilium*, Vol. 36, Paulist Press, New York, 1968, pp. 3-18. Metz defined "political theology" as "a critical corrective of contemporary theology's tendency to concentrate on the private individual, and at the same time to formulate the eschatological message in the circumstances of our present society" (p. 2). "The reversal of this privatizing tendency," Metz writes, "is the task of political theology" (p. 5).

[184]   See above pp. 72-73.

[185]   Cf. the articles in *Sacramental Reconciliation*, ed. Edward Schillebeeckx, *Concilium*, vol. 61, Herder & Herder, New York, 1971.

[186]   Cf. Peter de Rosa, *Christ and Original Sin*, Bruce, Milwaukee, 1967; A. M. Dubarle, *The Biblical Doctrine of Original Sin*, Herder & Herder, New York, 1965; Karl Rahner, *Hominization: The Evolutionary Origin of Man as a Theological Problem*, Herder, Freiburg, 1965; Piet Schoonenberg, *Man and Sin: A Theological View*, University of Notre Dame Press, Notre Dame, IN, 1965.

[187]   Patrick Kerans, *Sinful Social Structures*, Paulist Press, New York, 1974.

[188]   Cf. R. Pierard, *The Unequal Yoke: Evangelism, Christianity and Political Conservatism*, J. B. Lippincott, Philadelphia, 1970; D. O. Moberg, *The Great Reversal: Evangelism Versus Social Concern*, J. B. Lippincott, Philadelphia, 1972.

[189]   For an example taken from the Canadian church, see "The Fifteen Affirmations," in "Restating the Inherited Faith," *The United Church Observer*, vol. 37, June 1974, pp. 8-9.

[190]   See above p. 157.

[191]   Gustavo Gutierrez, *A Theology of Liberation*, Orbis Books, Maryknoll, NY, 1973, pp. 25-32; Gustavo Gutierrez, "Liberation Movements and Theology," *Concilium*, vol. 93, 1974, pp. 135-146.

[192]   "La conjoncture internationale, les églises et les chrétiens: une entrevue avec Gonzalo Arroyo," *Relations* (Montréal), vol. 34, juillet-août 1974, p. 216.

[193]   See above p. 152.

[194]   Cf. Rosemary Ruether, "A New Political Consciousness," *The Ecumenist* 8, May-June 1970, pp. 61-64.

[195]   Pierre Vallières, *White Niggers of America*, McClelland and Steward, Toronto, 1969.

The expression "the international imperialism of money" is taken from Pius XI's encyclical *Quadragesimo Anno,* (1931) # 109, and has been used more recently in Paul VI's encyclical *Populorum Progressio* (1967) # 26.

197   Rosemary Ruether, *Liberation Theology*, Paulist Press, New York, 1972; "Paradoxes of Human Hope: The Messianic Horizon of Church and Society," *Theological Studies*, June 13, 1972, pp. 235-252.

198   "In contemporary society, it is impossible to believe in a Christianity that is not at one with the movement to emancipate mankind": Edward Schillebeeckx, "Critical Theories and Christian Political Commitment," *Concilium*, vol. 84, 1974, p. 55. Cf. the entire article, ibid., pp. 48-61, and *The Understanding of Faith*, The Seabury Press, New York, 1974, pp. 124-150.

Chapter 10

199   Henri de Lubac, *Catholicism*, trans. L. C. Sheppard, Burns & Oates, London, 1962, especially pp. 49-62.

200   *Enchiridion Symbolorum*, ed. Denzinger-Schönmetzer, Herder, Freiburg, 1963, # 990-991, p. 295.

201   Peter Berger, *The Sacred Canopy*, pp. 23-28; *The Social Construction of Reality*, pp. 27, 101-102.

202   Herbert Marcuse, *Eros and Civilization*, Vintage Books, New York, 1962, p. 216.

203   For contemporary literature on eschatology, see Edward Schillebeeckx, "The Interpretation of Eschatology," *Concilium*, vol. 41, Paulist Press, New York, 1969, pp. 42-56.

204   For a popular presentation of deprivatized eschatology, see Gregory Baum, "Eschatology," *An American Catechism*, Chicago Studies, 12, Fall 1973, pp. 304-311.

205   See above pp. 95-98.

206   Ernst Bloch, *Thomas Münzer als Theologe der Revolution*, rev. ed., Suhrkamp Verlag, Frankfurt am Main, 1969.

207   Friedrich Engels, *Marx & Engels on Religion*, introduction by Reinhold Niebuhr, Schocken Books, New York, 1964, pp. 97-118.

208   Ibid, p. 102.

209   Ibid, p. 103.

210   Ernst Bloch, *Thomas Münzer*, p. 99.

211   Ernst Bloch, *Das Prinzip der Hoffnung*, 2 vols., Suhrkamp Verlag, Frankfurt am Main, 1969.

212   For Bloch's mature thought in English, see sections of his *Prinzip der Hoffnung*, published with a useful introduction by Harvey Cox in Ernst Bloch, *Man on His Own*, Herder & Herder, New York, 1970; also *A Philosophy of the Future*, Herder & Herder, New York, 1970, and *Atheism in Christianity*, Herder & Herder, New York, 1972.

213   Ernst Bloch, *Tübinger Einleitung in die Philosophie*, Suhrkamp Verlag, Frankfurt am Main, 1970, p. 230.

214   Ibid., p. 243.

215   Ernst Bloch, *Prinzip der Hoffnung*, pp. 82-84.

216   Ibid., pp, 178-180,

217   Cf. D. H. Meadows et al., eds., *The Limits to Growth*, New American Library, New York, 1972 and the critical reply, H. S. D. Cole, ed., *Thinking About the Future: A Critique of the Limits to Growth*, Chatto & Windus for the Sussex University Press, 1973.

218   Gutierrez, *A Theology of Liberation*, Orbis Books, Maryknoll, NY, 1973, pp. 220-225.

Chapter 11

219   See above pp. 23, 131.

220   Gregory Baum, *Essays in Critical Theology*, Sheed & Ward, Kansas City, 1994, pp. 4-10.

221   See above pp. 32-35.

222   See above p. 157.

223   *Gaudium et spes,* the conciliar document on the Church in the Modern World, in Joseph Gremillion, ed., *The Gospel of Peace and Justice*, Orbis Books, Maryknoll, NY, 1976, pp. 243-336.

224   See "From Word to Action,"(1976), "Ethical Reflection on the Economic Crisis" (182) and "Ethical Choices and Political Challenges," in *Do Justice! The Social Teaching of the Canadian Bishops*, Éditions Paulines, Montreal, 1987, pp. 314-321, 399-410, 411-434.

225   H. Stewart Hughes, *Consciousness and Society: The Reorientation of European Social Thought 1890-1930*, Vintage Books, New York, 1961.

226   Cf. Gustavo Gutierrez, *A Theology of Liberation*, Orbis Books, Maryknoll, NY, 1973.

227   The Medellin Documents, in Joseph Gremillion, ed. *The Gospel of Peace and Justice*, Orbis Books, Maryknoll, N.Y., 1976, pp. 445-476, 456.

228   "Justice in the World," World Synod of Bishops, 1971, in *The Gospel of Peace and Justice*, pp. 513-529, 514.

229   At the Puebla Conference (1979), the Latin American bishops offered their definition of the preferential option for the poor, "Final Document," # 1134-1165, in J. Eagelson and P. Scharper, eds, *Puebla and Beyond,* Orbis Books, Maryknoll, 1979, pp. 264-267. See Gregory Baum, "Option for the Powerless," *The Ecumenist*, 26 (Nov.-Dec. 1987) 5-11.

230   Gregory Baum, *The Priority of Labor: Commentary on 'Laborem exercens'*, Paulist Press, New York, 1982, and "The Church's Evolving Social Teaching," in *Theology and Society*, Paulist Press, New York, 1987, pp. 3-121.

231   *The Ecumenist*, 29 (spring 1991) 1-3

[232]   Gregory Baum, "Are We in a New Historical Situation," in Kevin Arsenaut et al, eds., *Stone Soup: Reflections on Economic Injustice*, Montreal: Paulines, 1997, 19-40.

[233]   John Paul II, *Memory and Identity*, Rizzoli, New York, 2005, p. 48.

[234]   I have become acquainted with the authors of the Frankfurt School mainly through commentaries such as Martin Jay, *The Dialectical Imagination*, Little, Brown & Co., Boston, 1973; T. B. Bottomore, *The Frankfurt School*, E. Horwood, London, 1984; Jay Bernstein, *The Frankfurt School: Critical Assessments*, Routledge, London, 1994.

[235]   Max Horkheimer and Theodor Adorno, *Dialectic of the Enlightenment*, Herder and Herder, New York, 1972.

[236]   See Gregory Baum, "The End of Innocent Critique," *The Ecumenist*, vol. 3, July-Sept. 1996, 58-63.

[237]   Gregory Baum, *The Priority of Labour: A Commentary no 'Laborem exercens'*, Paulist Press, New York, 1982, and Gregory Baum/Robert Ellsberg, eds. *The Logic of Solidarity: Commentaries on 'Sollicitudo rei socialis,'* Orbis Books, Maryknoll, NY, 1989.

[238]   Jean-François Lyotard, *La condition postmoderne*, Minuit, Paris, 1979, translated as *The Postmodern Condition*, Manchester University Press, Manchester, 1986; also Gregory Baum, *Essays in Critical Theology*, Sheed & Ward, Kansas City, 1994, pp. 77-95.

[239]   See below pp. 234-235.

[240]   Jean-François Lyotard, *The Postmodern Condition*, pp. 12-14.

[241]   Jean-François Lyotard/Loup Thébaud, *Just Gaming*, University of Minnesota Press, Minneapolis, 1985, pp. 5-8.

[242]   Samuel Huntington, *The Clash of Civilizations*, Simon & Schuster, New York, 1996. Gregory Baum, "The Clash of Civilizations or Their Reconciliation," *The Ecumenist*, 39 (Spring 2002), 12-17.

[243]   World Conference of Religion for Peace, www.wcrp.org

[244]   This expression is central in Johann Baptist Metz's political theology.

[245]   See above p. 152.

[246]   Richard Falk, *Religion and Humane Global Governance*, Palgrave, New York, 2001.

[247]   Karl Polanyi, *The Great Transformation*, Beacon Press, Boston, 1944.

[248]   Cf. Gregory Baum, *Karl Polanyi: On Ethics and Economics*, McGill-Queen's University Press, Montreal, 1996.

[249]   For a discussion of the social economy, see Eric Shragge and Jean-Marc Fontan, *Social Economy: International Debates and Perspectives*, Black Rose Books, Montreal, 2000.

[250]   Hans Küng, ed., *Global Ethic: The Declaration of the Parliament of the World Religions*, SCM Press, London, 1993.

[251]   Gregory Baum, *Amazing Church*, Novalis, Ottawa, 2005.

Index

Amazing Church

A Catholic Theologian Remembers a Half-Century of Change

GREGORY BAUM

Can the Catholic Church change its mind? Gregory Baum responds with a resounding "yes," exploring and analyzing key areas where, over the past fifty years, the Church has done just that. Affirming the universality of God's grace, human rights and religious liberty, the option for the poor, the validity of the ancient covenant with the Jews and a new openness to religious pluralism, official Catholic teaching has undergone profound transformations. Affected by a new historical situation and new reflection on scripture and tradition, the Church's official teaching has evolved in an extraordinary way.

The Catholic people are beginning to take for granted that the hierarchical Church is a learning as well as a teaching Church: it continually reviews its inherited teaching in dialogue with creative thought summoned forth by the Spirit.

For Baum, inconsistencies in the Church are not reason enough to mute his admiration of the development of its official teaching – a Catholicism that is truly at the service of humanity.

Awarded Second Place for History and an Honorable Mention for Popular Presentation of the Catholic Faith by the Catholic Press Association in 2006!

"This is a refreshing and challenging book, looking back and also seeing the possibilities of the present and future. Baum's optimism is evident in the pages where he shows how the Church's teaching has changed over the last several decades on several pivotal issues. The work gives hope that the Holy Spirit continues to work in our all-too-human enterprises. It also shows the importance of seeing matters in historical perspective."—*Judges' comments*

Available in Canada from
Novalis
1-800-387-7164
www.novalis.ca

Available in the United States from
Orbis Books
1-800-258-5838
www.orbisbooks.com

In this collection of essays edited by Gregory Baum, a host of internationally renowned scholars offers a theological assessment of our contemporary history. They examine some of the events (e.g., World War I, the Depression, the Holocaust, the globalization of the free market economy) and movements (e.g., the ecumenical movement, Christian feminism, Marxism, the environmental movement) of the twentieth century and assess how these have changed the face of theology.

Contributors are from a variety of Christian backgrounds and include Victor Consemius, Douglas John Hall, Bernard Dupuis, Joseph A. Komonchak, Donald Schweitzer, A. James Reimer, Rosemary Radford Ruether, Gary Dorrien, Virgilio Elizondo, Lee Cormie, Harvey Cox, Ulrich Duchrow, Robert J. Schreiter, Susan A. Ross, Dwight N. Hopkins, Linda E. Thomas, Stephen B. Scharper, and Michael J. Scanlon, O.S.A.

"A theological, sociological, and historical report on the relation of Christians to the twentieth century is bound to be illuminating. Add to this the name of the editor – Gregory Baum – and we have a text that is trustworthy and fascinating as well. Not to be missed at any cost."—*Robert McAfee Brown*

Available from
Novalis
1-800-387-7164
www.novalis.ca